A PUBLICATION OF THE WACHOVIA HISTORICAL SOCIETY

THE AMERICAN INDIAN
IN NORTH CAROLINA

Town Creek Mound, or Frutchey Mound, on Little River in Montgomery County

Photograph by courtesy of the State Department of Archives and History

THE AMERICAN INDIAN
IN NORTH CAROLINA

Douglas L. Rights

Second Edition

JOHN F. BLAIR, *Publisher*
WINSTON-SALEM, 1957

Library of Congress Catalog Card No. 57-9277

First Paperback Edition, 1988
Second Printing, 1991

Manufactured by BookCrafters
Chelsea, Michigan

To

My Indian Friends

That man to man, the warld o'er,
Shall brithers be for a' that.

B<small>URNS</small>

Preface

AN ATTEMPT is made in this volume to portray the character and manner of living of the American Indian in North Carolina, to identify tribes, and to trace tribal movements.

Although North Carolina possesses considerable authentic material relating to the story of the aborigines, references are scattered, early writings are not easily accessible, and studies that have been attempted, sometimes excellent in preparation, have often failed to examine the entire field, or have been lacking in details that contribute to interest and understanding.

After the explorers, far too few, who recorded their discoveries, still fewer authors have contributed supplementary material in the past century and a half. It was not until the latter part of the nineteenth century that linguists of the Bureau of American Ethnology discovered to what racial stock the Piedmont tribes belonged; that James Mooney, Charles C. Royce, and several other scholars made important contributions to our knowledge of the North Carolina Indians. It has been necessary in this attempt to furnish a representation of Indian life to draw largely from the records of the few explorers and from the investigations of the still fewer ethnologists in this particular field. Archaeology, although in its infancy in this state, has contributed a share.

The surviving Indians can add little. They are rapidly assuming the manner of life of their neighbors. The Catawba Indians, who still make their pottery in ancestral fashion, had never seen an ancient Catawba vessel made by their ancestors until this writer showed them one in a museum.

The information here presented has been assembled bit by bit at odd moments over a score of years. It lacks, therefore, the thorough annotation that belongs to historical research, and the careful literary finish that results from continuous study and writing. Historical accuracy has been sought, but effort has been made to prevent the book from becoming merely a string of references, or a technical study that beclouds the subject with an array of scientific data. Not only information about, but also acquaintance with, the Indian is sought. Quotations from the explorers give a flavor of pioneer days when direct contact with various tribes was possible; some early writings and later studies of considerable length are included for a better understanding of the Indian, although they make for dull reading.

The arrangement of material will appear unorthodox to some readers. The general plan is to present the tribes of North Carolina according to chronology of discovery and early contacts; to follow the historical treatment with ethnological notes, the brief contribution of archaeology, and a description of Indian antiquities. Just as it is with people, some of the chapters are long and some are short, and there seems to be no reason for adding or subtracting without cause.

The restriction of the field under survey to a single state will appear artificial. The tidewater Indians represented the extensive stock that inhabited a vast territory spreading from the Atlantic states to the Rocky Mountains; the Tuscarora became the Sixth Nation of the Iroquois Confederacy; the Siouan tribes formerly ranged also throughout Piedmont Virginia and South Carolina and were kinsmen of numerous strong tribes of the West; the Cherokee claimed territory now included in at least eight states of the Southeast. For intensive examination, however, the field has been limited to the area with which the writer is more familiar, although important references lead beyond the borders of North Carolina. This state furnishes a favorable field for study, for here was a meeting ground of the better-known cultures of the East, a laboratory for investigation of the leading tribes. The records of North Carolina will always form a valuable contribution to knowledge of the American Indian.

DOUGLAS L. RIGHTS

Winston-Salem
North Carolina

Acknowledgments

FRIENDLY ASSISTANCE from many sources has been helpful in the gathering of material for this volume. Among those who are due grateful recognition are the following:

Dr. John R. Swanton, Bureau of American Ethnology, Washington, for supplying important references to Southeastern tribes; Dr. Frank G. Speck, Professor of Anthropology, University of Pennsylvania, for notes on Siouan survivors; Neil M. Judd, Curator, Department of Archaeology, United States National Museum, Washington, for museum courtesies; the late Warren K. Moorehead, Andover, Massachusetts, for classifying material; Roy J. Spearman, of High Point, Dermid McLean, of Winston-Salem, Bill Baker and Bill Sharpe, of Raleigh, and others, for photographic work; Dr. C. C. Crittenden, Secretary, State Department of Archives and History, and Dr. A. R. Newsome, former Secretary of the North Carolina Historical Commission, for library references; Dr. Adelaide L. Fries, of Winston-Salem, for preparing index; Dr. Guy B. Johnson, Dr. Wallace E. Caldwell, Dr. J. B. Bullitt, Joffre Coe, and the late Colonel Joseph Hyde Pratt, of Chapel Hill, Burnham S. Colburn, of Asheville, H. M. Doerschuk, of Badin, Mrs. Margaret Siler, of Franklin, W. J. Morgan, of Brevard, Dr. Sanford Winston and Harry Davis, Director of State Museum, of Raleigh, James E. Steere, of Charlotte, John R. Shipley, of Winston-Salem, and other members of the Archaeological Society of North Carolina; Dr. Cornelius Osgood, Professor and Curator of Anthropology in Peabody Museum at Yale University, and Dr. Irving Rouse, of Yale, for bibliography; the late Burton Craige, Richard J. Reynolds, Charles M. Norfleet, Sr., Thurmond Chatham, William Pfohl, and Joseph T. Pfohl, of Winston-Salem; the late Jesse Scott, of Rocky Mount, Fred O. Scroggs, of Brasstown, the late Joseph E. Poole, of Asheboro, the late Richard Chatham, of Elkin, Earl Norman and Gates Huff, of East Bend, Oscar V. Poindexter, of Donnaha, Thomas S. Petree, of Danbury, Dr. W. P. Cumming, of Davidson College, the late Professor Collier Cobb, Dr. R. D. W. Connor, and Dr. Archibald Henderson, of Chapel Hill.

The Bureau of American Ethnology has been indispensable in furnishing information about the native tribes, through its publications and by correspondence.

The Department of Conservation and Development of North Carolina has generously responded with assistance.

I wish to acknowledge the careful editing of the manuscript by Ashbel G. Brice of the Duke University Press.

My gratitude is expressed to these, and to hundreds of farmers, whose fields I have roved, for helping assemble material for a contribution to knowledge of the American Indian in North Carolina.

D. L. R.

Introduction

THE AMERICAN INDIAN

WHENCE CAME the Indian?

The theory most favored is that the Indian came from Asia. Only fifty-six miles of open sea separate that continent from America. Investigations of the Alaskan shores, particularly those by Dr. Henry Collins and Dr. Ales Hrdlicka, of the Smithsonian Institution, reveal a trail of camping grounds with deep deposits in kitchen middens, some as much as twenty feet thick.

When came the Indian?

The Indian has been regarded as a recent comer to the American continent, but discoveries in the past few years have tended to set back the estimate. Dating by tree rings, discovered by Dr. Douglass, of Arizona, has given definite chronology of a thousand years and more to ruins in the West. Carved stones of Mexico are dated near the beginning of the Christian era. Investigations in Colorado and New Mexico have revealed the Folsom culture, with artifacts associated with bones of extinct animals, and the estimate goes back ten thousand years. Discoveries in the caves of the Sandia Mountains of New Mexico are believed to add another ten thousand years.

Investigations thus far in North Carolina give little evidence of great antiquity for Indian residence in this state.

How large was the Indian population?

According to Matthew W. Stirling, Chief of the Bureau of American Ethnology:

There are six times as many people living in New York City today as occupied all of North America north of Mexico when Columbus arrived. Ethnologists estimate the total population of this area at approximately 1,150,000. Of this number 846,000 were within the limits of the present United States, 220,000 were in Canada, 72,000 were in Alaska, and 10,000 in Greenland.

Within the limits of the United States east of the Mississippi, there were probably less than 300,000 Indian inhabitants when European colonization began. It has been remarked that there are more office-holders in Washington today than there were Indians in all of eastern America when Columbus landed.

What was the distribution of the Indian population?

Waves of immigration reached all parts of America. Climatic conditions and geographical features did much to determine density of population. Upper South America and Central America held the largest group and produced advanced social development, made possible by the cultivation of corn as supporting food crop. The culture of this area showed remarkable progress in architecture, skill in making ornaments of gold, silver, and stone, the preparation of an accurate calendar, the discovery of the term zero, and other evidences of achievements that win our admiration. California had a population estimated at 250,000. In the West the Cliff Dwellers and the Pueblo Indians left worthy monuments of their labors. In the Mississippi Valley and in the region southeast near the Gulf of Mexico there were large sedentary groups which have left notable earthworks[1] and skilfully made artifacts. Other parts of the East were more sparsely settled.

What was the contribution of the American Indian?

Pioneer life was much influenced by the Indian. The settlers found something to learn about clothing, traveling, woodcraft, and even fighting. The Indian gave the world three of its most valuable crops—corn, potatoes, and tobacco, and at least eighty other important products for food and medicine. The Indian is still the most colorful figure in our literature, and his arts are being studied with renewed interest. With an increasing population the Indian is still contributing. In our country today there are 400,000 Indians, 0.3% of the population; south of the Rio Grande, Indians

---

[1] There are thousands of mounds in the Middle Western area. Among the best-known earthworks in America are the Cahokia Mounds near East St. Louis, Illinois, the Serpent Mound in Ohio, numerous effigy mounds in Wisconsin, and mounds at Marksville, Louisiana, Etowah and Macon, Georgia, and Spiro, Oklahoma.

number 28.25% of the population. A report of 1943 stated that in the fighting forces of the Second World War there were more Indians per capita than any other racial group in the United States.

The reader who desires more detailed accounts of these broad aspects of Indian history may turn to the following: Frederick R. Burton, *American Primitive Music, with Special Attention to the Songs of the Ojibways* (New York, 1909); H. B. Collins, Jr., "Archaeology of St. Lawrence Island, Alaska," *Smithsonian Miscellaneous Collections*, XCVI (1937), 1-431; A. E. Douglass, "Tree Rings and Chronology," *University of Arizona Bulletin*, 1942; Frank C. Hibben, "We Found the Home of the First American," *Saturday Evening Post*, CCXVII (April 7, 1945), 11, 35-37; Ales Hrdlicka, "Origin and Antiquity of the American Indian," *Annual Report of the Smithsonian Institution for 1923* (Washington, 1925), pp. 481-494; J. H. Kempton, "Maize— Our Heritage from the Indian," *Annual Report of the Smithsonian Institution for 1937* (Washington, 1938), pp. 385-408; James Mooney and John R. Swanton, "The Aboriginal Population of America North of Mexico," *Smithsonian Miscellaneous Collections*, LXXX (1928), 1-40; Sylvanus Griswold Morley, "Archaeological Investigations of the Carnegie Institution in Washington in the Maya Area of Middle America during the Past Twenty-eight Years," *Proceedings of the American Philosophical Society*, LXXXVI (1943), 205-219; Frank H. H. Roberts, Jr., "Developments in the Problem of the Paleo-Indian," *Smithsonian Miscellaneous Collections*, C (1940), 51-116; Matthew W. Stirling, "America's First Settlers, the Indians," *National Geographic Magazine*, LXII (1937), 535-596; Matthew W. Stirling, "The Historic Method Applied to Southeastern Archaeology," *Smithsonian Miscellaneous Collections*, C (1940), 117-123; George C. Vaillant, *Indian Arts in North America* (New York, 1939); John Collier, *The Indians of the Americas* (New York, 1947); Paul S. Martin, George I. Quimby, and Donald Collier, *Indians before Columbus* (Chicago, 1947); Elizabeth Chesley Baity, *Americans before Columbus* (New York, 1951); Thomas R. Henry, "Ice Age Man, the First American," *National Geographic Magazine*, CVIII (1955), 781-806; National Geographic Society, *Indians of the Americas* (Washington, 1955).

Contents

Illustrations

THE AMERICAN INDIAN
IN NORTH CAROLINA

CHAPTER I

The Old North State

NORTH CAROLINA has been called Nature's Sample Case, a term believed to have been coined by Collier Cobb, of the University of North Carolina. The wide variety of its natural resources and products is not equaled elsewhere in the Union. Its geographical features include the highest mountains east of the Mississippi, a Piedmont area drained by innumerable streams, the sandy coastal plain, and extensive ocean strand.

The Blue Ridge Mountains form a barrier across the state in the west. Behind them are cross chains of mountains. Mt. Mitchell, the highest peak, rises 6,684 feet above sea level. The Great Smoky Mountains have a mean elevation of about 5,500 feet. In the area of the mountain division of the state, approximating 6,000 square miles, there are forty-three peaks which attain an elevation of over 6,000 feet. East of the Blue Ridge are several series of irregular ridges or spurs, of which the most prominent are the South Mountains and the Brushy Mountains. There are some small isolated chains or peaks, such as the Saura Town Mountains, Pilot Mountain, and King's Mountain. The Uwharrie Mountains, charted by early map-makers but not designated on recent maps, extend south from the center of the state. Nearly one-half of the area of the state lies between the Blue Ridge Mountains and the coastal plain. It is known as the Piedmont, a region of gentle hills and valleys. In this area are the rivers Roanoke, Neuse, Cape Fear, Yadkin, and Catawba with their numerous tributaries. The elevation varies from three hundred to one thousand feet above sea level. East of the "falls line" marked by the rapids in the rivers is the coastal plain, averaging about 150 miles in width, much of it level ground. Deep, sandy soil predominates. The gently flowing rivers Chowan, Roanoke, Tar, Neuse, and Cape

Fear, and smaller streams were easily navigated by the Indians. At the eastern extremity of the state there are several large sounds, a distinctive feature of the physiography of North Carolina, shut in behind the sandbanks that skirt the ocean. While the shore line of the ocean follows the sandbanks and wider areas, the state has few localities favorable for harbors. Too much sand has been carried out into the ocean. The stormy shallows off Cape Hatteras are known as the "Graveyard of the Atlantic."

Plant life in North Carolina ranges from the subtropical of the southeast to the hardwoods of the mountain peaks. Almost any kind of agricultural crops can be grown. Since the Indians of this region derived much of their subsistence from agriculture, the advantage of this favorable region for them is readily understood.

Geological formations vary widely and mineral deposits are diversified—gold, silver, copper, lead, graphite, and many other native minerals are found, and numerous precious gems, including the diamond, have been discovered. The Indians made little use of native metals, but discovered and used extensively varieties of stone and clay.

Aliquid omnium, something of everything, may describe nature's realm in the Old North State.

Varied also were the racial characteristics of the aborigines who possessed the land before the coming of European colonists. There was a diversity of linguistic stocks representing most of the main divisions east of the Mississippi. The chief cultures of eastern America found here a meeting ground.

The grouping of the tribes later found is strikingly defined according to the chief geological characteristics of the state. The four natural divisions include the tidewater region of seacoast and sounds, the coastal plain, the Piedmont plateau, and the mountain region. Along the coast were the Algonquian-speaking tribes, living in small, scattered settlements on the sandbanks and around the broken shore line of the sounds; on the coastal plain were the Tuscarora, a large, compact body of Iroquois exercising considerable authority, yet not so vigorous and aggressive as their kinsmen of the North; within the Piedmont area were numerous tribes of Siouan stock, who occupied with their cognate tribesmen of

Virginia and South Carolina a territory seventy thousand square miles in extent; in the Blue Ridge Mountains and farther west the Cherokee, another detached Iroquoian tribe, were securely intrenched.

North Carolina provided well for the necessities of the Indians. Sea food was abundant along the coast, the rivers teemed with fish, game was plentiful, and the soil was productive of cereals, vegetables, and fruits cultivated by the natives. Deposits of stone were available for making arrow points and other implements. The climate was mild and wholesome. The natural beauty of the region could not fail in its appeal. There is little wonder that different culture groups found their way here and that territory embraced by every county in the state has been frequented by Indians.

REFERENCES

Broadhurst, Sam D. "An Introduction to the Topography, Geology, and Mineral Resources of North Carolina," *Educational Series 2*, Bureau of Conservation and Development. Raleigh, 1952.

Cobb, Collier. *Common Rocks and Rock Minerals*. Chapel Hill, 1915.

North Carolina: Today and Tomorrow. Bureau of Conservation and Development. Raleigh, 1936.

Rights, Douglas L. "North Carolina as an Archaeological Field," *Bulletin of the Archaeological Society of North Carolina*, I (March, 1934), 5-7.

CHAPTER II

The Indians Meet the Spaniards

DE SOTO'S EXPEDITION

IN MARCH, 1540, De Soto and his army left winter quarters in northwest Florida and began the long march that led to the Mississippi, the final resting place of this intrepid explorer. He first traveled northeast, crossed several streams, and visited settlements of natives. The first of May he reached the province of Cofitachequi. The chieftainess, or her niece, welcomed the explorer, who made searching investigation of the Indian town according to Spanish custom with an eye for precious metals or other treasure. Pearls (Indian beads) were found in abundance. Objects of European origin were found also, including a dirk, beads, and metal axes, which De Soto supposed were former possessions of Ayllon, another Spaniard, who had attempted an ill-fated expedition some time before. (The "Jordan River," mentioned by Ayllon, has been identified as the Santee.) De Soto repaid the courtesy of the Lady of Cofitachequi by seizing her and obliging her to travel with him under guard when he continued his journey about twelve days after his arrival at the town. Direction of travel was now to the north through a hilly region.

The location of Cofitachequi has long been sought by historians. Silver Bluff on the Savannah has been the choice of many. Investigations, however, have pointed more to the east. From a survey of the territory and study of documents I am of the opinion that De Soto passed through Aymay (Hymahi) on upper Edisto River and next reached Cofitachequi in the Congaree River section near Columbia, South Carolina.

On Friday, May 21, the explorer arrived at Xualla, or Xuala, a large village on a plain between two rivers. The mountains were in sight, and the land appeared to furnish better prospects for gold. The chief was so prosperous that he gave the explorers whatever they asked—corn, dogs, baskets, and porters for service as pack-carriers.

It is probable that Xualla was located along the headwaters of streams near the boundary line of the Carolinas, and this may have been the first contact of Europeans with Indians within the confines of what is now the state of North Carolina. The name indicates that the tribe met was the Saura, pronounced Xualla (Shualla) by the Spaniards.

Tracing the line of march of De Soto has been attempted by succeeding generations of historians with varied results. As for the route of the explorer between the famous Cofitachequi and Guasula or Guasili, my opinion is that De Soto followed a ridge trail between Broad and Saluda rivers to reach Xualla, for which the vicinity of Greenville County, South Carolina, furnishes a likely location. The route then turned to the southwest and led through the rugged foothills of the Blue Ridge in the general direction taken by the Southern Railway in passing through Toccoa, Georgia. Beyond, the broad valley of the headwaters of the Chattahoochee and the mound village of Nacoochee suggest the location of Guasula.

Although I should like to see the route established without doubt across the Blue Ridge Mountains, the following difficulties stand in the way: A knowledge of the Spaniards' practice of exaggeration leads one to expect a more grandiose description of the Blue Ridge than *"muy alta sierra"*; the time limit for the march (Ranjel gives four days from Xuala to Guasili) would not permit a passage through the Appalachian mountain region; the mountain passes would not allow a ready march for De Soto's small army with considerable equipment and supplies including a drove of hogs, as any traveler familiar with the mountain trails in that section can testify. (De Soto sent two of his men north on a scouting trip. They brought back a buffalo hide. Possibly the scouts crossed the Blue Ridge.)

Against this dissenting opinion, however, there have been others that trace the explorer across the mountains of western North Carolina. James Mooney suggested Swannanoa Gap as the probable crossing, basing his opinion on the Cherokee name meaning trail of the Suali or Saura. Other careful studies have led to the decision that the Saura town was in the present Oconee County, South Carolina; that the trail extended from there across the Blue Ridge Mountains via Highlands to Franklin, and thence to Hiwassee Town at the mouth of Peachtree Creek, this town corresponding with Guasili. A large mound on this site was excavated in 1933-34 under the direction of the Smithsonian Institution—Civil Works Administration.

Here we must leave De Soto, as did also his captive "queen," who ran away from Xualla with one of his slaves, carrying with her a box of pearls, doubtless her own shell beads, much to the chagrin of the Spaniard.

Exploits of Juan Pardo

Twenty-six years later another Spanish expedition set out for the interior. Juan Pardo was the bold captain who led in this venture, assisted by his sergeant, Boyano; another officer, Escudero; and 125 soldiers. From the lower South Carolina coast at St. Helena they traveled northwest, reaching Aymay and Cofitachequi, where De Soto had camped a quarter-century before. Onward they pushed until they reached Xualla (Joara), where they built a fort. Here Boyano was left with thirty soldiers while the venturesome Pardo continued his scouting. The account of his explorations mentions Issa, Guatari, and Sauxpa, suggesting tribal names of Catawba, Wateree, and Saxapahaw, and gives a glowing account of the land and its inhabitants.

It is my opinion that Pardo journeyed from the coast to the headwaters of Edisto River, and thence to the Congaree before reaching the Saura. His turn to the east probably brought him to the Wateree (Guatari), then located on the Yadkin-Great Peedee River. His trail from Joara (Xualla-Saura) was that followed by De Soto. On his way he reached Tocar (Toccoa probably, where Toccoa Falls is located—the Siouan word *Tukar* meaning "to fall"), and Cauchi (Nacoochee).

The Spanish expeditionary force made several incursions into the hill country, lured by tales of gold irresistible to the Spaniards. Boyano's courage did not fail—even when an arrow caught him in the mouth. Pardo rejoined his force and led them on long excursions, but gained little save the glory of adventure. After his second return to the coast, his hard-pressed soldiers retreated after him. The waning power of Spain eclipsed further efforts to continue the conquest of the hinterland of Carolina.

CHICORA

In 1521 two Spanish vessels reached the coast of what is now South Carolina. The Spaniards carried away a great number of the Indians to be enslaved in the West Indies. The name of one of the Indians, Francisco of Chicora, furnishes the suggestion that Chicora was a tribal name equivalent to Shakori, the designation of a tribe known also as Saxapahaw, later found on the upper Haw River in North Carolina.

REFERENCES

Bourne, Edward Gaylord (ed.). *Narratives of the Career of Hernando de Soto*. Vols. I-II. New York, 1922.

Gregg, Alexander. *History of the Old Cheraws*. New York, 1867.

Heye, George C., with Hodge, F. W., and Pepper, George H. *The Nacoochee Mound in Georgia*. Contributions from the Museum of the American Indian, Heye Foundation, Vol. IV (1918), No. 3.

Mooney, James. "Myths of the Cherokees," *Nineteenth Annual Report of the Bureau of American Ethnology*, Washington, 1900, Part 1, pp. 3-548.

Ross, Mary. "With Pardo and Boyano on the Fringes of the Georgia Land," *Georgia Historical Quarterly*, XIV (1930), 267-285.

Ruidiaz y Caravia, Eugenio. *La Florida su conquista y colonización por Pedro Menéndez de Aviléz*. Vols. I-II. Madrid, 1894.

Setzler, Frank M., and Jennings, Jesse D. *Peachtree Mound and Village Site, Cherokee County, North Carolina. With Appendix: Skeletal Remains from the Peachtree Site, North Carolina*, by T. D. Stewart. Bulletin No. 131, Bureau of American Ethnology. Washington, 1941.

Stirling, M. W. "Smithsonian Archeological Projects Conducted under the Federal Emergency Relief Administration, 1933-34," *Annual Report of the Smithsonian Institution for 1934*, Washington, 1935, pp. 371-400 ("North Carolina: Peachtree Mound and Village Site," pp. 392-394).

Swanton, John R. *Early History of the Creek Indians and Their Neighbors.* Bulletin No. 73, Bureau of American Ethnology. Washington, 1922.

————. "Tracing De Soto's Route," *Exploration and Field Work of the Smithsonian Institution in 1934,* Washington, 1935, pp. 77-80.

CHAPTER III

The Indians Meet the English

EXPEDITION OF DISCOVERY

BY A GRANT from Queen Elizabeth authority was given Sir Walter Raleigh to undertake discovery and the planting of a colony in "such remote heathen and barbarous lands, countries and territories not actually possessed by any christian Prince, nor inhabited by christian people." For the purpose of discovery Raleigh sent from England on April 27, 1584, two small ships, the *Tyger* and the *Admirall*, commanded by the captains Philip Amadas and Arthur Barlowe.[1]

On the second of July the vessels sailed into shoal water and two days later reached the coast. The voyagers coasted 120 miles, entered an inlet which they supposed to be a river, and cast anchor beyond the sand bars in the quiet waters of the sound. After a prayer of thanksgiving the sailors manned the boats and rowed to the sandbanks, where they landed and with accustomed ceremony took possession of the country in the name of England's Queen.

Three days later they espied a small boat being rowed toward the ships that lay anchored near the shore. While two boatmen remained with the boat, a third landed and walked along the beach nearer the ships. The captains Amadas and Barlowe, accompanied by others of their crew, rowed to land to meet the stranger. After addressing the Englishmen in a language they did not understand, the native accompanied them on shipboard. He was given a shirt, a hat, and some other things, also a taste of wine and meat, which he liked very well. After an inspection of both ships the Indian returned to his boat, rowed a short distance away, and began to fish. In less than half an hour he had caught a boatload of fish, which he brought to the shore and divided into

[1] The narrative follows closely Hakluyt's *Voyages*.

two parts, making signs that one part was for each ship. Then he departed.

The next day forty or fifty Indians came in boats. The Englishmen described them as "very handsome, goodly people, and in their behavior as mannerly and civil as any of Europe." Among the visitors was Granganimeo, brother of the chief, Wingina. The latter could not come since he had recently been twice wounded in battle and was compelled to remain at the chief town of the tribe, five days' journey distant. Granganimeo's attendants spread a mat on the ground. He sat at one end of the mat, four other Indians sat at the opposite end, and the remainder stood at a respectful distance. The Englishmen reported that when they sat down by invitation beside Granganimeo, "he made all signs of joy and welcome, striking on his head and his breast, and afterwards on ours, to show we were all one, smiling and making show the best he could of all love, and familiarity." He alone addressed the explorers, who presented him with gifts.

Shortly after this visit the Englishmen began trading with the Indians, exchanging European merchandise for furs. Granganimeo was much pleased with a bright tin dish, and after punching a hole in the rim he hung it about his neck in the manner of a gorget or breastplate, making signs that it would defend him against his enemies' arrows. The tin dish was bartered for twenty skins worth twenty crowns, and a copper kettle brought fifty skins worth fifty crowns. The Indians secured hatchets, axes, and knives, and would have traded for swords if the Englishmen had been willing.

A few days later Granganimeo brought along his wife, his daughter, and several of his other children. The wife was described as being very well favored, of small stature, and very bashful. She wore a long leather cloak or robe, presumably of deerskin, with the furry side next to her body, and an apron or skirt of like material. About her forehead she had a band of white "coral," the same kind of shell beads with which her husband decked himself more profusely. In her ears were "bracelets of pearls, hanging down to her middle, and those were the bigness of good pease," doubtless strings of shell beads. Other women of

Plate 1

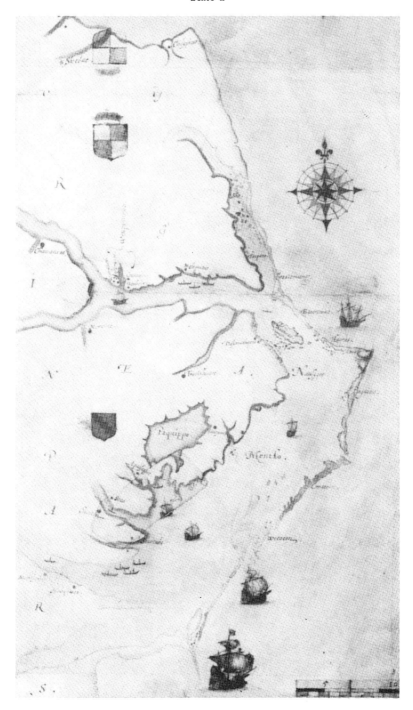

Map of Carolina by John White

Original in the British Museum; copy by courtesy of the North Carolina Museum of Art

Plate 2

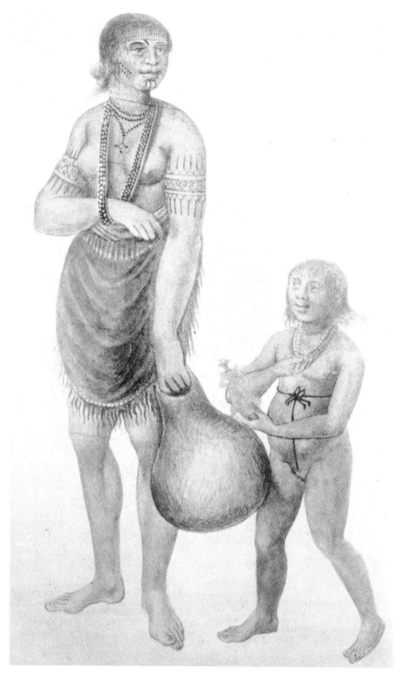

"A chief lady of Pomeiock" or "A chiefe Herowans wife of Pomeoc
and her daughter of the age of 8 or 10 years"

John White pictures in the British Museum. Photograph by courtesy of the Smithsonian
Institution, U. S. National Museum

Plate 3

"A Weroan or great lord of Virginia—The manner of their
attire and painting themselves when they goe to their generall
huntings or at their solemne feasts"

John White pictures in the British Museum. Photograph by courtesy of the Smithsonian
Institution, U. S. National Museum

Plate 4

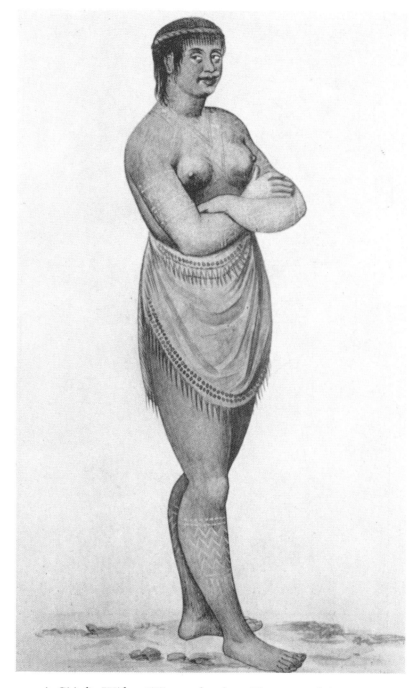

A Chief's Wife—"The wyfe of an Herowan of Secotan"

John White pictures in the British Museum. Photograph by courtesy of the Smithsonian
Institution, U. S. National Museum

Plate 5

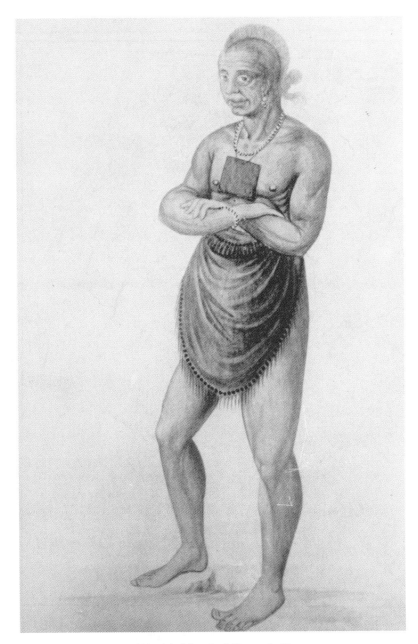

"A chief lord of Roanoke"

John White pictures in the British Museum. Photograph by courtesy of the Smithsonian
Institution, U. S. National Museum

Plate 6

Map Showing Location of Indian Villages Visited by
Sir Walter Raleigh's Colonists

By courtesy of Maurice A. Mook and the *Journal of the Washington Academy of Sciences*

Plate 7

An Indian Village—"The Town of Pomeiock"

John White pictures in the British Museum. Photograph by courtesy of the Smithsonian
Institution, U. S. National Museum

Plate 8

The Conjurer or the Flyer

"They be verye familiar with deuils, of whom they enquier what their enemys
does, or other suche thinges. They shaue all their heads, sauing their crest, which
they weare as other doe and fasten a badge of their office. . . . They weare a
bagg by their side."—Hariot

John White pictures in the British Museum. Photograph by courtesy of the Smithsonian
Institution, U. S. National Museum

Plate 9

"Their manner of fishing in Virginia"

John White pictures in the British Museum. Photograph by courtesy of the Smithsonian Institution, U. S. National Museum

Plate 10

"Their manner of praying with their rattles about the fire"
John White pictures in the British Museum. Photograph by courtesy of the Smithsonian
Institution, U. S. National Museum

Plate 11

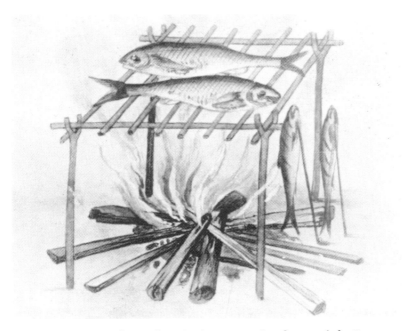

"The broyling of their fish ouer the flame of fier"

John White pictures in the British Museum. Photograph by courtesy of the Smithsonian
Institution, U. S. National Museum

"Theire sitting at meate"

John White pictures in the British Museum. Photograph by courtesy of the Smithsonian
Institution, U. S. National Museum

Plate 12

"Their dances which they use at their feasts"

Plate 13

"The town of Secota," Secoton, or Secotan, Showing Plantings
of Early and Late Corn in the Fields

John White pictures in the British Museum. Photograph by courtesy of
the North Carolina Museum of Art

Plate 14

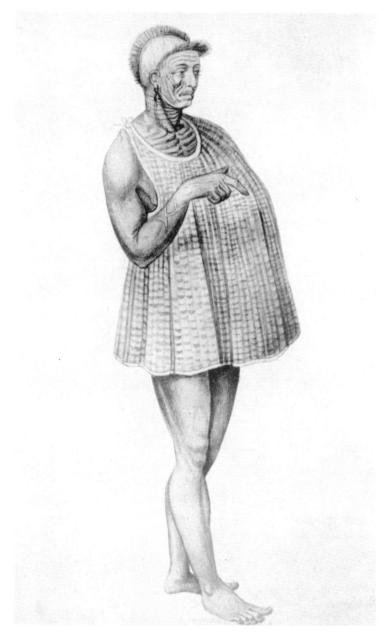

"One of the religious men of the town of Secota"

John White pictures in the British Museum. Photograph by courtesy of the Smithsonian
Institution, U. S. National Museum

Plate 15

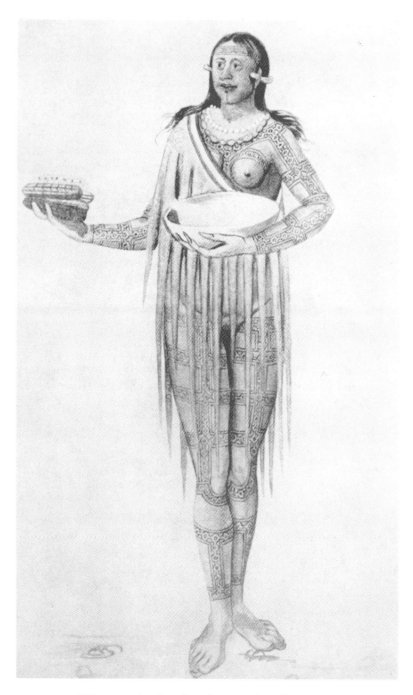

Woman with Bowl and Ears of Indian Corn

John White pictures in the British Museum. Photograph by courtesy of the Smithsonian
Institution, U. S. National Museum

Plate 16

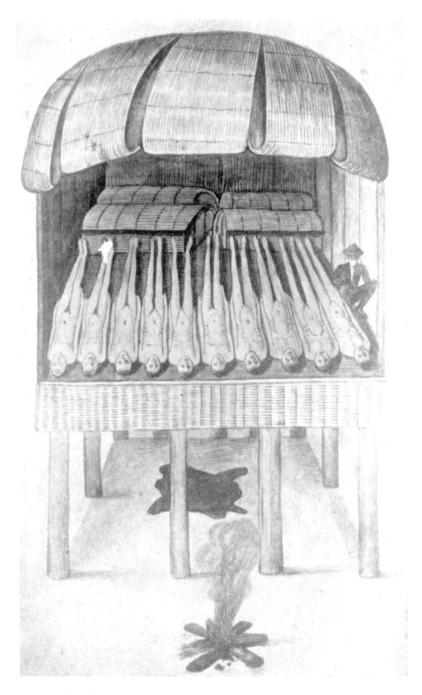

"The Tombe of their Cherounes or chiefe personages"

John White pictures in the British Museum. Photograph by courtesy of the Smithsonian
Institution, U. S. National Museum

high rank wore pendants of copper in either ear, as did some of Granganimeo's children. Some of the braves had as many as five or six of these copper ornaments suspended from their ears. As a headpiece Granganimeo wore a broad plate of copper, which he would not allow to be removed. The Englishmen observed that the dress of the men was similar to that of the women, "only the women wear their hair long on both sides, and the men but on one," and that their hair was "black for the most part," though the explorers stated that they saw children that had "very fine auburn, and chestnut-colored hair."

A possible explanation of this last statement may be found in the information gathered from the Indians that twenty-six years before a ship had been wrecked on the coast and its crew of white people saved. After they had remained a few weeks with the natives in the region of Ocracoke, they attempted to sail away in two Indian canoes which had been lashed together, using shirts for sails. The boats were later found stranded on the shore, but no other trace of the castaways was discovered.

The canoes used by the Indians were dugouts, and the manufacture of them was described as follows:

The manner of making their boats is thus; they burn down some great tree, or take such as are wind-fallen, and putting gum or rosin upon one side thereof, they set fire into it, and when it has burnt it hollow, they cut out the coal with their shells, and ever where they would burn it deeper or wider they lay on gums, which burn away the timber, and by this means they fashion very fine boats, and such as will transport twenty men.

In trade the chief's brother was faithful to his word. Sometimes he obtained goods on credit, and always met his obligations on time. As a token of friendship he provided bountifully for his new acquaintances. The explorers reported: "He sent us every day a brace or two of fat bucks, conies, hares, fish, the best in the world. He sent us divers kind of roots, and fruits very excellent good, and of their country corn, which is very white, fair and well tasted."

Such friendly treatment gave the newcomers assurance and encouraged them to further exploration. Eight of the travelers went twenty miles to an island which the natives called Roanoak. At the north end of the island was a village of nine houses built of "cedar," probably framework of small trees or boughs covered with cedar bark and twigs. Around the village was a palisade formed by tree trunks set in the ground. Granganimeo's wife, in the absence of her husband, received the travelers kindly and took great care to provide for their comfort. Food was served in earthen pots, and chips of wood were provided for plates. While the meal was being enjoyed, several Indians with bows and arrows arrived from a hunting trip. The white men took alarm at the sight of weapons, but the Indian hostess chased the hunters away after having her attendants break the bows and arrows to pieces. When for safety the voyagers chose to sleep in their boat some distance from the shore, she was grieved at their seeming distrust, sent them provisions in earthen pots and five mats for a covering against rain, and posted numerous men and women to sit all night along the shore as guards. The white men had good reason to report that they found these people "most gentle, loving, and faithful, void of all guile and treason, and such as live after the manner of the golden age."

The explorers soon learned, however, that the Indians were by no means pacifists. They observed their armor and weapons of war: bows, arrows of small canes tipped with a sharp shell or tooth of a fish, clubs headed with the sharp horn of a stag or other beast, and breastplates made of small pieces of wood fastened together. They learned of tribal warfare, cruel and bloody, that wasted the country. Beyond the region of these Indians, called Secotan, there was another called Pomiouk, where the chief was in league with the ruler of the adjoining land called Newsiok, situated on the goodly river "Neus" (Neuse). The Secotan cherished "mortal malice" against the tribes of these two provinces for many injuries and slaughters committed in the past. The white men were urged by their Indian friends to join in a campaign against the inhabitants of Pomiouk with the promise of much booty, but were uncertain whether this proposal was prompted by desire for revenge against an ancient enemy or by love their hosts bore them. They did not put the matter to a test.

After a sojourn of about two months in the country that yielded so many delights to the explorers, they set sail for England. The closing lines of their record of discovery state: "We brought home also two of the savages, being lusty men, whose names were Wanchese and Manteo."

The Englishmen have given us a story of their discoveries that yields never-failing interest. It is to be regretted that we have no record of the impressions of the two Indian braves, the first American tourists to reach England. Imagination follows them as they wandered through crowded streets of London, as they gazed upon Westminster and the Tower, and as they were presented to the Queen. The Englishmen found a strange New World. How utterly strange must have been the Old World to these dwellers of an Indian village on the Carolina coast! Their impressions we cannot learn. We do know, however, that after their sojourn in England and their subsequent return home, one of these Indians proved himself a true friend of the English, and the other a bitter enemy. Out of the same environment and experiences sometimes issue strangely contrasting results.

THE FIRST COLONY

The report of the first expedition was received in England with great enthusiasm. The Queen was delighted, and proudly bestowed the name "Virginia" upon the newly discovered country. Sir Walter Raleigh hastened to make preparations for the first colony.

Sir Richard Grenville commanded the fleet that sailed from England on April 9, 1585. Among the 108 colonists were Ralph Lane, appointed governor; Thomas Hariot, historian and scientist; Philip Amadas, captain of the first expedition; Manteo and Wanchese, returning natives. After a voyage by way of the West Indies the fleet sighted Cape Fear on June 23, and three days later anchored at Wocokon (Ocracoke). On July 3 they sent word of their arrival to Wingina at Roanoke. Two scouting parties were sent out. One party visited Croatoan on the sandbanks; the other set out for the mainland and reached Indian settlements in the following order: July 12, Pomeiok; July 15, Aquascogoc; July 15, Secotan. In this same order the probable locations of these towns were on Gibbs Creek, Hyde County; southwest on the coast of the same county; and on the north bank of Pamlico River in Beaufort County. The great lake they found, called Paquipe, was evidently Mattamuskeet.

On their return occurred the first unfriendly encounter with the natives, reported as follows: "The 16th, we returned thence, and one of our boats, with the admiral, was sent to Aquascogoc, to demand a silver cup which one of the savages had stolen from us, and not receiving it according to his promise, we burned and spoiled their corn, all the people being fled." Foreshadowed in this unhappy event was the long series of conflicts between incoming settlers and Indians that spread through territory now included in every state of the Union.

The fleet anchored at Hatteras on the twenty-seventh, and two days later Granganimeo, with Manteo, came to welcome the colonists.

Governor Lane began a series of explorations. He became convinced that a much better location could be found for the new colony. He was lured also by the expectation of finding precious metals, a prospect made more attractive by the fanciful tales of the Indians. Many of his men were ill-fitted for pioneer life and were not satisfied to settle down to hard work. Consequently, instead of building a strong base at Roanoke, he spent most of his time treasure hunting, depending on the Indians to furnish corn and to aid in fishing in order to provide sufficient food for his men. This task became burdensome to the Indians and was the cause of later troubles, aggravated by the imprudent and unfriendly conduct of some of the colonists.

On the mainland north of Albemarle Sound, including what are now the counties of Currituck, Camden, Pasquotank, and Perquimans, was the Indian province Weapomeiok, ruled by the chief Okisco. This was visited early in August.

The Chowan Indians lived along the river bearing their name. One of their villages, called Ohanoak, situated on high land with good cornfields adjacent, was probably in Hertford County. The chief village, Chawanook, was not far from the junction formed by Bennett's Creek, on the east side of the river. Lane estimated the number of warriors of this town to be seven hundred, certainly an exaggeration. The chief of the tribe, Menatonon, was described as being "a man impotent in his limbs, but otherwise for a savage a very grave and wise man." He gave Lane directions for travel by river and overland to Chesapeake Bay. His description of the abundance and fineness of the pearls of that region sounded alluring to the Governor, to whom he presented a string of black beads, probably the dark-colored shell beads called wampum. His son, Skyco, was retained by Lane as a prisoner and proved to be a valuable hostage.

Roanoke River, called Moratuc, was visited next. The Indians gave a strange description of the source of this river, which may have been a myth, or a yarn to deceive the travelers, or a veritable tale misunderstood by reason of difference in speech—or a mixture of all three. The river, they said, sprang out of a rock standing so near the sea that in storms the waves beat into the spring and made its water salty. Another mysterious tale was of the strange country inland called Chaunis Temoatan, which yielded a great abundance of metal called *wassador*, supposed by Lane to be copper. These stories, especially the *wassador* narrative, greatly impressed the travelers.

Lane, with forty men, voyaged up the river. The Moratoc Indians,[2] who dwelt along the stream, were strangely absent from their town, and not a grain of corn could be found. It was learned that Wingina, who had changed his name to Pemisapan after the death of his brother, had aroused the inland natives to enmity against the newcomers.

When the explorers were 160 miles upstream, according to the liberal estimate of the Governor, their food supply was nearly exhausted. Lane proposed a direct return, but his men desired to make a more thorough exploration and, if possible, to take some of the Mangoaks of that region prisoners. The cherished hope of

[2] These have been thought to be of Iroquoian stock, possibly Nottoway Indians, remnants of which tribe lingered on the state border until as late as 1825, when there were forty-seven members of the tribe living in Southampton County, Va. There is another possibility that they were affiliated with the Tuscarora. Strong supporting evidence has been given by Maurice A. Mook that the Moratoc were of Algonquian stock, and this view has been favored by other competent authorities.

finding some of the fabulous *wassador* among the Indians seemed to have inspired the whole party. But the Indians were wary. They did not appear until the boats were far down the river. Manteo gave his friends timely warning, for, when the Governor's party was preparing to land and meet the Indians in friendly conference, a shower of arrows fell on the boats. That night the travelers camped on a barren shore and dined on emergency rations of "dog's porridge." The day following, their only food was soup of sassafras leaves. Lane recorded that the next day, Easter Eve, "was fasted very truly." The hungry voyagers landed at Roanoke on Easter Day.

Ensenore, father of Pemisapan, was friendly to the colonists. The Chowan chief, whose son was held captive at Roanoke, also exercised a helpful influence with the Indians of Weapomeiok, and persuaded their chief to send a delegation to Lane, professing allegiance to the English. In council, because of the good graces of Ensenore, Pemisapan agreed that the natives should plant sufficient corn for the colonists. This resolution was most welcome to the white men, whose food supply was at the vanishing point and who were seemingly unable to provide for themselves even sufficient food to ward off starvation. Unfortunately for them, Ensenore died soon after their return from the futile search for *wassador*. Ill will between colonists and natives henceforth persisted.

Pemisapan straightway conspired with the neighboring tribes to destroy the settlers. Wanchese was a partner in the conspiracy. The plan proposed called for the assembly of a large number of warriors at Dasamonguepeuc on the mainland west of the island, under guise of a ceremonial feast in honor of the dead. A score of Indians were appointed to make a night attack on Lane and his principal men. Stronger forces were to be ready to move over and attend to the other colonists, who were to be found in scattered groups seeking food about the island. In order to break up the colonists into detached groups, the Indians refused to provide food and secretly broke or robbed the weirs where the colonists caught fish. These efforts were successful; famine threatened. A score of colonists went to Croatoan, a dozen to Hatteras, and another party of sixteen or twenty to the mainland.

The plot was revealed to Lane by his prisoner, the son of the Chowan chief. Once when the youth attempted to run away Lane had fettered him and threatened to cut off his head. The boy was released at the request of Pemisapan, who made him a confidant, thinking he would harbor mortal enmity against his captors. However, the Governor treated Skyco kindly and the men made a favorite of him. He repaid them by revealing the plot, which was confirmed by one of Pemisapan's men.

The time set for the uprising was June 10. By the last of May the Indians were assembling at Roanoke while larger numbers were waiting on the mainland. Lane resolved to break up the plot without further delay. He planned to seize all the boats at nightfall and to move to the mainland for attack the following day. The Indians on the island were to be prevented from leaving, and any invaders were to be seized. At sunset the guardsmen began to bring in the boats. They met a canoe setting out from shore, overturned it, and cut off the heads of two Indians. A savage cry from land apprised them that the act of violence was discovered. At this alarm the Indians seized their bows and the colonists rushed to their weapons. In a brief skirmish three or four natives were slain; the rest fled into the woods.

The next morning the Governor and a strong detachment of men rowed to the mainland. A message was sent by one of Pemisapan's men, who met the party when they landed, telling that Lane was going to Croatoan to complain of one of the Indians who had sought to carry away the Governor's prisoner the night before, and demanding that Pemisapan go along. The chief, with several principal warriors, received the message, suspected no deception, and awaited the Governor. When the Englishmen arrived at the meeting place, Lane gave the signal for attack with the cry, "Christ our victory!" The invaders opened fire upon their surprised enemies and speedily gained a victory. The chief, shot in the first volley, fell to the ground as dead, but suddenly sprang up and ran for cover, receiving a second shot in flight. Lane's Irish servant and an English officer pursued him. The Governor feared that he had lost both the chief conspirator and his man, until he met the Irishman coming out of the woods with Pemisapan's head in his hands.

The date of this conflict was the first of June. On the nineteenth the colonists returned to England with the fleet of Sir Francis Drake.

HARIOT'S NARRATIVE

Thomas Hariot, in *A Briefe and True Report of the New-found-land of Virginia,* published in 1587 a description of some of the principal resources of the new country and of the nature and manners of its inhabitants. He listed merchantable commodities including flax, hemp, pitch, tar, turpentine, pearl, dyes used by the natives, furs, copper, and two kinds of grapes for wine, one of which can be recognized as the scuppernong. He catalogued the forest products and gave a fair description of the animals, fish, and fowls. He mentioned the native foods, beans, melons, fruits, and nuts, and among vegetable products included the three most important contributions the Indians have made to the world's agriculture: corn, potatoes, and tobacco, known respectively as *pagatour, openauk,* and *uppowoc.* Although Indian corn had already been widely cultivated in Europe, tobacco, introduced by the Spaniards, was as yet little known in England. The supply carried back by Lane's expedition served to popularize smoking. Sir Walter Raleigh's experiment with the pipe was quickly followed by other persons of rank. Tobacco soon passed from the luxury stage to popular demand. Within two years after the return of the expedition Hariot wrote this account of the product that has made North Carolina famous the world over:

There is an herb which is sowed apart by itself, and is called by the inhabitants Uppowoc. . . . The leaves thereof being dried and brought into powder, they use to take the fume and smoke thereof by sucking it through pipes made of clay, into their stomach and head, from whence it purges superfluous phlegm and other gross humours, and opens all the pores of the body, by which means the use thereof not only preserves the body from obstructions, but also (if any be, so that they have not been of too long continuance) in short time breaks them, whereby their bodies are notably preserved in health, and know not many grievous diseases, wherewithal we in England are often times afflicted.

This Uppowoc is of so precious estimation amongst them, that they think their gods are marvelously delighted therewith; whereupon sometime they make hallowed fires, and cast some of the powder therein for a sacrifice; being in a storm upon the waters, to pacify their gods, they cast some up into the air and into the water; so a weir for fish being newly set up, they cast some therein and into the air; also after an escape from danger, they cast some into the air likewise; but all done with strange gestures, stamping, sometime dancing, clapping of hands, holding up of hands, and staring up into the heavens, uttering therewithal, and chattering strange words and noises.

We ourselves, during the time we were there, used to suck it after their manner, as also since our return, and have found many rare and wonderful experiments of the virtues thereof, of which the relation would require a volume by itself; the use of it by so many of late, men and women of great calling, as else, and some learned physicians also, is sufficient to witness.

The potato, which was introduced into England by the expedition, soon became a staple crop. In Ireland its use has been indispensable, and it has become popularly known as the Irish potato.

Hariot's notes on the inhabitants are summarized as follows:

Their towns were small, with few near the coast. Some numbered ten or twelve dwellings; some twenty; the largest, thirty. The houses were constructed of small poles made fast at the top in round form, covered with bark or mats woven from rushes. The length, which was commonly double the breadth, varied from twelve to twenty-four feet.

In some places a chief governed only one town; in others, more; the greatest number of towns under authority of one chief was eighteen, the combined fighting strength of which was estimated at over seven hundred warriors.

The language of each tribe differed from the others.

They conducted warfare with surprise attacks and were fond of deceitful strategy. The time of attack was usually just before dawn. They disliked fighting in the open and were experts at taking to their heels.

Compared with the English, they were simple and ignorant of many things considered important by the white men, esteeming trifles of great value. But in their own manner of living they were ingenious.

They believed in many gods which they called Mantoac (first

English reference to Manitou, or Great Spirit),[3] of different sorts or degrees, with one chief god. Sometimes they represented their gods by images of human shape, which they housed in appropriate shrines where they worshiped, prayed, sang, and made offerings. They believed in immortality. The white men found them ready to listen to religious discourse and to respond in their simple way to Christian appeal. In sickness, crop failure, and other distress they called upon their white neighbors for prayer.

The white men who did such marvelous things were a mystery to them, and they knew not whether to call them gods or men. Strange powers were ascribed to the newcomers, especially when pestilence followed in the wake of their visits. (Evidently the Indians were very susceptible to diseases introduced by the whites.) When the medicine men sucked blood out of their patients' bodies, a usual method of treatment, these sorcerers sometimes claimed that the strings of blood were strings with which invisible bullets were tied and cast.[4]

Although Hariot conceded that some of Lane's company toward the end of their stay showed themselves too fierce in slaying the Indians in some of the towns for causes that might easily have been borne, yet he excused the rash deeds, claiming that such action was justly deserved by the natives.

THE JOHN WHITE PICTURES

Preserved in the British Museum are seventy-six water-color drawings made by John White, a member of Lane's expedition. These, the earliest illustrations of the Carolina country and its inhabitants, furnish valuable information for the antiquarian.[5]

---

[3] F. W. Hodge (ed.), *Handbook of American Indians North of Mexico.* Bulletin No. 30, Bureau of American Ethnology, Parts 1 and 2 (Washington, 1907, 1910). See *Manito.*

[4] *Ibid.* See *Medicine and Medicine Men.*

[5] The original pictures are in the British Museum. The United States National Museum has acquired photostats giving excellent reproductions except for color and has kindly permitted their use in supplying illustrations in this volume. Lantern slides of the drawings have been shown in this country by Sir John Forsdyke, Director and Principal Librarian of the British Museum, in lectures on "The First English Settlement in America." The original John White maps also are in the British Museum. Through the courtesy of Dr. W. P. Cumming copies obtained by him in London have been furnished for reproduction.

The Lost Colony

On April 26, 1587, Sir Walter Raleigh sent out another colony in charge of John White, whom he appointed governor. The colonists numbered 150. Of their names 121 were recorded, including 17 listed as women and 9 as boys and children. Two Indians, Manteo and Towaye, returned with them. On July 22 they arrived at Hatteras. They had planned to make their settlement on Chesapeake Bay, and paused at Roanoke Island only for the purpose of finding fifteen men who had been left there the year before, but the treacherous commander of the fleet, Simon Ferdinando, forced them to remain where they landed.

They found on the island the bones of one of the fifteen men, whom the Indians had slain. Later they learned from the friendly Croatoan how the party had been attacked in the following manner by thirty inhabitants of Secotan, Aquascogoc, and Dasamonguepeuk: Eleven of the men were approached by two Indians, who made friendly signs for two of the white men to come unarmed to meet them. One of the Indians embraced one of the white men while the other Indian drew a club which had been concealed beneath his coat and killed the Englishman with a blow on the head. A sudden attack was then made by the entire party of Indians against the colonists, who, under a shower of arrows, retreated to a house. The house was set afire by the attackers and the inmates were driven to battle outside. An hour's skirmish followed wherein the Indians had a great advantage, dodging nimbly about and shooting from behind trees. After another white man had been slain and others wounded, the besieged colonists retreated to their boat and fled. They found the four remaining white men some distance away where they had gone to seek oysters, and, having received them into the boat, proceeded to a small island near Hatteras. After a brief stay they left, never to be seen again.

On July 23 the Governor and some of his men went to the north end of the island. They found Lane's fort razed to the ground, but all the houses standing. The ruins of the fort and the outer rooms of the houses were overgrown with "melons of divers sorts" (probably gourds) on which the deer were feeding. Immediately orders were given that every man should be employed either in repairing the houses found standing or in building new ones.

Five days later one of their number, George Howe, was slain by the Indians. The natives were hidden among the high reeds where they sometimes killed sleeping deer. They espied Howe wading in the water, lightly clad, and armed only with a forked stick which he was using in catching crabs. He had strayed two miles from his companions. The Indians shot him in the water, inflicting sixteen wounds with their arrows, and then clubbed him to death. After this deed of violence the Indians, a remnant of Wingina's men dwelling then at Dasamonguepeuk, with whom Wanchese kept company, hastily fled to the mainland.

On July 30 a score of men led by Captain Stafford went with Manteo by water to the island of Croatoan. This island is thought to have been the long sandbank which includes Cape Lookout. The islanders were presumably the Hatteras Indians. When the party landed, the Indians showed hostility, but Manteo called to them in their language and they quickly approached, throwing away their bows and arrows. The welcome was cordial, and friendly entertainment was offered, the visitors being asked only not to gather or spoil the corn in the fields, for there was little of it to be had. Promise was given to the Indians that their request would be complied with, and they were assured that the visit was for the purpose of renewing the old love and of promoting friendship. Invitation to visit the town was accepted by the colonists, and a feast was prepared for them. The Indians expressed an earnest desire that a badge or other token be given them to wear so that when they were away from their island they might be known to the colonists. They said that for want of such identification some of their men had been hurt by Lane's company the year before, and they showed the visitors one of their men who still lay lame on this account. No blame was attached by them to the white men who had mistaken the Croatoan for one of Wingina's men.

The next day a council was held. A proposal was made that the Croatoan convey a message of forgiveness to the tribes of Secotan, Aquascogoc, and Pomeiok, and ask for a pledge of friendship. To this the Indians gladly consented, saying that within seven days they would bring the chiefs of those provinces to Roanoke for conference. After hearing from the Indians the story of the fate of Lane's fifteen men and dispatching what business was at hand, the colonists returned to the fleet at Hatteras.

By August 8 no word had been received from the Indians. The Governor decided to wait no longer, but to seek at once revenge for the mistreatment of Lane's men and for the death of George Howe. The same night he passed over to the mainland with twenty-five men, including Manteo, and in the darkness before dawn his party attacked a band of Indians encamped near the shore. The Indians fled into the reed thickets, where one was shot down. Unfortunately, the Governor had been deceived. He had attacked a band of the friendly Croatan, who had come to gather from the fields the corn, tobacco, and pumpkins left in haste by Wingina's men after they had slain George Howe. Manteo was grieved at this sad blunder, but imputed the harm done to the folly of the Indians in not coming to the Governor on the day appointed. The colonists gathered all the corn, peas, pumpkins, and tobacco they found ripe, left the rest unspoiled, and returned to Roanoke, taking with them several Indians, including the wife of Menatoan, whose little child was strapped on her back, near victims of the unfortunate episode.

On August 13, by command of Sir Walter Raleigh, Manteo was christened at Roanoke, and given the title Lord of Roanoke and of Dasamonguepeuk, in reward for his faithful service. This is the earliest record of a Protestant service and of the conferring of an English title on American soil.

On August 18 the first white child of English parents was born in America. A daughter was born to Ananias Dare and his wife Eleanor, the Governor's daughter. On the following Sunday the little girl was baptized and given the name Virginia Dare. This scant record is all the definite knowledge we have of the most famous baby in American history. The mystery of her fate must be left with the mysterious race found upon our shores, the American Indians.

On August 27, soon after these events, Governor White returned to England to obtain necessary supplies.

When the Governor reached England, he found the people excitedly preparing to resist the invasion threatened by the great fleet from Spain, called the Invincible Armada. All available ships were ordered to the defense of the country. Sir Walter Raleigh, extremely busy with wartime duties, managed by great effort to prepare a small expedition for the relief of the colonists, but the government forbade the expedition to leave. Raleigh, however, by his strong influence did succeed in sending out two small ships in April, 1588, but they were attacked by the Spanish and forced to return. Only after the momentous conflict was over and the Invincible Armada had been shattered was there an opportunity for sending relief to the colony. In March, 1590, Governor White at last set out as passenger on a merchantman bound for the West Indies. Not until August 15 did the ship reach Hatteras.

Hope was afforded by the sight of smoke rising from the island. After a day spent in reconnoitering, the two boats of the relief party encountered rough waters, and seven of the men were drowned in the attempt to reach Roanoke. The party arrived after dark, guided by the light of a great fire in the woods near the north end of the island. They sounded a trumpet, sang familiar English songs, and called out in friendly tones; but there was no answer. At daybreak they landed and found the grass and trees still smoldering, a burnt-out forest fire. Freshly trodden footprints of Indians appeared in the sand. A circuit was made of the north end of the island until the place was reached where the Governor had left the colony. On a tree near the shore were carved the letters C R O. The inscription signified to the Governor where he should find the colonists, as he had secretly agreed with them that if they departed they should not fail to write or carve on the trees or posts of the doors the name of the place to which they went, for at the time of his departure the colony was preparing to move fifty miles into the mainland. In case of distress they were to carve a cross above the letters or name—but no such sign was found.

The houses had been torn down and the place enclosed with a strong palisade of trees. On one of the main trees or posts at the right side of the entrance the bark had been removed, and five feet from the ground in fair capital letters was engraved *CROATOAN*, without any cross or sign of distress. Within the fort were found bars of iron, pigs of lead, and heavy shot scattered about, almost overgrown with grass and weeds. Five chests, three of them belonging to White, which had been carefully hidden, were found despoiled, evidently the work of unfriendly Indians. The Governor grieved at the loss of his books, pictures, maps, armor, and other spoiled possessions, but rejoiced to have found what seemed to him a certain token of the colonists being safe at Croatoan, which, he stated, was "the place where Manteo was born, and the savages of the island our friends."

The captain agreed to take White to Croatoan, but the dangers of the coast deterred the seamen from further navigation in those parts. The ships returned to England, leaving the Lost Colony to its fate.

REFERENCES

Connor, R. D. W. *The Beginnings of English America: Sir Walter Raleigh's Settlements on Roanoke Island.* Raleigh, 1907.

Green, Paul. *The Lost Colony.* Chapel Hill, 1937. (A Dramatization.)

Hakluyt, Richard. *Voyages.* London, 1589-1600.

Hariot, Thomas. *A Briefe and True Report of the New-found-land of Virginia.* London, 1588.

Hodge, F. W. *Handbook of American Indians North of Mexico.* Bulletin No. 30, Bureau of American Ethnology, Parts 1 and 2. Washington, 1907, 1910.

Lorant, Stefan (ed.). *The New World: The First Pictures of America, Made by John White and Jacques Le Moyne.* New York: Duell, Sloane, and Pearce, 1946.

Mook, Maurice A. "Algonkian Ethnohistory of the Carolina Sound," *Journal of the Washington Academy of Sciences,* Vol. XXXIV, Nos. 6 and 7 (June 15 and July 15, 1944).

Porter, Charles W., III. "Fort Raleigh," *North Carolina Historical Review,* XX (1943), 22-42.

CHAPTER IV

Decline of the Coastal Tribes

THE ALGONQUIAN STOCK

THE INDIANS met by the Englishmen of Sir Walter Raleigh's expeditions belonged to the great linguistic stock known as Algonquian. Their tribes were scattered throughout a vast triangular-shaped territory extending from the North Carolina sandbanks to the St. Lawrence River, and from the Atlantic Ocean to the Rocky Mountains. The coastal tribes occupied the southern point of the triangle. They were mainly sedentary and agricultural. "The eastern Algonquian probably equaled the Iroquois in bravery, intelligence, and physical powers, but lacked their constancy, solidity of character, and capability of organization, and do not appear to have appreciated the power and influence they might have wielded by combination. . . . There seems, indeed, to have been some element in their character which rendered them incapable of combining in large bodies, even against a common enemy."[1]

For a half century or more after Raleigh's expeditions the Indians of the North Carolina seaboard were left to themselves. No further efforts were made to renew the settlement at Roanoke, and the colony at Jamestown was too far distant to involve relationships with the Carolina natives. About 1650, however, Virginians began to push south into the Albemarle region.

A VIRGINIA EXPEDITION

In September, 1654, a young fur trader of Virginia, with three companions, visited Roanoke Island, arriving by boat. The Indian chief of that region received them cordially and showed them the ruins of the fort erected by Sir Walter Raleigh's colonists. The

[1] Hodge, *Handbook of American Indians North of Mexico*, Part 1. See *Algonquian*. For a careful study of the Algonquian-speaking tribes of North Carolina, see Mook, "Algonkian Ethnohistory of the Carolina Sound," *loc. cit.*

Indians of Roanoke and others of neighboring tribes entered into a treaty of peace with the English.

As proof of their good intentions, a delegation of the Indians visited Francis Yardley at his Virginia home. The leader of the band, upon seeing and hearing the children of the settlement read and write, asked that his son might be taught "to speak out of the book, and to make a writing." He was invited to bring the boy to school, and at his departure he expressed himself as being desirous to serve the God the Englishmen served and to have his child brought up as a Christian. He promised to return with him in "four moons." The chief, arriving in Yardley's absence, was mistreated by the settlers, but was saved from personal injury through the kindness of his host's wife. Upon his return Yardley arranged with the chief to purchase lands along three great rivers in Carolina territory and sent men to select the tracts, to build a comfortable house for the chief, and to pay him two hundred pounds English money. It was agreed that the lands thus acquired should become a possession of England, and the chief solemnly carried out the transaction with the neighboring Indians by delivering to them "a turf of earth with an arrow shot into it." The Indians at once vacated these lands.

While Yardley's men were building the new house, the chief invited some of them to visit the Tuscarora. Two of the men went along with a party of the Indians, and after two days' travel they came to the hunting quarters of a Tuscarora chief, who, with 250 men, received them kindly. He invited the visitors to journey to his town, where he told them there resided a rich Spaniard who had been with the Tuscarora for seven years. Yardley's men were also invited to go farther inland where, it was said, copper was to be found in great abundance. The white men saw much copper among the Tuscarora, including plates which they claimed were a foot square.[2] They also stated that one of the Indians had two gold beads in his ears, as big as "rounceval peas."[3] The travelers were desirous of further exploration, but as their interpreter became ill, and as there was strife between the Tuscarora

[2] Use of copper among the natives has been noted in all areas of North Carolina. (See below, Chapter XX.)

[3] No objects of gold used by Indians have been found in this state, except for this reference.

and a great nation called Cacores, the journey was considered too hazardous.

The Cacores were described as "a very little people in stature, not exceeding youths of thirteen or fourteen years, but extremely valiant and fierce in fight, and above belief swift in retirement and flight, whereby they resist the puissance of this potent, rich, and numerous people." This tribe of valiant little men may have been the Shoccoree, or Shakori, living westward, probably in the region of Haw River. Saxapahaw is another rendering of their name. It is interesting to note that in lower Randolph County on Cedar Creek, within Shoccoree territory, several graves were disturbed by waters of a freshet in 1929, revealing skeletal remains of Indians of small stature whose teeth indicated that they were past middle age.

The travelers learned also that "there is another great nation by these called Haynokes, who valiantly resist the Spaniard's northern attempts." These are thought to have been the Eno Indians, neighbors of the Shoccoree. Further reference will be made later to these two tribes. It is probable that they were formerly located farther south on the line of march of the Spanish explorers.

A party of forty-five Indians accompanied their friendly white companions to Virginia. The chief brought along his wife and son, whom he wanted baptized. The only present they delivered was the "turf of earth with an arrow shot into it." The boy was accordingly baptized, and as Yardley devoutly stated, was "left with me to be bred up a Christian, which God grant him grace to become!"

George Fox Preaches to the Indians

George Fox visited Carolina in 1672. The Governor and his wife received the minister charitably, but a doctor of the province began a dispute. In the words of Fox:

And truly his opposing us was of good service, giving occasion to the opening of many things to the people concerning the Light and Spirit of God, which he denied to be in every one; and affirmed it was not in the Indians. Whereupon I called an Indian to us, and asked him, "Whether or no, when he did lie, or do any wrong to any one, there was not something in him that did so reprove him for it?" He said

"There was such a thing in him that did so reprove him; and he was ashamed when he had done wrong, or spoken wrong." So we shamed the doctor before the governor and people. . . .

I went from this place among the Indians, and spoke to them by an interpreter, shewing them, "That God made all things in six days, and made but one woman and one man; and that God did drown the old world because of their wickedness. Afterwards I spoke to them concerning Christ, shewing them, that he died for all men, for their sins, as well as for others; and had enlightened them as well as others; and that if they did that which was evil he would burn them; but if they did well they should not be burned. There was among them their young king and others of their chief men, who seemed to receive kindly what I said to them. . . .

[Another service] There was at this meeting an Indian captain, who was very loving; and acknowledged it to be truth that was spoken. There was also one of the Indian priests, whom they called Pauwaw [origin of "pow-wow"?], who sat soberly among the people.

SUBJECTION

The early settlers in the Albemarle region were well received, but the first friendly dealings were followed by occasional hostility which retarded the growth of the settlement. The Indians could not offer resistance sufficient to drive back the newcomers, and the settlers prevailed. Soon the coastal tribes became subject to their white neighbors. Decline of these tribes was rapid, largely because of the evil effects incurred by contact with the white man's civilization. Their annals are short and simple.

HATTERAS INDIANS

These Indians occupied the sandbanks in the neighborhood of Cape Lookout. They have been long considered no other than Manteo's people, the friendly Croatoan, and there is good evidence that they afforded a refuge for the Lost Colony and that survivors of the colony were incorporated into their tribe. Smith and Strachey of Virginia heard about 1607 that the colonists of 1587 were still alive. John Lawson's history, published in 1709, says of the Hatteras Indians:

These tell us that several of their ancestors were white People, and could talk in a Book, as we do; the truth of which is confirmed by grey Eyes being found frequently amongst these Indians, and no others.

They value themselves extremely for their Affinity with the English, and are ready to do them all friendly offices.

When this was written, shortly after 1700, the Hatteras had only one town, Sand Banks, and numbered but sixteen fighting men, indicating a population of about eighty.

True to their affinity, they were allied with the English during the Tuscarora War. The journal of the provincial council of May 29, 1714, carried the report that the Hatteras Indians had lately escaped from the enemy Indians and were at Colonel Boyd's house. Colonel Boyd was ordered to supply the Indians with corn until they could return to their own habitation. Later the Indians appealed for "Some Small reliefe from ye Country for their services being reduced to great poverty." They were allowed sixteen bushels of corn for their needs to be supplied out of the public store.

In 1731 Governor Burrington listed them among the six nations at that time in the province, none of which, except the Tuscarora, contained more than twenty families.

In May, 1761, the Rev. Alexander Stewart, a missionary of the Society for the Propagation of the Gospel, wrote of his visit to Hyde County, including this mention:

I likewise with pleasure inform the Society, that the few remains of the Altamuskeet [Mattamuskeet], Hatteras & Roanoke Indians (whom I likewise mentioned in a former letter) appeared mostly at the chapel & seemed fond of hearing the Word of the true God & of being admitted into the church of our Lord Jesus Christ. 2 men and 3 Women & 2 children were baptized by me. I could have wished the adults were better instructed, but their sureties & a northern Indian among them, who had been bred up as a christian, promised to take that care.

Two years later the same clergyman made another voyage to Hyde County and reported:

The remains of the Attamuskeet, Roanoke and Hatteras Indians, live mostly along the coast, mixed with the white inhabitants, many of these attended at the Places of Public Worship, while I was there & behaved with decency seemed desirous of instruction & offered themselves & their children to me for baptism. & after examining some of the adults I accordingly baptized, 6 adult Indians, 6 Boys, 4 Girls & 5 Infants & for their further instruction (at the expence of a society called Dr. Bray's associates, who have done me the honor of making me Superintendent of their schools in this Province, have fixed a school mistress among them, to teach 4 Indian & 2 negro boys & 4 Indian girls to read & to work & have supplied them with Books for that purpose & hope that God will open the eyes of the whites everywhere that they may no longer keep the ignorant in distress but assist the charitable design of this Pious Society & do their best endeavours to increase the kingdom of our Lord Jesus Christ.

The possibility that members of the tribe migrated to Robeson County, where several thousand so-called Croatan Indians now reside, seems very remote.

CHOWAN

The Chowan Indians, whose name signifies "Southerners," were still a strong tribe when settlers began to move into the Albemarle region about 1650. Their name was well known, as the following reference from early records of Virginia indicate.

On August 27, 1650, a Virginia exploring party set out from Fort Henry to reach the Tuscarora settlements. The company included Edward Bland, Abraham Wood, Sackford Brewster, Elias Pennant, two white servants, and an Appamattox Indian guide. On the way they secured a Nottoway Indian guide named Oyeocker. Some distance west of Meherrin River they came to an Indian trail. Their narrative states:

At this path our Appamattuck Guide made a stop, and cleared the Westerly end of the path with his foote, being demanded the meaning of it, he shewed an unwillingness to relate it, sighing very much. Whereupon we made a stop untill Oyeocker our Other Guide came up, and then our Appamattuck journied on; but Oyeocker at his coming up cleared the other end of the path, and prepared himselfe in a most serious manner to require our attentions, and told us that many years since their late great Emperour Appachancano came thither to make War upon the Tuscarood, in revenge of three of his men killed, and one wounded, and brought word of the other three murthered by the Hocomawananck Indians for lucre of the Roanoke they brought with them to trade for Otter skins. There accompanied Appachancano severall petty Kings that were under him, amongst which there was one

King of a Towne called Pawhatan, which had long time harboured a grudge against the King of Chawan, about a young woman that the King of Chawan had detayned of the King of Pawhatan: Now it happened that the King of Chawan was invited by the King of Pawhatan to this place under pretence to present him with a guift of some great vallew, and there they met accordingly, and the King of Pawhatan went to salute and embrace the King of Chawan, and stroaking of him after their usual manner, he whipt a bowstring about the King of Chawans neck, and strangled him; and how that in memoriall of this, the path is continued unto this day, and the friends of the Pawhatans when they passe that way, cleanse the Westerly end of the path, and the friends of the Chawans the other. And some two miles from this path we come unto an Indian Grave upon the East side of the path: Upon which Grave there lay a great heape of sticks covered with greene boughs, we demanded the reason of it, Oyeocker told us, that there lay a great man of the Chawans that dyed in the same quarrell, and in honor of his memory they continue greene boughs over his Grave to this day, and ever when they goe forth to Warre they relate this, and other valorous, loyall Acts, to their young men, to animate them to doe the like when occasion requires.

In 1663 the Chowan entered into a treaty with the English and "submitted themselves to the Crown of England under the Dominion of the Lords Proprietors." This treaty was faithfully observed for a decade, but in 1675 the Susquehanna War broke out in Virginia. Through incitement of the Indians of Virginia the Chowan violated their treaty. A year of warfare followed with serious loss to the settlers. Later the Chowan were forced to surrender all of their land on the south side of Meherrin River and were assigned a reservation on Bennett's Creek. Here they struggled along for a hundred years. Many petitions were made to the council for a survey, but nearly fifty years passed before the request was granted. Their lands gradually dwindled from twelve square miles, as first assigned, to six square miles about 1707. At this time they had only one town with about fifteen fighting men.

They were allied with the colonists during the Tuscarora War. Chief John Hoyter petitioned the council in 1714 for a survey of the six-mile reservation, stating that the Indians had been fighting on

Eight Expiditions agt the Indyan Enemy of this province and during the time they were in ye Countys Service they Suffered Considerable loss in their plantations & Stocks loosing Seaventy five head of hoggs a Mare & Colt their Corne destroyed by all wch & ye wearing out of their clothes they are reduced to great poverty,

and asked that some allowance be made for their services and losses.

In 1712 Missionary Giles Rainsford of the English Church wrote:

I had several conferences with one Thomas Hoyle King of the Chowan Indians who seem very inclinable to embrace Christianity and proposes to send his son to school. . . . I readily offered him my service to instruct him myself. . . . where I lodge being but three miles distant from his Town. But he modestly declined it for the present till a general peace was concluded between the Indians and the Christians. I found he had some notions of Noahs flood which he came to the knowledge of and exprest himselfe after this manner—My Father told me I tell my Son.

Three years later Rainsford reported: "I have been five months together in Chowan Indian Town & made myself almost a Master of their language." In this same letter he offered to serve as missionary among them.

In 1718 and 1720 petitions were filed by Chief Hoyter complaining that the settlers were continually intruding upon the lands of the Indians and that the limits of the territory had never been determined. In the former petition he also asked for payment due one of his tribesmen by a settler for an Indian slave of the Core Sound region. In 1723 a reservation of 53,000 acres was laid out for the Tuscarora and the Chowan.

By the year 1731 the tribe had dwindled to less than twenty families. Two years later the council gave them permission to be incorporated with the Tuscarora. In 1752 Bishop Spangenberg wrote from Edenton, "The Chowan Indians are reduced to a few families, and their land has been taken away from them." A report of Governor Dobbs in 1755 stated that the tribe consisted of two men and five women and children who were "ill used by their neighbors."

Dr. Richard Dillard has described a shell mound in the former Chowan region:

One of the largest and most remarkable Indian mounds in Eastern North Carolina is located at Bandon on the Chowan, evidently the site of the ancient town of the Chowanokes which Grenville's party visited in 1585, and was called Mavaton. The map of James Wimble, made in 1729, also locates it about this point. The mound extends along the river bank five or six hundred yards, is sixty yards wide and five feet deep, covered with about one foot of sand and soil. It is composed almost exclusively of mussel shells taken from the river, pieces of pottery, ashes, arrowheads and human bones. . . . Pottery and arrowheads are found in many places throughout this county, especially on hillsides, near streams, etc.

WEAPOMEIOK

North of Albemarle Sound were the Weapomeiok, whose chief town was located within the present Pasquotank County. Their towns mentioned by the explorers were Weapomeiok, Pasquenoke or Women's Town, Chepanoc, Mascoming, and Metachkwem, all ruled by Okisco. Shortly after 1700 the Indians of this region were listed as Yeopim with six people, Pasquotank with one town on Pasquotank River and ten fighting men, Poteskeet with one town on North River and thirty fighting men, and Perquiman, a total of about two hundred inhabitants. (Most of the estimates of tribes in decline are listed in John Lawson's *History of North Carolina*.)

The first deed on record in North Carolina, which bears the date 1662, reads:

Know all men by these presents that I, Kilcacenen, King of Yeopim have for a valeiable consideration of satisfaction received with the consent of my people sold, and made over to George Durant a Parcell of land lying and being on Roneoke Sound and on a river called by the name Perquimans. . . .

The document is signed with the mark of Kilcocanen or Kistotanen, the chief.

MACHAPUNGA, BAY RIVER, PAMLICO, AND CORANINE

The Machapunga, or Mattamuskeet, dwelt in Hyde County. Their name signifies "bad dust," or "much dust," probably an allusion to the sandy region they inhabited in the neighborhood of Lake Mattamuskeet. Ralph Lane's party visited their settlements. In 1701 they had one town and thirty fighting men. They joined the Tuscarora against the colonists. Governor Pollock reported in 1713 that the Mattamuskeet and Coranine

of late have done us great mischief, having killed and taken our people since my last to you, about 45 at Croatan Roanoke Island, and Alligator River, these being about 50 or 60 men of them got together between Matchepungo River and Roanoke Island which is about 100 miles in length and of considerable breadth, all in a manner lakes, quagmires, and cane swamps, and is, I believe, one of the greatest deserts in the world, where it is almost impossible for white men to follow them. They have got likewise boats and canoes, being expert watermen, wherein they can transport themselves where they please.

In 1761 they were listed as having seven or eight fighting men.

Near by were the Bear River, or Bay River, Indians, listed in 1701 as having one town called Raudaugua-quank with fifty fighting men, and the Pampticough (Pamlico) with one town called Island and fifteen fighting men. These tribes were likewise allies of the Tuscarora.

The Coranine, or Coree, lived in the region of Core Sound, which preserves their name. Governor Archdale described them as a bloody and barbarous people. Lawson listed them in 1701 as Connamox with two towns, Coranine and Raruta, having twenty-five fighting men. They had a prominent part in the Tuscarora War, fighting against the colonists. In 1715, with other enemy Indians, they were allowed to settle at Mattamuskeet and the council requested the governor "to Commission & Impower Some person and to remit accounts thereof," for which service he was to be allowed 2 shillings 6 pence per day.

John Lawson gave the following story of early warfare between these Indians and the Machapunga:

The Machapungas were invited to a Feast by the Coranines; (which two Nations had been a long time at War together, but had lately concluded a Peace). Thereupon, the Machapunga Indians took advantage of coming to the Coranine's Feast, which was to avoid all suspicion, and their King, who, of a Savage, is a great Politician and very stout, ordered all the Men to carry their Tomahauks along with them, hidden under their Match Coats; which they did, and being acquainted when to fall on, by the Word given, they all (upon this design) set forward for the Feast, and came to the Coranine town, where they had gotten Victuals, Fruit and such things as make an Indian Entertainment, all ready to make these new Friends welcome, which they did, and after Dinner, towards Evening, (as it is customary amongst them) they went to dancing, altogether; so when the Machapunga King saw the best opportunity to offer, he gave the Word and their Men pulled their Tomahauks from under the Match Coats and killed several and took the rest Prisoners, except some few that were not present and four or five that escaped. The Prisoners they sold as Slaves to the English. At the time this was done, those Indians had nothing but bows and Arrows, neither side having Guns.

On Harkers Island, in Core Sound, there is a shell mound that marks the feasting place of Indians in former days. This was in Coranine territory, and may have been the scene of the fateful feast described by Lawson. The mound is roughly circular in outline, one hundred yards or more in diameter. Its height rises to ten feet or more near the center. Considerable excavation has been made. Five miles of road on the island have been paved with shells from the mound and many loads have been transported in barges to Hyde County for fertilizer. Clam and oyster shells predominate, with frequent occurrence of conch shells. The greater portion of the shells have been opened, and such shells as the conch have been broken, apparently for extraction of food. In addition to shells there are bones of fish, carapaces of turtles, etc. The layers are well defined, often marked by fire pits showing charcoal and ashes. On these levels are found broken pieces of clay pots, pebbles, and animal bones. Intermingled with the shells have been found also stone tools, arrowheads, and other artifacts of the Indians. Several skeletons of Indians have been found in the mound. With one was a necklace of animal teeth strung together. There are other mounds of shells in the vicinity, but the Harkers Island mound is probably the largest on the Carolina coast.[4]

[4] This mound was visited by the author in 1931. One of the islanders produced a skull taken from the mound.

NEUSE INDIANS

Near the mouth of Neuse River were the Neusiok, or Neuse Indians, evidently Iroquois and affiliated with the Tuscarora. In 1701 they had two towns, Chattooka and Rouccoonk, with fifteen fighting men.

WOCCON

Lawson stated that the Woccon lived two leagues from the Tuscarora, and placed them on his map near lower Neuse River. They had two towns, Yupwareremau and Tooptatmeer, with 120 fighting men (about 1701), or a total of about 500 inhabitants. A vocabulary of 150 words of their language was preserved by Lawson, which identifies them as being of Siouan stock. Some early references indicate that they were allied with the Tuscarora; however, the nine warriors of the Wareperes, listed in Barnwell's Indian army campaigning against the Tuscarora, were in the company of Siouan allies of the eastern Carolinas, and their name is suspiciously like Yupwareremau, the designation of a Woccon town. I am inclined to believe that they were the Waccamaw, who gave their name to a lake and river of southeastern North Carolina. Their population was the largest recorded of all eastern Carolina tribes except the Tuscarora. It is hard to account for the complete disappearance of so large a body. In 1715 the Waccamaw were not far from the Winyaw, who lived near the junction of the Waccamaw and Peedee rivers. If a guess may be ventured, here is another clue to the mystery connected with the origin of the large body of descendants of Indians now living in Robeson County, commonly called Croatan. The Siouan tribes, Waccamaw, Peedee, Winyaw, Cape Fear, and other native tribes of the region drained by rivers of the same tribal names, together with remnants of the Saura (Cheraw), who lived for some time on the Peedee, could find a natural inland retreat to the swampy regions of the Robeson County area, where they would be more secure than in the exposed neighborhood of the settlements.

THE CAPE FEAR INDIANS

As early as 1661 some New Englanders attempted to make a settlement near the mouth of the Cape Fear River on lands claimed to have been purchased from the Indians. The cause of their withdrawal from that region was ascribed by John Lawson to trouble with the Indians. He related that the colonists sent away some of the children of the tribesmen "under pretense of instructing them in learning and the principles of the Christian religion, which so disgusted the Indians that tho' they had no guns, yet they never gave over until they had entirely rid themselves of the English, by their Bows and Arrows."

These settlers had disappeared before 1663, when another party of Englishmen from Barbados arrived to explore the same region. On October 16 they anchored in Cape Fear River. Several Indians came on board the ship and brought a "great store of fresh fish, large mullets, young bass, shads, and several other sorts of very good, well-tasted fish." The Englishmen spent two months in exploring the Cape Fear and its branches. The first Indian town they visited was called Necoes. A report of discoveries recorded a distance of fifty leagues traveled upstream. The narrative states that in the region of the lower Cape Fear four Indians in a canoe met the explorers and sold them several baskets of acorns. After the purchase one of the Indians followed for some distance along the shore and from a high bank shot an arrow which narrowly missed one of the men and stuck in the upper edge of the boat. Four of the party were left to guard the boat while the rest set out to overtake the bowman. They heard some of the Indians "sing" some distance away in the woods and advanced to attack, but, alarmed by the sound of two gunshots, they hurried back to the boat, where they found their men safe. These explained that when another Indian had appeared creeping along the bank, they had fired at him with small shot, but evidently had done him no harm, since he ran away.

Presently two Indians with bows and arrows appeared, crying, "Bonny, bonny," a salutation that may have been intended for the Spanish *bueno*, an indication of former contact with Spaniards. The bows and arrows were taken from the Indians, and they were given beads, to their content. They showed great concern about the arrow sticking in the boat, but made signs to show that they knew nothing about it. According to the narrative, farther downstream was found the canoe of the Indian who had done the shooting. The men cut the canoe in pieces and then pulled down his hut, broke his pots, platters, and spoons, tore the deer skins and mats to pieces, and took away a basket of acorns.

Farther downstream the Englishmen met more Indians, who again gave the "bonny" greeting. Two of them persisted in swimming out to the boat and persuaded the travelers to go ashore, where it was "bonny." The account of the visit states:

As soon as we landed, several Indians, to the number of near forty lusty men, came to us, all in a great sweat, and told us Bonny: we showed them the arrow-head in the boat-side, and a piece of the canoe we had cut in pieces. Whereupon the chief man amongst them made a long speech, threw beads into our boat, which is a sign of great love and friendship, and gave us to understand that, when he heard of the affront which we had received, it caused him much worry; and that he and his men were come to make peace with us, assuring us, by signs, that they could tie the arms and cut off the head of the fellow who had done us that wrong. And, for a further testimony of their love and goodwill towards us, they presented us with two very handsome, proper, young Indian women, the tallest that we ever saw in this country, which we supposed to be the king's daughters, or persons of distinction among them. These young women were so ready to come into our boat, that one of them crowded in, and would hardly be persuaded to go out again. We presented the king with a hatchet and several beads, and made presents of beads also to the young women, the chief men, and the rest of the Indians as far as our beads would go. They promised us, in four days, to come on board our ship, and so departed from us.

At a distance of three leagues downstream the party arrived at a place where nine or ten canoes were assembled. When they went ashore, they found that most of the Indians gathered there were those with whom peace had been made shortly before. On December 1, near Crane Island, they made a purchase of "the river and land of Cape Fair" from Wat-Coosa and such other Indians as appeared "to be the chief of those parts."

These Cape Fear Indians may have been of Siouan stock. By the year 1715 they were listed as having five villages and a population of 206. They were mentioned in a report of the Albany Conference in 1751 as being a small, friendly tribe which the government of South Carolina desired to be at peace with the Iroquois.

REFERENCES

Bland, Edward. *The Discovery of New Brittaine*. London, 1651.

The Colonial Records of North Carolina. Edited by William L. Saunders. Vols. I-III. Raleigh, 1886.

Dillard, Richard. "Indian Tribes of Eastern Carolina," *North Carolina Booklet,* Vol. VI, No. 1, Raleigh, 1906.

Fries, Adelaide L. (ed.). *Records of the Moravians in North Carolina.* Vol. I. Raleigh, 1922.

Hawks, F. L. *History of North Carolina.* Vol. II. Fayetteville, N. C., 1858.

Hodge, F. W. *Handbook of American Indians North of Mexico.* Bulletin No. 30, Bureau of American Ethnology, Parts 1 and 2. Washington, 1907 and 1910.

Lawson, John. *History of North Carolina.* London, 1714; second ed., 1718; reprints: Raleigh, 1860; Charlotte, 1903; Richmond, 1937.

Mook, Maurice A. "Algonkian Ethnohistory of the Carolina Sound," *Journal of the Washington Academy of Sciences,* Vol. XXXIV, Nos. 6 and 7 (June 15 and July 15, 1944).

Mooney, James. *Siouan Tribes of the East.* Bulletin No. 22, Bureau of American Ethnology. Washington, 1894.

Strachey, William. *The historie of travelle into Virginia Britannia.* Hakluyt Society Publications, Vol. VI. London, 1849.

CHAPTER V

The Tuscarora

Iroquois of the Coastal Plain

THE ALBEMARLE region attracted a steady flow of settlers from Virginia; French settlements were begun along Pamlico River; Swiss and German immigrants, led by Baron Christopher de Graffenried, founded New Bern. As the white population increased, extending settlements steadily inland, the Indians saw their former habitations and hunting grounds rapidly diminishing. The lands occupied by the settlers were usually secured under form of purchase, but surveys were indefinite and the land deals were not always approved by the various tribes that inhabited the country. The Indians resented the steady encroachment upon their territory. They visited the settlements unmolested, some finding employment with the colonists, and they enjoyed generally friendly relations with their new neighbors, but they were people of the forest and could not adapt themselves easily to the white man's manner of living. Incursions into their territory and the clearing of the land alarmed them and aroused in them ill will against the newcomers.

Unscrupulous men of the colony were guilty of gross abuses against the Indians, although the government sought to be friendly. Instructions of the Lords Proprietors to the governor in 1676 read, "Cultivate friendship with the Indians." Governor John Archdale wrote to George Fox in 1686:

We at present have peace with all the nations of Indians, and the great fat king of the Tuscaroras was not long since with me, having had an Indian slain in these parts. He was informed it was by the English; but upon inquiry I found out the murderer, who was a Chowan Indian, one of their great men's sons, whom I immediately ordered to be apprehended; but the Chowan Indians bought his life of the Tuscarora king for a great quantity of wampum and bags. This

Tuscarora king was very desirous to cut off a nation of Indians called the Matchepungoes; which I have prevented, and hope I shall have the country at peace with all the Indians and one with another. . . . This Tuscarora king seems to be a very wise man as to natural parts. Some of the Indians near me are so civilized as to come into English habits, and have cattle of their own; and I look upon their outward civilizing as a good preparation for the Gospel, which God in his season, without doubt, will cause to dawn among them.

John Lawson wrote of the Carolina Indians that they were

really better to us than we have been to them, as they always freely give us of their victuals at their quarters, while we let them walk by our doors hungry, and do not often relieve them. We look upon them with disdain and scorn, and think them little better than beasts in human form; while with all our religion and education, we possess more moral deformities and vices than these people do.

The weaker tribes along the coast were soon forced to give way before the tide of incoming settlers, although not without some opposition. The Tuscarora, a strong, numerous people more removed, at length prepared to make desperate resistance. Mention of this tribe has already been made in the earlier stories of the settlement. In July, 1670, John Lederer passed through their territory. He reported his visit to their town, Katearas, on the Eruco River, a place of great Indian trade and the seat of the "haughty Emperour" called Kaskufara, or Kaskous. Lederer stated:

His grim Majestie, upon my first appearance, demanded my gun and shot; which I willingly parted with to ransom myself out of his clutches; for he was the most proud imperious barbarian that I met with in all my marches. The people here at this time seemed prepared for some extraordinary solemnity: for the men and women of better sort had decked themselves very fine with pieces of bright copper in their hair and ears, and about their arms and neck, which upon festival occasions they use as an extraordinary bravery: by which it would seem that this country is not without rich mines of copper. But I durst not stay to inform myself further in it, being jealous of some sudden mischief towards me from Kaskous, his nature being bloudy, and provoked upon any slight occasion.

The impression made upon Lederer and other travelers indicates the fierce, aggressive nature of the Tuscarora (the name means "Hemp Gatherers"). They were of Iroquoian stock, having in ancient times become separated from their kinsmen of the north, the Five Nations. The Cherokee of the southern Appalachian mountains were of the same stock. Without question the Southern Indians retained much of the bold, warlike character that made their northern kinsmen feared by Indians and colonists throughout North America east of the Mississippi.

The Nottoway and Meherrin Indians, located on rivers of their name along the Virginia border, were of the same linguistic stock, as were probably the Neusiok, or Neuse River Indians.

John Lawson has given a detailed description of the North Carolina Indians, which will be reviewed later. Much of this information relates to the Tuscarora; therefore little more will be said of their description. When Lawson prepared his account of these people, he little dreamed that he was soon to be a victim of their cruel tortures.

According to their tradition, the Tuscarora possessed in early times the "country lying between the sea shores and the mountains, which divide the Atlantic states." Lawson listed them in 1701 as having fifteen towns and about twelve hundred fighting men (about five thousand total population), giving the names of their towns as follows: Haruta, Waqui, Contah-nah, Anna Ooka, Conauh-Kare, Harooka, Una Nauhan, Kentanuska, Chunanetts, Kenta, Eno, Naur-hegh-ne, Oonossoora, Tosneoc, Nonawharitse, and Nursoorooka. He also stated that "the Tuskeruro's are most numerous in North Carolina, therefore their Tongue is understood by some in every Town of all the Indians near us." They seem to have included large subdivisions within the tribe. At this time their territory embraced the country drained by Neuse River and its tributaries Contentnea and Trent, from near the coast to the vicinity of the present Wake County, and lands along the Tar-Pamlico River and possibly the Roanoke, while their hunting quarters extended nearly to Cape Fear. The important municipalities Raleigh, Smithfield, Goldsboro, Wilson, Rocky Mount, Tarboro, Greenville, and Kinston are located in former Tuscarora territory.

The half century of apparent friendship drew to a close. In the year 1710 Tuscarora emissaries made an appeal to the provincial government of Pennsylvania, presenting eight belts of wampum as an evidence of the earnestness of their plea. Their petition stated that in view of the large number of their people being seized and sold into slavery, and of others being killed in defending their children and friends, they desired to remove to a more friendly region where they would be free from evil encroachments. Their claims were recognized as just; five years earlier the Pennsylvania council, alarmed at the traffic in Indian slaves lest it should lead to an uprising of the Pennsylvania Indians, had decreed to prohibit further importation of Indian slaves from Carolina.[1] (South Carolina seems to have been the chief offender in this slave traffic.) Answer to the petition was delayed, and in the meantime the situation in eastern North Carolina became precarious. A dissatisfied faction of the colonists, led by a deposed unscrupulous official, Carey, were blamed for inciting the Indians to extreme measures. De Graffenried ascribed as one of the causes of the Tuscarora War "the harsh treatment of certain surly and rough English inhabitants who deceived them in trade, would not let them hunt about their plantations, and under this excuse took away from them their arms, munitions, pelts or hides, yes, even beat an Indian to death."

On their side the Indians were quick to resent an injury and harbored unending resentment against their aggressors. They waged wars among themselves with extreme cruelty, especially to captives. The fury of their vengeance spared not the innocent and defenseless who happened to be in their way, although it must be said that the Indians also suffered like wrongs perpetrated by their neighbors. The introduction of liquor made matters worse. Under its influence the Indians were driven to commit deeds of violence that would have been avoided by sober conduct. The Tuscarora carried on extensive rum-trading with the tribes

[1] For references to Indian slavery, see R. D. W. Connor, *History of North Carolina* (Chicago, 1919); A. W. Lauber, *Indian Slavery in Colonial Times within the Present Limits of the United States* (New York, 1913); Clarence H. Poe, "Indians, Slaves and Tories: Legislation Regarding Them," *North Carolina Booklet*, Vol. IX, No. 1 (Raleigh, 1909); and Sanford Winston, "Indian Slavery in the North Carolina Region," *Bulletin of the Archaeological Society of North Carolina*, III (April, 1936), 3-9.

farther inland. Of this sort of traffic with Indians to the west, Lawson wrote:

Now they have it brought to them by the Tuskeruros and other Neighbour Indians, but the Tuskeruros chiefly, who carry it in Rundlets several hundred Miles, amongst other Indians. Sometimes they cannot forebear breaking their Cargo, but sit down in the Woods and drink it all up, and then hollow and shout like so many Bedlamites. . . . But when they happen to carry it safe (which is seldom without drinking some part of it, and filling it up with water) and come to an Indian Town, those that buy rum of them have so many Mouthfulls for a Buck-Skin, they never using any other Measure; and for this purpose the Buyer always makes choice of his Man, which is one that has the greatest Mouth, whom he brings to the Market with a Bowl to put it in. The Seller looks narrowly to the Man's Mouth that measures it, and if he happens to swallow any down, either through wilfulness or otherwise, the Merchant or some of the other Party does not scruple to throw the Fellow down, exclaming against him for false Measure. Thereupon, the Buyer finds another Mouthpiece to measure the rum by; so that this trading is very agreeable to the Spectators, to see such a deal of quarreling and controversy, as often happens about it, and is diverting.

DE GRAFFENRIED'S NARRATIVE

Baron Christopher de Graffenried secured for a colony of Swiss and Germans a tract of land at the junction of Neuse and Trent rivers. This settlement was called New Bern. The Indian name for the region was Chattoka, or Cartouca. The Baron claimed to have paid three times for the land: to the Lords Proprietors, to the surveyor-general, and to the "Indian King Taylor."[2]

In September, 1711, Surveyor-General Lawson invited the Baron to join him in a scouting expedition up Neuse River. The inducement of finding a quantity of good wild grapes did not win De Graffenried to consent to the journey, but the hope of discovering a shorter way to Virginia by river navigation was sufficient persuasion. The adventurers were accompanied by two slaves and two Indians. The river was low and travel was easy. Lawson had insisted that a horse should be taken along. One of the Indians rode the horse and by chance or treachery came to the

[2] A considerable portion of De Graffenried's narrative is given because the story is illuminating in its descriptions of Indians on the warpath.

Indian village Catechna. This name has been preserved as Contentnea. The Indians seized the horse and gave orders that the river-travelers should be detained. The boat had reached a location three days' travel upstream not far from an Indian village called Zurutha. The prisoners were forced to march by night through woods and swamps until three o'clock in the morning, when they arrived at Catechna. The chief, named Hancock, called a council, which decided that the prisoners should not be bound as criminals, and towards noon he brought them some food "in a lousy fur cap," bread made of Indian corn, and cold boiled venison.

Another council was held that night, which was attended by a great number of neighboring Indians with their chiefs. The assembly was held in a broad, open space especially prepared for festivities and executions. Chief Hancock presided, and the other chiefs sat with him in a ring around the great fire. Both prisoners were assigned places in the circle and sat upon mats made of woven reeds. At a sign from the chief, the orator of the assembly made a long speech with much gravity. One of the youngest members of the council was appointed to represent and defend the interests of the council and of the Indian nation. The presiding chief proposed the questions, which were vigorously debated. Consultation and decision followed.

The first question was: What was the cause of the journey? The answer was: for pleasure, to get grapes, to see if it were convenient to reach the Indians by water to bring goods to them, and to have good business with them. To this the chief complained that the travelers had not paid their respects to him and that they had not informed him of their project. Next came the complaint that the Indians had been badly treated and detained by the settlers, something no longer to be endured. Among others Lawson was accused in this charge. He defended himself as best he could. After considerable dispute and deliberation it was decided that the prisoners should be set free and allowed to return home next day.

On the following morning there was delay in securing the boat, and in the meantime another examination was held in the chief's lodge two miles away. The same promise of freedom was granted as before. Unfortunately, the chief of Cartuca was there, and reproached Lawson for something. A quarrel arose—that spoiled everything. Shortly afterwards several angry chiefs suddenly seized the travelers, roughly handled them, and set them forcibly in their former places. The angry Indians snatched the prisoners' hats and wigs, which they threw into the fire, and some of the young fellows plundered their pockets. A council of war condemned both to death. They remained sitting on the ground until morning. At daybreak they were led to a great assembly. De Graffenried by chance met an Indian who spoke English and asked him the cause of the condemnation. He replied with a disagreeable face: "Why had Lawson quarreled with Core Tom, and why had the prisoners threatened that they would get revenge on the Indians?" De Graffenried made great efforts to persuade the Indian that a mistake had been made, saying that he regretted Lawson's imprudence in quarreling with Core Tom, and as to threatening, it was a misunderstanding, or else Lawson's complaining of the slaves' having disturbed his rest the first night, whereupon De Graffenried had threatened the slaves for their "impudence." A quarter of an hour later the prisoners were led out and bound hand and foot. The Baron thus described the scene:

In the middle of this great space we sat bound side by side, sitting upon the ground, the Surveyor-General and I, coats off and bare headed; behind me the larger of my negroes; before us was a great fire and around about the fire the conjurer, that is, an old gray Indian, a priest among them, who is commonly a magician, yes, even conjures up the devil himself. He made two rings either of meal or very white sand, I do not know which. Right before our feet lay a wolf skin. A little farther in front stood an Indian in the most dignified and terrible posture that can be imagined. He did not leave the place. Ax in hand, he looked to be the executioner. Farther away, before us and beyond the fire, was a numerous Indian rabble, young fellows, women, and children. They all danced in the most abominable postures. In the middle was the priest or conjurer, who, whenever there was a pause in the dance, made his conjurations and threats. About the dance or ring at each of the four corners stood a sort of officer with a gun. They beat time with their feet and urged on the other dancers and when a dance was over shot off their guns. Besides this, in a corner of the ring, were two Indians sitting on the ground, who beat upon a little drum and sang, and sang so strangely to it, in such a melody, that it would provoke anger and sadness rather than joy. Yes, the Indians themselves, when tired of dancing, would all run away suddenly into the forest with frightful cries and howling, but would soon come back out of the forest with faces striped black, white, and red. Part of them, besides this, would have their hair hanging loose, full of feathers, down, and some in the skins of all sorts of animals: In short in such monstrous shapes that they looked more like a troop of devils than like other creatures; if one represents the devil in the most terrible shape that can be thought of, running and dancing out of the forest. They arranged themselves in the old places and danced about the fire. Meanwhile there were two rows of armed Indians behind us as a guard, who never left their post until all was over: Back of this watch was the council of war sitting in a ring on the ground very busy in consultation.

Towards evening the dancing ceased and the Indians began to gather wood for their several fires. The narrative states, "But especially they made one at some distance in the forest which lasted the whole night and was so great that I thought the whole forest was afire."

De Graffenried counted all lost and sought the consolations of prayer. Strengthened and more composed, he addressed the throng of Indians, knowing that one of them spoke English, and giving promise and assurance of reward for his delivery. He noticed that one of the Indians, who proved to be of the tribe from which the land of New Bern had been purchased, was affected and spoke earnestly with others. The warrior's plea was effective in gaining delay. The Indians dispatched runners with messages to the neighboring Tuscarora villages, and to a chief of great renown, Tom Blount. The messengers returned about three o'clock in the morning with their replies. An Indian came after awhile and released De Graffenried, who knew not whether it meant death or freedom. The Baron wrote: "Oh how dumbfounded I was when, some paces from the old place, the Indian said to me in my ear, in broken English, that I should not fear, they would not kill me, but that they would kill General Lawson. This went to my heart."

The fettered slave was also released, but was never seen again. The unfortunate Lawson was executed. Of his fate, De Graffenried stated:

To be sure I had heard before from several savages that the threat had been made that he was to have his throat cut with a razor which was found in his sack. The smaller negro, who was left alive, also testified to this; but some say he was hanged; others that he was burned. The savages kept it very secret how he was killed. May God have pity on his soul.

A letter of Major Gale, dated November 2, 1711, stated that if the reports of the Indians were true, the executioners stuck the unfortunate prisoner "full of fine small splinters of torchwood, like hogs' bristles, and so set them gradually on fire."

We cannot review this fearful tragedy without a sense of deep regret that this man who had dealt long and intimately with the Indians of Carolina, who understood them so well and portrayed them so admirably, and who often spoke so kindly of them, should have met such a cruel fate at their hands.

The Tuscarora War

The execution of Lawson was the first of the hostilities that marked the outbreak of the Tuscarora War. While De Graffenried was still a prisoner, the murderous bands of Indians started on the warpath. Their plot had been carefully and secretly made. Allied with the Tuscarora under Chief Hancock were the Coree or Coranine, Pamlico, Machapungo or Mattamuskeet, Bear or Bay River Indians, and others. The warriors scattered according to their tribal territory, and foraying parties were dispersed over the country to attack the settlers along the Pamlico, Neuse, and Trent rivers and in adjacent territory. Five hundred warriors advanced stealthily to rush upon the unsuspecting settlers. The frontiersmen were wholly unprepared. They had become accustomed to dealing generally unmolested by the Indians, who were frequently employed as servants. There was no warning until in the early morning hours of September 22 the war whoop sounded its signal of peril.

The fury of the murderous invaders spared none who came in their path. Men, women, and children were killed, and atrocities of savage warfare were committed. Houses were plundered and set afire. The massacre continued for three days, spreading death and destruction through the lately peaceful settlements. In the up-river country 130 victims lay dead, 60 or more around New Bern, and many others in regions beyond. This was the most terrible disaster that ever befell the colony in Indian warfare.

MORE ABOUT DE GRAFFENRIED

On the day after Lawson's execution the Indians told De Graffenried of their intentions to make war on North Carolina, and of their especial desire to surprise the people along the Pamlico, Neuse, and Trent rivers, and Core Sound. For this reason they would not allow him to leave until this expedition had been carried out. A few days after the massacre they returned, first from Pamlico and later from Neuse and Trent rivers, with their plunder, bringing women and children captives. The Indian who lodged De Graffenried brought back a boy, the son of one of the Baron's tenants. Weeping bitterly, the little fellow told of how his father, mother, and brother—all the rest of the family—had been slain by this same Indian.

A band of sixty colonists came out against the Indians. Although they did not come near enough to the Indian settlement to enable the prisoner to see them, De Graffenried knew there were Germans in the party because the alarmed Indians made mocking exclamations, "Ja! ja!" In haste the old men, women, and children were sent to a safe place in the swamps while the warriors went out to meet their foes. After a brief skirmish the colonists were driven back. The Baron told how the Indians celebrated their victory:

So these wild warriors or murderers who were in great glory came in triumph home; and we also went out of our place of concealment in the evening, and traveled the whole night through, back again to our old quarters in Catechna. They made great fires of rejoicing, especially in the place of execution, on which occasion they hung up three wolf hides, representing as many protectors or gods. At the same time the women made offerings of their ornaments, such as necklaces of wampum, which is a kind of coral of calcined mussels, white, brown, and gold colored.

In the midst of the ring was a conjurer acting as their priest, who made all sorts of strange motions and adjurations; and the rest danced in a ring about the fire and the above mentioned skins.

Two days later the Indians led De Graffenried two hours' distance from the village, gave him a piece of Indian bread, and allowed him to journey home afoot. He had not been badly treated by his captors. His account states:

I can here also not forget the generosity and sympathy of a good widow, who, immediately at my arrival and during my captivity, always brought me food, so that there was never any lack of food with me. But the most remarkable thing was, as soon as she had seen that when I was bound young fellows plundered me (among other things, my silver rings were taken from my shoes and these were held on by a small cord only), she took some of her pretty brass buckles through which she had drawn her hair bands on her forehead and fastened them on my shoes, and had no rest until she had discovered what Indian had taken my buckles, and had traded with him and gotten them. She came running back full of joy and put the silver buckles on my shoes. This was indeed a great kindness from a savage, enough to bring conviction to many Christians. I must say here to the shame of Christians, that all in all, the Indians are much more generous. I have observed many good things from them, such as—they do not swear, keep their word exactly whatever they promise, do not quickly quarrel in their games, are not so avaricious, there is not so much haughtiness; among their young people also, I have not noticed anything improper. . . . The bad thing about them is that their rage is furious.

They seldom offend the Christians without having some motive for it, and, the greatest part of the time, the abuse comes from the Christians, who deal roughly with them. I spoke with several Indians about their cruelty, but an Indian King, a man of good sense, answered me in comparing the Indian with a snake: Leave it alone, coiled up as it is, do not hurt it, and it will hurt no living creature,—but disturb its rest and it strikes and bites.

Here is to be observed, that when the above mentioned savage warriors or rather murderers came in with their booty and prisoners, the priest and the leading women seized the poor prisoners, compelled them to go into the dance, and if they did not wish to dance they caught them under the arms and dragged them up and down, as a sign that these Christians were now dancing to their music and were subject to them.

And so these heathenish ceremonies may be considered a sort of sacred litany or divine worship. In the morning I observed at times that they sang a serious little song instead of a prayer; and when they are in great danger, the same.

DEFEAT

Urgent appeal for help resulted in the sending of a detachment of soldiers from South Carolina under command of Colonel Barnwell. He arrived at New Bern with his militiamen in January, 1712, accompanied by five hundred Indian allies. This heterogeneous army had been recruited largely from the wasted tribes to the south and west of the Tuscarora. Some of them still fought with bows and arrows, as indicated by the mention of bowmen in Captain Bull's company. This captain made a circuit while the patchwork troops were straggling north and brought in recruits from the tribes situated near the line of march. Two days were required for the crossing of Cape Fear River on logs and rafts. The friendly Indians of the expedition were listed by Colonel Barnwell as follows:

In Capt. Steel's Troop

30	White men
158	Yamasses
155	Essaws [Catawba and kindred tribes]
182	Capt. Bull's

Including Captain Bull, Major Mackey, and Colonel Barnwell, the total reached 528. The companies were composed as follows:

Yamasse Company

Yamasses	87
Hog Logees	10
Apalatchees	56
Corsaboy	5
	158

Essaw Capt. Jack's Company

Watterees	28	
Sagarees	20	[Sugaree]
Catabas	40	
Saterees	27	[Santee]
Waxaws	27	
Congrees and Sattees	13	
	155	

Capt. Bull's Company

Watterees	28	[?]³
Pedees	18	
Weneaws	24	
Cape Fear	11	
Hoopengs	11	
Wareperes	9	
	117	[?]

Added to Capt. Bull's Company

Saraws	42
Saxpahaws	22
	181

The crossing was made on January 28 at a place where the Saxapahaw, formerly of Haw River, had lately settled. Colonel Barnwell stated that the Saxapahaw, "called by some Shacioes," had been forced to desert this settlement in the beginning of the month by reason that the Tuscarora of this town fell upon them and killed sixteen of them because they refused to join in the war against the English; that "they had just come among the Wattomas [Waccamaw], when I came and were going to pay their tribute" to the governor and to beg his protection. Colonel Barnwell added, "But I desired them not to do it until our return, and go with me, they seeming to me brave men and good."

Most numerous were the Yamassee of South Carolina, a tribe of Muskhogean stock. The Catawba Indians had been urged by the Carolina authorities to join the expedition with the promise that they would be supplied with goods "cheaper than formerly" if the campaign were successful. The Catawba and other Siouan tribes needed little persuasion, for they had long been at enmity with the Iroquois of the north and were glad to strike a blow at the proud Tuscarora. There was prospect of much booty, including prisoners whom they could sell as slaves. Colonel Barnwell numbered his men before crossing Neuse River and complained that many of the Indians had deserted—only sixty-seven of Captain Bull's two hundred recruits remained.

³ There is evidently an error in naming this tribe.

The Tuscarora and their allies had erected a palisade enclosing two log houses, called Fort Narhantes. The name Fort Barnwell identifies the region today. On January 30 Colonel Barnwell's men stormed the stronghold and captured it, meeting strong resistance. The commander complained that while "we were putting the men to the sword, our Indians got all the slaves and the plunder, only one girl we got." The Carolinians lost 7 white men, and 32 were wounded; of their allied Indians, 6 were killed and 28 wounded. The Tuscarora loss was 52 men and at least 10 women killed, and 30 prisoners. De Graffenried called the fortified place Core Town, and he is responsible for the assertion that the Indian allies of the colonists "drove the King and his Indians out of the same after they had slain several, got into such a frenzy over it that they cooked and ate the flesh of one of the Carolina Indians that had been shot down." The reference indicates that the Coranine were prominent among the defenders of Fort Narhantes. It is the only reference to cannibalism found in the records of the Indians of North Carolina.

Colonel Barnwell advanced his forces to Catechna, Chief Hancock's quarters, where Weetock, Bay River, Neuse, Core, and Pamlico Indians were said to be joined with the Tuscarora. Two attacks against the fort were repulsed, and Barnwell entered into a truce with the defenders on condition that they liberate the white prisoners held there.

Then Colonel Barnwell returned to New Bern expecting to receive honors and rewards from the North Carolina government. Little was forthcoming. Under pretense of peace he assembled a number of friendly Indians at Core Town and carried them away to South Carolina to be sold into slavery. De Graffenried wrote: "This so unchristian act very properly embittered the rest of the Tuscarora and Carolina Indians very much, although heathens, so that they no longer trusted the Christians."

The resentment of the Indians caused them to renew border warfare and to carry on repeated attacks along Neuse and Pamlico rivers. Again the North Carolina government called for aid and again South Carolina responded. Colonel Moore, with 33 militiamen and 900 Indians, set out to join the North Carolina forces.

A considerable body of the Tuscarora had not been involved

in the hostilities. Most of these were of the northern towns of the tribe under the leadership of able Chief Tom Blount. The aid of these Indians was sought by the government, and agreement was made with them that they should seize and deliver the participants in the massacre. Fair promises were made for the security and future welfare of these friendly Tuscarora. Before anything resulted from these plans, Colonel Moore arrived on the scene. In March, 1713, his motley army moved against Chief Hancock's fortified town at Catechna, called Necheroka, or Nahucke, in what is now Greene County near Snow Hill. The siege was begun on March 20 and continued three days. The Tuscarora fought desperately. De Graffenried wrote: "The savages showed themselves unspeakably brave, so much so that when our soldiers had become masters of the fort and wanted to take out the women and children who were under ground, where they were hidden along with their provisions, the wounded savages who were groaning on the ground still continued to fight." Colonel Moore stated that 392 prisoners were taken, 192 scalps were secured in the fort, 200 Indians were killed or burned in the fort, and 166 persons were killed or captured outside —a total loss of 950. The colonists lost 22 killed and 36 wounded; their Indian allies, 35 killed and 58 wounded. The prisoners were taken by their captors to South Carolina and sold as slaves.[4]

This was a crushing blow for the Tuscarora. They fled to another fort called Cahunke, or Cohunche, but did not tarry long. They were soon fleeing northward to join their kinsmen as the sixth nation of the Iroquois Confederacy. Their passage through Pennsylvania gave the name to Tuscarora Creek and Valley in Wyoming County. The northward flight of the Tuscarora continued for years. Loskiel stated that in 1766 seventy-five halted for a stay at the Moravian mission station at Friedenshuetten, Pennsylvania. This remnant of a once proud race was described as lazy and "refusing to hear religion." It is recorded that they were so alarmed at the first sight of snow that they left their huts

[4] "It is known that the prisoners of Col. Barnwell and Col. Moore were all sold as slaves, even the northern markets being canvassed for a market for them; indeed, the *Boston News Letter* of 1713 contained an advertisement offering these very Indians for purchase" (F. W. Hodge, *Handbook of American Indians*, Part 2, p. 844).

and sought refuge with the missionaries. Perhaps it was not merely the sight of snow, but the sight of a Pennsylvania snow that alarmed them, as some of us can testify that the light snows of eastern Carolina are little to be compared with Pennsylvania blizzards.

After the close of the war the friendly Tuscarora and remnants of other tribes in eastern North Carolina were united under authority of Chief Tom Blount. The reservation first assigned to them was on the Pamlico River, but as this location left the few survivors exposed to raids from Indians south of them, another reservation was selected in the present Bertie County along the Roanoke River. Some of this region is still known as "Indian Woods."

It was here that Bishop Spangenberg visited them in 1752. His diary entry for September 15, written at Edenton, notes:

The Indians in North Carolina are in a bad way. The Chowan Indians are reduced to a few families, and their land has been taken from them. The Tuscaroras live 35 miles from here, and are still in possession of a pretty piece of land. Those that are still here are much despised, and will probably soon come to an end. I asked one whether the Five Nations were their brothers, and he crooked two fingers, linking them together like a chain. Brother Antes asked the same question of others, and one of them crooked his arm and linked it into that of the other, and then embraced him.

Spangenberg's diary under date of September 25 states:

We also visited the Tuscaroras, who live on the Roanoke. They have a tract of good land, secured to them by Act of Assembly; I should judge that it contains twenty or thirty thousand acres. It is twelve miles long, but not wide.

Their interpreter, Mr. Thomas Whitemeal, was kind to us, took us to them, showed us their land, and introduced us to them. He was at one time a Trader among them, understands their language fairly well, and speaks it with ease. Now he is one of the richest men in the neighborhood, and is respected by everybody.

The Indians have no king, but a Captain elected from among them by the whites. There are also several Chiefs among them.

The Tuscaroras are few in number, and they hold with the Six Nations against the Catawbas, but suffer much on this account. They live in great poverty, and are oppressed by the whites.

Mr. Whitemeal is their Agent and Advocate, and stands well with them.

Hitherto no one has tried to teach them of their God and Saviour.

They told us that if we saw the Catawbas we should tell them that there are plenty of young men among the Tuscaroras who knew the way to the Catawba town, and that they could go and return in about twenty days. That so far they had kept quiet and had not gone into the Catawba country except to hunt a little, and they would do no more unless they were disturbed,—then they knew the way to the Catawba town.

We were courteously treated by the Indians, and they sent greetings by us to the Shawanos [Shawnee] on the Susquehannah.

The last chief of the Tuscarora in North Carolina was Samuel Smith, who died in 1802.

During the Revolution the greater part of the tribe in the North espoused the cause of the colonists. Their settlements were raided, their lodges burned, and their crops destroyed. A large part of them sought refuge in Niagara County, New York. A reservation was finally granted to them in New York State, the home of the surviving members of the tribe in the United States.[5] About the year 1802 the North Carolina legislature allowed $13,722 in return for a lease on the lands in this state. It may be said to the credit of North Carolina that the government attempted to deal fairly with the Indians. Hawks says in this connection:

Finally they joined their countrymen in New York; but their descendants still retained the title to the lands granted to them, regularly collected their rents by their agents, were protected and sustained by the legislature in their just claims, and when obliged, in some instances, to resort to law, a solemn adjudication of the highest tribunal in the State was made in their favor; so that they were never robbed of one foot of their lands; and though their title is now extinct, yet it was all bought and honestly paid for at full value. There is not a State in the confederacy that has dealt more honestly with the natives than North Carolina; and, with the exception of the unhappy war of 1711, into which the poor savage was deluded by designing and bad men, not one in which more uniformly amicable relations subsisted between the whites and the Indians than in North Carolina.

[5] The author's grandparents on their wedding journey bought a beaded pincushion and other souvenirs from Tuscarora survivors at Niagara Falls.

The amount received from the sale of the North Carolina lands was used by the Secretary of War to purchase 4,329 acres of land to add to their reservation in New York. The Tuscarora who adhered to the cause of Great Britain in the Revolution were granted lands on Grand River reservation, located now in Ontario. The two branches in the north numbered in 1910 a population of about 780. An educational report of 1932 stated that there were 402 inhabitants of the Tuscarora reservation in Niagara County. "In some sports Indian pupils excel white children; the Tuscarora Indian basketball team had not lost a game to a white team of similar school age."

The names of their clans are still remembered: Bear, Wolf, Turtle, Beaver, Deer, Eel, and Snipe. Today they are all professed Christians. A native Tuscarora, Elias Johnson, furnished much information as to legends and history of his tribe. One of the descendants of Chief Blount is said to have married into the royal family of Hawaii.

There are traditions that some of the Tuscarora remained in the South, and that some survivors were relocated in North Carolina.

A recent story tells of a student of sociology who visited the Tuscarora on their reservation in New York State. He was seeking information about their recreational pursuits.

"What do you do for amusement?" he asked.

"We go to the movies," was the reply.

"What kind of movies do you see?"

"Indians and cowboys."

"Do you enjoy the pictures?"

"Yes; we always get beat, but we like to go just the same."

———

Chief Tom Blount deserves honorable mention as a friend of the colonists. Amid the perils of the Tuscarora War he remained friendly to the settlers, and it was doubtless through his influence that a considerable number of Tuscarora warriors did not engage in that conflict. He is mentioned no less than sixty times in the Colonial Records of North Carolina. On November 4, 1712, a treaty signed by Chief Blount and five lower chiefs pledged aid to the colonists. The original copy of this treaty has been preserved. Governor Pollock wrote of him, "I have great reason to believe that he is real and hope we shall find him so." The Governor's belief was apparently well founded.

REFERENCES

Barnwell, John. "Journal," *Virginia Magazine of History and Biography*, VI (1898), 42-55.

The Colonial Records of North Carolina. Edited by William L. Saunders. Vol. I. Raleigh, 1886.

De Graffenried, Thomas P. *History of the De Graffenried Family Including the Landgrave's Own Story*. New York, 1925.

Fries, Adelaide L. (ed.). *Records of the Moravians in North Carolina*. Vol. I. Raleigh, 1922.

Hawks, F. L. *History of North Carolina*. Vol. II. Fayetteville, N. C., 1858.

Hodge, F. W. *Handbook of American Indians North of Mexico*. Bulletin No. 30, Bureau of American Ethnology. Part 2. Washington, 1910.

Lawson, John. *History of North Carolina*. London, 1714.

Lederer, John. *Discoveries*. London, 1672.

Loskiel, George Henry. *History of the Mission among the Indians*. German ed., Barby, 1789; English ed., London, 1794.

Norment, Mary C. *The Lowrie History*. Wilmington, N. C., 1875.

CHAPTER VI

Discoveries of John Lederer

A GERMAN DOCTOR, John Lederer, of whom little is known, may be called the Father of Explorers in the Piedmont. On May 20, 1670, he left James River, Virginia, with a Major Harris, "twenty Christian horse," and five Indians, and marched westward. On account of a disagreement, on June 5 all turned back except Lederer and a Susquehanna Indian guide, Jackzetavon. Four days later the traveler and his guide arrived at Sapony, an Indian town situated near Staunton River, south of the present Lynchburg. The Indians received Lederer kindly and went so far as to offer him a particular favor, a chief's daughter in marriage. The doctor wrote: "But I, though with much a-do, waved their courtesie, and got my passport, having given my word to return to them within six months." If the bride-to-be tarried upon this promise of a return, she is still waiting.

The next town visited was the Occaneechee village[1] on an island at the junction of Staunton and Dan rivers, described as a well-fortified habitation provided with abundant crops of corn. The tribe was governed by two chiefs, "one presiding in arms, the other in hunting and husbandry." According to the traveler's narrative, "they hold all things, except their wives, in common," and "their costume in eating is, that every man in his turn feasts all the rest; and he that makes the entertainment is seated betwixt the two kings; where having highly commended his own chear, they carve and distribute it amongst the guests."

On the day following Lederer's arrival, a Rickohockan ambassador attended by five Indians, warriors from beyond the Blue Ridge, was received and the same night invited to a tribal dance. In the midst of the festivities the lodge was suddenly darkened and all the visiting Indians were barbarously murdered.

[1] Lederer was evidently in error as to direction.

Lederer and his guide, frightened by the tragedy, slipped away in haste the next morning, June 14. They traveled south-southwest for two days, sometimes by a beaten path and sometimes over hills and rocks, and reached the Eno Indians at their village not far from the present Hillsboro.[2] The settlement was described as follows:

The country here, by the industry of these Indians, is very open and clear of wood. Their town is built round a field, where in their sports they exercise with so much labour and violence, and in so great numbers, that I have seen the ground wet with sweat that dropped from their bodies: their chief recreation is slinging of stones. They are of mean stature and courage, covetous and thievish, industrious to earn a penny; and therefore hire themselves out to their neighbours, who employ them as carryers or porters. They plant abundance of grain, reap three crops in a summer,[3] and out of their granary supply all the adjacent parts. These and the mountain-Indians build not their houses of bark, but of watling and plaister. . . . Some houses they have of reed or bark; they build them generally round: to each house belongs a little hovel made like an oven, where they lay up their corn and mast, and keep it dry. They parch their nuts and acorns over the fire, to take away their rank oyliness; which afterwards pressed, yeeld a milky liquor, and the acorns an amber-colour'd oyl. In these, mingled together, they dip their cakes at great entertainments, and so serve them up to their guests as an extraordinary dainty. Their government is democratick; and the sentences of their old men are received as laws, or rather oracles, by them.

Though centuries have passed, this region retains some of its ancient characteristics. Not far from Eno Town the young braves of North Carolina and Duke universities still carry on ball play with much labor and violence, the government of the country is still Democratic, and the three crops a year are possible for farmers who space corn plantings properly.

The Eno Indians as described by the narrative seem to have declined considerably from the strong tribe called Haynoke mentioned in the Yardley letter, who once valiantly resisted the northern advance of the Spaniard.

[2] The Archaeological Society of North Carolina investigated the Eno River valley at Hillsboro and located the site of an Indian village.

[3] The John White pictures show the corn planting of the Indians with early and late corn in the same field.

Fourteen miles west-southwest Lederer found the Shackory Indians dwelling upon a rich soil. These seem to tally with the Shakori (Shoccoree), or Saxapahaw, sometimes called Sissipahaw, dwelling on Haw River in the neighborhood of Haw Fields.

More than forty miles southwest, in what is probably now a valley location in Randolph County, were the Watary Indians, possibly the Wateree. Lederer wrote of them:

> This nation differs in government from all other Indians of these parts: for they are slaves, rather than subjects to their king. Their present monarch is a grave man, and courteous to strangers: yet I could not without horrour behold his barbarous superstition, in hiring three youths, and sending them forth to kill as many young women of their enemies as they could light on, to serve his son, then newly dead, in the other world, as he vainly fancyed. These youths during my stay returned with skins torn off the heads and faces of three young girls, which they presented to his majestie, and were by him gratefully received.

On June 21 Lederer took up a westerly course which he traveled for thirty miles and came to Sara. This settlement was described as being near the mountains or hills which received from the Spaniards the name Suala, a reminder of Xualla, applied by De Soto to the Indians found on the southern border of the state. The name Uwharrie, designating a river and a range of small mountains, may be a survival. From these mountains the Indians procured minerals for making paint to adorn their faces. These Saura Indians occupied the Yadkin River valley near the famous crossing at Trading Ford. The little boys of the village brought into play their bows and arrows, using Lederer's horse for a target, as unruly boys of our day might direct their peashooters or slingshots at some strange animal. The Indians did not exercise rigorous parental restraint; hence Lederer went to the rescue of his steed and spurred the animal out of danger, but not before one of the Indian boys, angered because the visitor interrupted the target practice, nearly sent an arrow through the rider's body. The traveler made another hasty getaway.

On June 25, three days later, he reached Wisacky, or Waxhaw, in the neighborhood of the present Union County. On the day following he arrived among the Usheryes,[4] or Catawba, and came to a village more populous than any he had previously met. These Indians were at war with the Oustack Indians, probably the Westoes, described as warriors greatly feared by their enemies. Of the Catawba, the narrative states:

The Ushery-women delight in feather ornaments, of which they have a great variety; but peacock[5] in most esteem, because rare in those parts. They are reasonably handsome, and have more of civility in their carriage than I observed in the other nations with whom I conversed; which is the reason that the men are more effeminate and lazie.

These miserable wretches are strangely infatuated with illusions of the devil: it caused no small horrour in me, to see one of them wrythe his neck all on one side, foam at the mouth, stand bare-foot upon burning coals for near an hour, and then recovering his senses, leap out of the fire without hurt or signe of any.

The terrors of the way apparently gave the German doctor a case of the jitters. Since he had heard that bearded men, whom he judged to be Spaniards, dwelt two and one-half days' journey to the southwest, and that the northwestern territory was overrun by the tribe we know as Cherokee, he decided to return by an eastern route. After an arduous journey through the sand hills and pine barrens of eastern Carolina, including a brief halt at a Tuscarora stronghold, he passed on through the Meherrin and Nottoway villages and arrived on July 18 in familiar territory where he was "not a little overjoyed to see Christian faces again."

––––––––

Lederer offered this advice to prospective traders with the Indians:

[4] Lake Ushery, described by Lederer and shown on his map, does not fit into Carolina geography. Mooney suggested that he reached the Catawba River in flood season, and mistook flood waters for a lake. Lederer's description of an extensive marsh between the Saura and the Catawba might refer to rain-soaked country of the Yadkin watershed; it was the time of summer freshets. Dr. William P. Cumming, of Davidson College, has an explanation of Lederer's Lake Ushery that merits consideration: that the lake is derived from the traveler's imagination in attempting to put into his picture a mythical body of water of the southeast, which beguiled other cartographers.

The rivers charted on Lederer's return through eastern Carolina—Eruco, Torpaeo, and Rorenock alias Shonan—correspond with Neuse, Tar, and Roanoke or Chowan.

[5] Feathers of some Carolina wild fowl were probably wrongly identified by Lederer; there were no peacocks.

If you barely designe a home-trade with neighbour-Indians, for skins of deer, beaver, otter, wild-cat, fox, racoon, etc. your best truck is a sort of course trading cloth, of which a yard and half makes a matchcoat or mantle fit for their wear; as also axes, hoes, knives, sizars, and all sorts of edg'd tools. Guns, powder and shot, etc. are commodities they will greedily barter for: but to supply the Indian with arms and ammunition is prohibited in all English governments.

In dealing with the Indians, you must be positive and at a word: for if they perswade you to fall anything in your price, they will spend time in higgling for further abatements, and seldom conclude any bargain. Sometimes you may with brandy or strong liquor dispose them to an humour of giving you ten times the value of your commodity; and at other times they are so hide-bound, that they will not offer half the market-price, especially if they are aware that you have a designe to circumvent them with drink, or that they think you have a desire to their goods, which you must esteem to slight and disparage.

To the remoter Indians, you must carry other kinde of truck, as small looking-glasses, pictures, beads and bracelets of glass, knives, sizars, and all manner of gaudy toys and knacks for children, which are light and portable. For they are apt to admire such trinkets, and will purchase them at any rate, either with their currant coyn of small shells, which they call roanoack or peack, or perhaps with pearl, vermilion, pieces of christal; and towards Ushery, with some odde pieces of plate or bullion, which they sometimes receive in truck from the Oestacks.

REFERENCES

Cumming, William P. "Geographical Misconceptions of the Southeast in the Cartography of the Seventeenth and Eighteenth Centuries," *Journal of Southern History*, VI (1938), 532-557.

Gregg, Alexander. *History of the Old Cheraws*. New York, 1867.

Hawks, F. L. *History of North Carolina*. Vol. II. Fayetteville, N. C., 1858.

Lederer, John. *Discoveries*. London, 1672.

Rights, Douglas L. "The Trading Path to the Indians," *North Carolina Historical Review*, VIII (1931), 403-426.

Swanton, John R. *Early History of the Creek Indians and Their Neighbors*. Bulletin No. 73, Bureau of American Ethnology. Washington, 1922.

CHAPTER VII

A Trading Ford Tragedy

ABRAHAM WOOD was a prominent trader of Fort Henry, now Petersburg, Virginia. He sought to open up the back country for more extensive Indian trade.[1] In May, 1673, he sent out a scouting expedition consisting of two Englishmen and ten Indians. They met a party of Tomahitan Indians[2] from the mountain country to the west, who agreed to lead the way to their settlements. The white men were James Needham, a gentleman of some prominence in the colony, and Gabriel Arthur, an illiterate youth possessing courage and adaptability. With their Indian escort they traveled to the island home of the Occaneechee at the confluence of Dan and Staunton rivers. The island-dwellers were a strong tribe, fierce and warlike, and their power was feared by neighboring tribes. So great was their influence that the religious ritual of the Indians for miles around was in their tongue. They controlled the back-country trade, forcing traders to pass through their island gateway to the hinterland of the Piedmont, and compelling the westward Indians to transport their furs via Occaneechee Town. Their advantage in trade resulted in prosperity that later caused their downfall.

Needham and Arthur left Occaneechee with a lone Appamattox Indian, as the island tribesmen allowed none of the other Virginia Indians of the party to accompany the travelers. Their nine days' journey west and by south, across nine rivers and creeks, carried them over the Trading Path traveled three years before by Lederer. They arrived at Sittaree, probably the Catawba capital at the mouth of Sugar Creek, which derives its name from the Sugaree Indians, kindred of the Catawba. Here they left the

---

[1] This narrative is recorded in Abraham Wood's letter published by Alvord and Bidgood in *First Explorations of the Trans-Allegheny Regions*.

[2] See *Early History of the Creek Indians and Their Neighbors*, by John R. Swanton.

beaten path and set out for the mountains.[3] They crossed the Blue Ridge and journeyed west, sighting the Great Smoky Mountains on their right.

At the end of fifteen days they arrived at the Tomahitan town, which seems to have been located on the river now called Tennessee. The two venturers and the lone horse that survived the rough travel were courteously and curiously inspected by the inhabitants, who had never before seen a horse. Needham returned to Fort Henry to report the success of the journey to his patron. Arthur was left to learn the language of the Tomahitan.

Abraham Wood was overjoyed at the report of his scout, and on September 20 sent him back accompanied by twelve Tomahitans who had returned with him. No news came to Wood after the party left Eno Town until January 27, when rumors were received that Needham had been killed by the Tomahitans. Thereafter reports followed thickly, brought by Indians who spoke vaguely of the affair lest they should bring suspicion on themselves. In February came Henry Hatcher, an English trader, who stated that he had been at Occaneechee when Needham started out on the second journey. Needham had been stopped there by the Indians, and only upon persuasion of Hatcher was he allowed to pass. Hatcher was certain that Needham had been killed, and he had heard the Occaneechee lay the blame on the Tomahitan party, but he had met an Occaneechee Indian, called Indian John, or Hasecoll, who had Needham's pistols and gun in his possession.

Not until Gabriel Arthur returned on June 18 was the mystery cleared. It was then learned that Needham traveled from Eno Town to Sarrah, a Saura Indian town,[4] with the Tomahitan and several Occaneechee, including Indian John. This last-named Indian had been paid for his services on the former journey, and was to be rewarded again on his return. As the party crossed Sarrah River (Uwharrie?), an Indian let his pack fall into the water, for which he was rebuked by Needham. Indian John took Needham to task and continued quarreling all day until the party

---

[3] The trail that suggests itself runs through Hickory Nut Gap by Chimney Rock and across the Blue Ridge.
[4] This was the village visited by Lederer.

reached Yattken Town at Yattken River[5] (first mention of the Yadkin). The crossing was made before nightfall and camp was pitched for the night, in all probability within sight of the famous Trading Ford. Indian John continued to rail at Needham until the latter seized his sword, threw a hatchet upon the ground, and challenged the Indian whether or not he meant violence. Indian John snatched up a rifle and fired a bullet into Needham's brain. The Tomahitan escort attempted a rescue, but too late, and began to lament the murder. Before the startled Indians the culprit brandished his knife, ripped open the body of the victim, tore out his heart, and held it aloft as he turned to the east and vented his rage at the English.

The young man, Arthur, who had been left with the Tomahitan, had a series of remarkable adventures rivaling any pioneer exploits on record. Most of these were engaged in beyond the borders of North Carolina, however, and do not come within the geographical limits of these stories. Our narrative is resumed where we find him in May, 1674, on his way back to the trading post.

The chief of Tomahitan and eighteen other Indians of the tribe, laden with packs of furs, traveled with Arthur and proceeded unmolested until they came to the Yadkin River settlement frequented by the Saura Indians, the scene of Needham's murder. Evidences of the crime were discovered when they saw some of the unfortunate Englishman's possessions scattered about on the ground. Four Occaneechee were lying in wait for them and made a night attack, frightening away the Saura townsmen and all the Tomahitan except one who had been a former captive among the Spaniards. With this companion Arthur took to the bushes, and although the Occaneechee hunted for their victim by aid of the bright moonlight, he was not discovered. In the morning Arthur came out of hiding and hired four Saura Indians of the village to carry to Eno the packs deserted by the fleeing Tomahitans. From Eno he traveled with his Indian companion, coming by nightfall within sight of the Occaneechee town. They forded the river and

[5] The meaning of the word *Yadkin*, derived from *Yattken*, or *Yattkin*, a Siouan Indian word, is unknown. In Siouan terminology it may mean "big tree," or "place of big trees."

crossed the island by night. On June 18 they reported to Abraham Wood.

REFERENCES

Alvord, Clarence W., and Bidgood, Lee. *The First Explorations of the Trans-Allegheny Regions by the Virginians.* Cleveland, 1912.

Rights, Douglas L. "The Trading Path to the Indians," *North Carolina Historical Review,* VIII (1931), 403-426.

Swanton, John R. *Early History of the Creek Indians and Their Neighbors.* Bulletin No. 73, Bureau of American Ethnology. Washington, 1922.

CHAPTER VIII

Lawson's Long Trail

On December 28, 1700, John Lawson set out from Charleston, South Carolina, on a long journey that was to follow a horseshoe-shaped course from the South Carolina coast around through the Piedmont country and eastward to the North Carolina coast. The first stages of his journey were in South Carolina territory. His descriptions of the Indians in this region, however, give information of Siouan tribes related to the North Carolina Piedmont stock, and are helpful for a better understanding of this great body of native inhabitants. Lawson is among the best of the early writers on the subject of the Indians. He explained why so few authentic accounts of the aborigines had been prepared, giving as his reason that most of the early travelers were "persons of the meaner sort, and generally of very slender education." We have Lawson to thank for excellent pen pictures of native tribes.

In the party leaving Charleston were six Englishmen, three Indian men, and an Indian woman, the wife of the guide. The voyage was made in what Lawson called a "large Canoe," past Sullivan's, Bell's, Dix, Bull's, and Raccoon islands to the mouth of the Santee River.

Near the entrance of the river a noise that sounded like an exchange of firearms proved to be the crackling of cane swamps fired by the Sewee Indians for the purpose of driving out game they were hunting. The Sewee had declined rapidly since their first contact with the colonists. Smallpox and rum had been the chief agents in their destruction. Further decline of the tribe had been hastened by an ambitious enterprise. They determined upon a bold resolution to take their wares direct to the foreign market, having seen the English ships sailing in from the east with their cargoes of merchandise for trade. They fitted out a large fleet of canoes laden with food, supplies, and merchandise, and embarked.

Their mat sails caught a favoring wind, but scarcely had it borne them out of sight of land when a sudden tempest swamped many of their frail vessels. The surviving mariners of the Sewee fleet were supposed to have been taken up by an English ship and carried away to be sold into slavery in the West Indies.

The Sewee Indian guide, whom Lawson called Scipio, fell from grace, and was left drunk among the Santee Indians next encountered.

The Santee settlements extended for miles along the river, although the nation was not nearly so strong as formerly. They were described as a "well-humored and affable people." The bottom lands of the Santee River furnished them with abundant crops of corn, which they stored in cribs set on posts six or eight feet above ground and daubed well with mud to keep out "the smallest insect." Cribs of this kind had been previously noted and frequently raided by Spaniards on the march. The Indians did not practice thieving with one another—only foreigners were to blame.

The travelers helped themselves to supplies at a hunter's cabin, leaving some small present in return, a custom in vogue. In this wayside refreshment Lawson mentioned Indian peas, beans, oil, chinquapin, corn, barbecued peaches, and peach bread. The last named has been until recent years often concocted by the rural folk of the Carolinas, who called it peach leather. Next day in a Santee settlement the party was given another treat, "fat barbacu'd Venison, which the Woman of the Cabin took and tore in pieces with her teeth, so put it into a mortar, beating it to Rags, afterwards stews it with Water, and other Ingredients, which makes a very savoury Dish."

Dignitaries of the tribe, their "King" and a "No-nosed Doctor" wearing a coat made of turkeys' feathers, appeared to pay their respects. Lawson found out from them many things of interest concerning their tribes: The chief had power to put to death any of his people who had committed a fault, although usually among Indians murder could be avenged by a relative of the victim unless gifts were acceptable to satisfy the avenger; the Indians were skilful in medical treatment, although he observed that the natives generally were credulous and notoriously cheated by their priests and conjurers; their burial customs were lengthy and involved. In regard to funerary rites, Lawson gave detailed information which would probably apply to other Siouan tribes, of mourning ceremonies, funeral oration, bestowal of possessions of the deceased, removal of flesh from the bones, etc. He stated that in some instances a pile of stones marked the tomb where an Indian was slain, and each passing warrior added another stone to the pile in respect for the deceased.

While here Lawson saw an Indian seven feet in height, the tallest he had yet discovered. This Santee was a renowned hunter whose method of following the deer may have been practiced widely. The hunter dressed in a deer skin surmounted by an antlered head of the animal. Thus appareled he could venture near a feeding herd or mingle with them. The story is carried rather far when the assertion is made that Indians disguised as deer have been so skilful that two hunters have stalked the same herd unknown to each other and one of them has been mistaken by the other for a deer and shot.

During a halt at a small settlement the travelers met another medicine man who told something of the little-known Hooks and Backhooks, Indians of Winyaw River, the lower Peedee.

Santee Jack was hired as guide in the place of the delinquent Scipio, and was straightway fortified with a stroudwater blanket.

Hills were now to be seen and the land was fertile. Game was abundant; the hunter brought in turkeys, opossums, and two polecats—the last named much esteemed by the natives. Beasts of prey lurked in the forests. Santee Jack was described as a good hunter and a well-humored fellow. He used a single ball for a shot and missed only two in forty. Lawson stated that when an Indian bought a gun that did not shoot to his liking, he would take the barrel out of the stock, cut a notch in a tree, place the barrel therein and bend it straight, sometimes shooting away a hundred loads before bringing the gun to shoot according to his desire.

Near the confluence of the Wateree and Congaree rivers, on the latter stream, they arrived at the Congaree town. This location is in the present Richland County. The town consisted of not over a dozen dwellings, although there were scattered settlements along the stream. The men were all away hunting in preparation for a feast, having left at home only women, who were busily engaged in gaming, keeping score of their winnings with piles of Indian corn. The gamesters received the travelers hospitably. The visitors were guests in the lodge of her royal highness, the chief's wife. These women smoked much tobacco and had pipes cut out of stone.

The Congaree had been much reduced by war, but had suffered far more from the ravages of smallpox. As with the Sewee and other tribes of the Carolinas, their treatment for smallpox was the well-known sweat bath. Patients remained in a heated lodge until they perspired freely, and then dashed outside and jumped into the river. It may have been possible that for some maladies this treatment was curative; for smallpox it was usually fatal to patients.

A new guide was hired, but although the travelers were up early the next day, according to Indian custom he would not set out until the sun was an hour or two high and had dried the dew. The guide maintained such a rapid pace, "walking like a Horse," that his patrons had to load him with a heavy pack of clothes and bedding in order to keep pace with him. On the way the same Indian shot at a "tyger," evidently a panther.

About sixty miles from the Congaree village the travelers reached the Weteree Chickanee Indians, or the Wateree, located near the river that today bears their name, not far from the present town of Great Falls. These Indians were more numerous than the Congaree. They were poor in trade goods, some of them using bows and arrows for lack of guns. Lawson called them the laziest Indians he had ever seen, since they possessed in a superlative degree this trait common to most Indians. They were so ingenious in pilfering that Lawson complained, "They will steal with their feet."

A few miles farther on the party arrived at the Waxhaw town, evidently near the creek of that name in the region which Lederer had reached thirty years before. Indians of this tribe were large of stature. They were called Flat Heads by their neighbors on account of their practice of strapping children on a cradle-board and placing a weight on the heads of the infants. It is asserted that this treatment made the children's eyes stand farther apart, which, the Indians believed, strengthened the sight and enabled the Flat Heads to discover game at greater distances.

This commendation is given of a cook of Lawson's host:

At our Waxhaw Landlord's Cabin was a woman employed in no other business than Cookery; it being a house of great Resort. The fire was surrounded with Roast Meat, or Barbakues, and the Pots continually boiling full of Meat, from Morning until Night. This She-cook was the cleanest I have ever seen among the Heathens of America, washing her hands before she undertook to do any Cookery; and repeated this useful Decency very often during the day. She made us as White-bread as any English could have done, and was full as neat and expeditious, in her affairs.

Another visitor put in his appearance. "There arrived an Ambassador from the King of Sapona, to treat with these Indians about some important affairs. He was painted with Vermillion all over his body, having a very large Cutlass stuck in his girdle, and a Fusee in his Hand." The emissary was from the Saponi Indians then living at Trading Ford on the Yadkin, with whom Lawson was to tarry later.

All the visitors were invited to share the festivities of the Waxhaw in commemoration of the plentiful harvest of corn gathered the summer before. The scene of the festal ceremonies was a large lodge built for the occasion, shaped like an immense haystack, thatched with sedge and rushes instead of being covered with bark as were ordinary dwellings. Some of the chief men of the village were assigned to dwell in the lodge and take care of it. It served as a state house in which public affairs were deliberated in council. The English visitors sat near the chief, and Lawson was assigned the position between the chief and the war captain of the tribe. The lodge was "as Dark as a Dungeon and as hot as one of the Dutch Stoves in Holland." A fire of split canes was burning in the middle of the floor, constantly replenished by a man employed in that particular occupation. Offerings of food were brought in by the Indians, everyone bringing something for the banquet. When the eatables were assembled, the hungry dogs were kicked out. After the dog-kicking ceremony a drum was beaten to summon attendance. The drum had been manufactured by stretching a dressed deerskin over an earthen pot.

Presently came in five men dressed up in Feathers, their Faces being covered with Vizards made of Gourds, round their Ancles and Knees were hung bells of several sorts, having Wooden Falchions in their Hands (such as Stage Fencers commonly Use); in this dress they danced about an hour, shewing many strange gestures, and brandishing their Wooden Weapons, as if they were going to fight each other; often walking very nimbly around the room without making the least noise with their bells (a thing I much admired at) again turning their bodies, arms and legs into such frightful postures, that you would have guessed they were quite raving mad. At last they cut two or three high capers and left the room. In their stead came in a parcel of women and girls, to the number of Thirty odd, every one taking place according to her degree of stature, the tallest leading the dance, and the least being placed last; with these they made a circular dance, like a ring, representing the shape of the fire they danced about; many of these had great Horse Bells about their legs, and small Hawks Bells about their necks. They had Musicians who were two Old Men, one of whom beat a Drum, while the other rattled with a Gourd, that had corn in it to make a noise withal; to these instruments they both sung a mournful ditty; the burthen of their song was In Remembrance of their former Greatness, and the Numbers of their Nation, the famous exploits of their renowned ancestors and all actions of moment that had (in former days) been performed by their forefathers.

The good "she-cook" who conducted the barbecue stand at Waxhaw was not missing in the jubilation, as the narrative relates:

Their way of Dancing is nothing but a sort of stamping motion much like the treading upon Founders Bellows. Their Female Gang held their dance for above six Hours, being all of them like a White Lather of a running Horse that has just come in from his race. My Landlady was the ring leader of the Amazons, who, when in her own House, behaved herself very discreetly and warily, in her domestic affairs, yet custom had so infatuated her, as to almost break her heart with dancing amongst such a confused Rabble. During this Dancing the spectators do not neglect their Business, in working the loblolly Pots, and other meat that was brought thither; more or less of them being continually eating, whilst the others were dancing.

The humor of this description must not blind us to the character of this festival, which was a ceremony of thanksgiving, enacted with sincerity and not without rhythmic charm. The

Plate 17

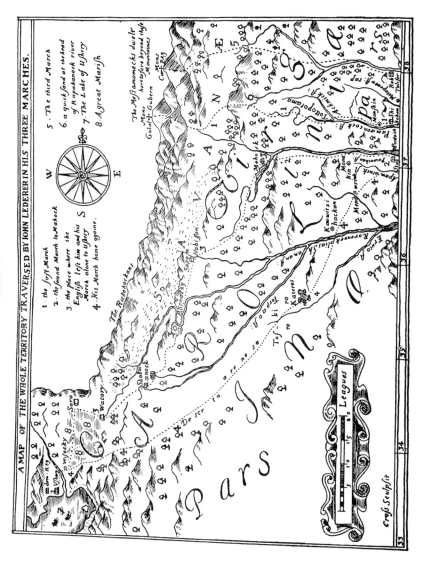

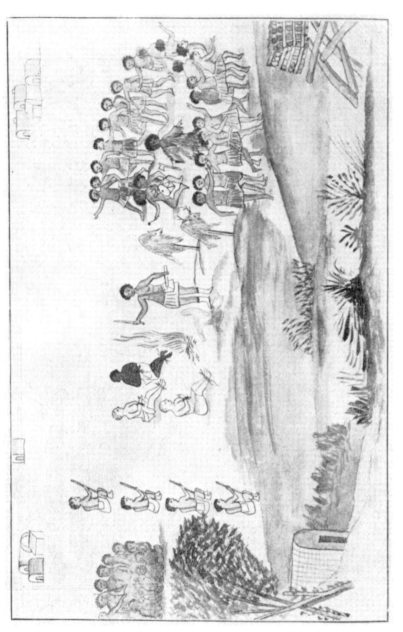

John Lawson Awaiting His Death

Photograph by courtesy of the State Department of Archives and History

Plate 19

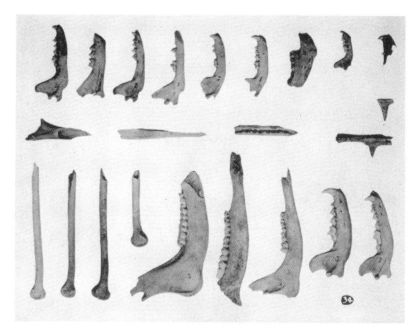

Bones of Wild Fowl and Animal Teeth from Donnaha Village Site
on Yadkin River

Photograph by Roy J. Spearman

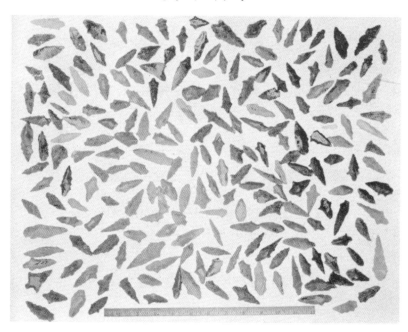

Arrowheads from Site in Randolph County, Made of Igneus Stone
Quarried Nearby

Photograph by Roy J. Spearman

Plate 20

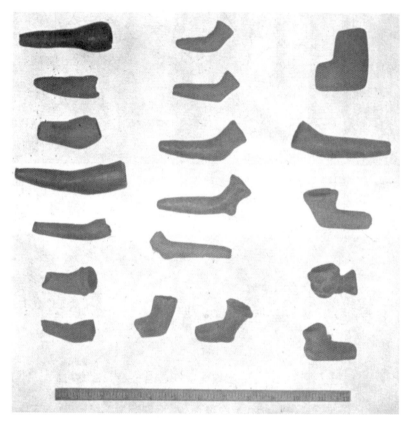

Series of Clay Pipes, Piedmont North Carolina

Photograph by Roy J. Spearman

Plate 21

Large Chipped-Stone Implements

Photograph by Roy J. Spearman

A Cache of Rhyolite Blades from Davidson County

(These were plowed up in a cornfield.)

Photograph by Roy J. Spearman

Plate 22

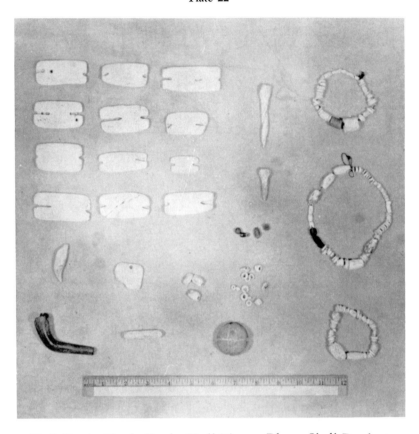

Shell Beads, Trade Beads, Shell Pins or Plugs, Shell Pendant,
Animal Tooth, Trade Pipe and Broken Stem, and
Paint Cup (Bottom View)—Keyauwee Site

Photograph by Roy J. Spearman

Plate 23

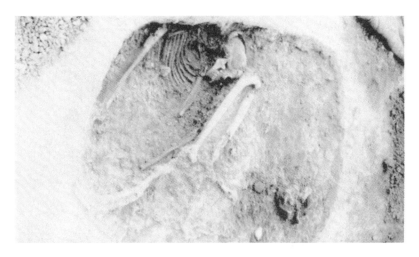

Burials at Keyauwee Village Site

Keyauwee Village Site, Randolph County

Plate 24

Rock Formations on Top of Ridge's Mountain in Randolph
County near Keyauwee Village Site

Photograph by the Author

Plate 25

Arrowheads and Scrapers Made from Quartz Crystals

Photograph by Herman Dezern

Plate 26

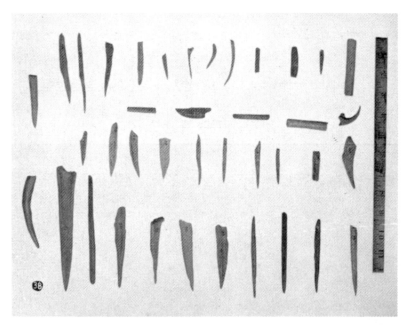

Tools and Fragments of Bone and Antler, Tubes from Bones
of Wild Fowl, Antler Arrow Point, a Tooth, and a Claw from
Donnaha Village Site

Photograph by Roy J. Spearman

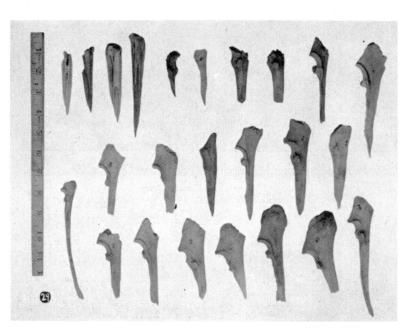

Bone Tools from Donnaha, Yadkin River
(Deer and turkey bones predominate.)

Photograph by Roy J. Spearman

Plate 27

Pilot Mountain

Photograph by Jim Keith

Pinnacle of Pilot Mountain

Photograph by courtesy of the North Carolina Department of Conservation and Development

Plate 28

Stone Disk, or Plate, Found below Badin on Yadkin River

Upper row (left to right): Pottery Vessels from the Dan,
Catawba, and Yadkin Rivers

Lower: Cone-shaped Pottery Vessel Found within the City
Limits of Winston-Salem

Photograph by Roy J. Spearman

Plate 29

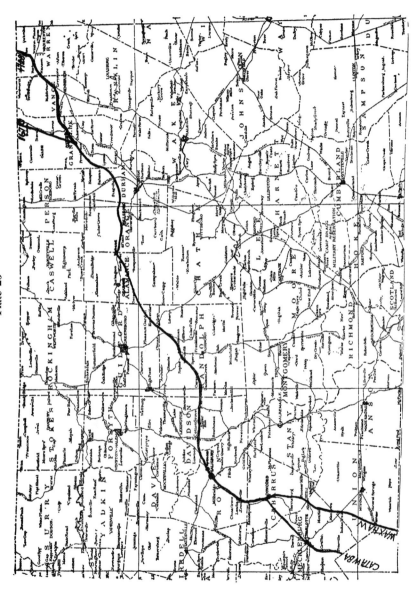

The Trading Path to the Indians, Traced on a Map of Present-Day North Carolina

Plate 30

Large Urn, Twenty-one Inches in Height, Found at Steelman's Place on the Yadkin River in Yadkin County, Broken into Seventy-five Pieces; Smaller Vessel, with Impression of Leaf on Bottom, Found at Donnaha, Yadkin County

Photograph by Roy J. Spearman

Plate 31

Large Pottery Vessel Found by H. M. Doerschuk in Richmond
County along the Yadkin-Great Peedee River

Plate 32

Stamped-Ware Pottery Vessel, Twenty-one Inches in Height,
from Richmond County, Yadkin-Great Peedee River

Photograph by courtesy of H. M. Doerschuk

patriotic theme was evident in the musical recital of ancestral deeds of renown and of the ancient glory of a fast-dying race destined soon to vanish from the earth.

The travelers now turned to the Esaw Indians, "a very large Nation containing many thousands of people." These were the Catawba and affiliated tribes. Several towns were passed, each having a council house like the one at Waxhaw. At a lodge by the way they met one of the war captains. When the captain departed, his host scratched him on the shoulder, which was considered a sign of compliment.

The Catawba towns were numerous, and accommodations were easily obtained. While being entertained by a Catawba warrior, one of the party was treated by his host for lameness. The Indian took an instrument fashioned like a comb, made of split reeds with fifteen teeth of rattlesnakes, and scratched the afflicted limb until the blood came, bathing the affected part with warm water before and after the incision. He then procured some sassafras root, heated it between two stones, and with it bound up the wound. In a day or two the lameness disappeared.

After passing through numerous towns of the Sugaree Indians in the neighborhood of the present Sugar Creek, the party arrived at the lodge of the Catawba chief. Here they met a Scotsman, John Stewart, of James River, Virginia, who had traded with the Catawba for many years. He had brought along seven horses loaded with English goods to trade with the Indians. As it was reported that the Seneca Indians were making inroads into Carolina, he feared to return home alone and had waited for the Lawson party. He had heard of their travels twenty days before they arrived. This is an indication of the speed with which news spread from tribe to tribe. His company was quite acceptable to the party.

The chief of the Catawba was doubtless located at the principal village of the tribe situated on the Catawba River near the mouth of Sugar Creek. From this village the travelers resumed their journey over the famous Trading Path, which led northeast near the present location of Charlotte, Concord, and Salisbury. As they passed along, they observed seven heaps of stones in a single day, each cairn representing the tomb of a Southern Indian who had been slain by the "Sinnagers," or Seneca, of the dreaded Iroquois confederacy. The Indian guide added a stone to each heap. Immense flocks of pigeons, such as are known to have visited the Piedmont region until after the middle of the nineteenth century, afforded a pleasant hunt. While one of the travelers went with a Saponi Indian, who attended trader Stewart, to look for horses that had wandered back toward the Catawba town, the others joined in the pigeon hunt. In speaking of the amazing number of birds in these flocks, Lawson commented:

You may find several Indian Towns of not above seventeen Houses, that have more than 100 gallons of Pigeon Oil or Fat, they using it with Pulse or Bread as we do Butter. . . . The Indians take a light and go among them in the night, and bringing away with them some thousand, killing them with long poles as they roost in the trees. At this time of year, the flocks as they pass by, obstruct the light of the day.

After several days of delightful travel through a country described as "delicious," the party arrived at Trading Ford on the Yadkin River. The travel journal comments:

We reached the pleasant Banks of Sapona River, whereon stands the Indian Town and Fort, nor could all England afford a pleasanter Stream, were it inhabited by Christians, and cultivated by ingenious Hands. These Indians live in a clear Field, about a Mile square, which they would have sold me because I talked sometimes about coming into those parts to live. This pleasant River may be sometimes larger than the Thames at Kingston, keeping a continual pleasant Noise, with it reverberating on the bright Marble rocks. It is beautiful with a numerous train of Swans, and other sorts of Water Fowl, not common though extraordinarily pleasing to the Eye. The forward Spring welcomed us with her innumerable train of small Choristers, which inhabit those fair banks; the Hills redoubling, and adding sweetness to their Melodious tunes, by their shrill echoes. One side of the River is hemmed in with Mountainy Ground, the other side proving as rich a soil to the eye of a knowing person with us, as any this Western World can afford.

This delightful prospect may today be easily surveyed by travelers. Although the backwater of High Rock Lake now covers the river valley, in dry seasons the islands may be seen immediately southeast of the No. 70 highway bridge and the Southern Railway trestle of the Yadkin crossing. At the lower end of the islands is the historic Trading Ford. The Dukeville power station is located near the west end of the ford. The extensive, level river valley was once the home of the Indian tribes. This section is called the Jersey Bottoms after the Irish settlers from New Jersey who settled in the vicinity.[1] Although the river bottoms are under water much of the time, in the dry season many stone implements such as arrowheads, axes, pestles, etc., and fragments of pottery have been gathered from the lake bed. A small settlement in this neighborhood retained the name Sapona for many years, the only memorial of the locality which recorded a connection with the Indians who once possessed the land, except the names Trading Ford and Yadkin, which still persist.

These Saponi Indians had been met by Lederer in Virginia. They had later moved to one of the islands at the forks of Staunton and Dan rivers to become close neighbors of the Occaneechee. Forced to move again, they migrated to the Trading Ford location, which had been previously vacated by the Saura, who had lived here as late as 1673, when Needham and Arthur were on the trail, but had since deserted the Yadkin and had sought a home on Dan River.

The Saponi chief, a friend of the English, while on an expedition assisting them in pursuing an enemy tribe had lost an eye by the accidental explosion of gunpowder. He gave the travelers a friendly reception and lodged them in his house. Lawson commented, "Our Indian King and his wife entertained us very respectfully."

About ten days before, the Saponi had taken five prisoners of the terrible Seneca Indians. These captives were being held for execution in the following manner:

The fire of pitch-Pine being got ready and a Feast appointed, which is solemnly kept at the time of their acting this Tragedy, the sufferer has his body stuck thick with lightwood splinters, which are lighted by so many candles, the tortured person dancing round a great Fire, till his strength fails, and disables him from making them any further pastime. Most commonly these wretches behave themselves (in the Midst of their Tortures) with a great Deal of Bravery and Resolution, esteem-

---

[1] The family of Daniel Boone settled on the Yadkin River about twenty miles above this site.

ing it satisfaction enough, to be assured that the same Fate will befall some of their tormentors, whenever they fall into the Hands of their Nation.

A delegation of Totero, or Tutelo Indians, came down from the "Westward Mountains." These Tutelo begged that the lives of the Seneca be spared, stating that recently some of the Northern Indians had taken Tutelo prisoners and had released them. The petitioners felt that out of gratitude they should intercede for the prisoners at Saponi Town. The Saponi chief, with consent of the council, delivered the prisoners to the Tutelo for safe conduct home.

These visitors were of the tribe that had formerly lived in the foothills of the Blue Ridge near the headwaters of Dan River in Virginia. They had migrated to one of the islands near the Occaneechee, had been forced to retreat, and had subsequently settled in Carolina territory. Their location at the time of this visit has not been identified. Various sites on the upper Yadkin such as Donnaha near Pilot Mountain and other locations nearer the headwaters of the river invite consideration.

Another delegation of the same Indians came down. They were described as being "tall likely men, having great quantities of Buffaloes, Elks, and Bears, with other sort of Deer amongst them, which strong Food makes large, robust bodies." Upon inquiry they produced some "Bezoar Stone," a concretion found in the stomachs of deer and other ruminants, supposed to have a medicinal value. One of the Tutelo, a notable hunter, affirmed that the powder of the stone blown into the eyes strengthened the sight and the brain exceedingly.

At this time the Saponi, Tutelo, Keyauwee, and several other small tribes, much reduced in numbers and hard pressed by their enemies, were combining their scattered forces and planning to retreat eastward to the white settlements for protection. The Saponi chief wished to sell Lawson the Yadkin land occupied by his tribe.

One morning while his host, the chief, went to look after his beaver traps in the near-by creeks, Lawson and his companions went sightseeing. He reported:

Taken with the Pleasantness of the Place, we walked along the Riverside, where we found a very delightful Island, made by the River, and a Branch, there being several such plots of Ground environ'd with this Silver Stream, which are fit pastures for Sheep, and free from any offensive Vermin. Nor can anything be desired by a contented mind, as to a Pleasant situation, but what may be found here; every step presenting some new object which still adds Invitation to the Traveller in these Parts.

Near the town Lawson examined several of the "sweat houses" used by the villagers. These houses were made of stones and shaped like a large oven. Use was made of them in treating disease, especially cases involving rheumatic pains, with which the Indians were often afflicted because of much exposure in hunting, making war, and otherwise traveling about.

Before taking their departure the travelers witnessed a violent storm. The wind blew down the palisade of the town, and threatened to carry lodges, visitors, and all into the river. We are informed that in the darkness of the stormy night the one-eyed chief,

who pretends much to the art of Conjuration, ran out in the most violent Hurry, and in the middle of the Town fell to his Neckromantick Practice; tho' I thought he would have been blown away or killed, before the Devil and he could have exchanged half a dozen words; but in two Minutes the Wind had ceased and it became as Great a Calm, as I ever knew in my Life. As I much admired at that sudden alteration, the old man told me the Devil was very angry and had done thus, because they had not put the Sinnagers to Death.

Thus Lawson concludes the journal of his experiences with the Saponi Indians at Trading Ford.

As the travelers set out from the Indian town they saw some of the locusts, "the same sort that bears Honey," which still grow abundantly in the Piedmont and are sought for by boys. Several small creeks were passed, one of which today bears the name of Swearing Creek. A legend persists that the creek was so named because the traders along the famous Path bound themselves to secrecy under oath at this crossing that they would not reveal information of the transactions which were carried on in the regions of Trading Ford and beyond. Eight miles from Trading Ford the travelers "passed over a very pretty River, called Rock River, a fit name, having a ridge of high Mountains running from its Banks to the Eastward and disgorging itself in the Sapona River." This stream now bears the name of Abbotts Creek, and the high ridge near its mouth is known as Flat Swamp Mountain. Sapona River was the name applied by Lawson to the Yadkin.

After covering a distance of more than fifteen miles, the travelers pitched camp. Their slumbers were disturbed by a nocturnal prowler, a wolf that made repeated visits until finally driven away. The trail led near the location of the present settlements of Silver Hill and Cid. At noon on the second day the Highwaree (Uwharrie) River was crossed. Lawson noted the abundant outcropping of stone along this stream. The description of the Keyauwee Town next visited is given in some detail:

Five miles from this River to the N. W. stands the Keyauwee's Town. They are fortified in with Wooden Puncheons, like Sapona, being a people much of the same Number. Nature hath so fortify'd this Town with Mountains, that were it a Great Seat of War, it might easily be made impregnable, having large cornfields joining to their Cabins, and a Savanna near the Town, at the foot of these Mountains, that is capable of keeping some hundreds of heads of Cattle. And all this environ'd round with very High Mountains, so that no hard Wind ever troubles these inhabitants. These high clifts have no grass growing on them, and very few trees, which are very short and stand at a great distance from each other. The earth is a red Colour. . . . These Indians make use of red ore to paint their Faces withal, which they get in the Neighboring Mountains. . . . At the top of one of these Mountains is a cave that 100 Men sit very conveniently to dine in; whether natural or artificial I could not learn. . . . Near the Town is such another Current as Heighwaree.

In spite of these specific details of description, the location of the Keyauwee Town remained a mystery for probably a century. The nearest attempt at identification was the suggestion of James Mooney, eminent ethnologist, that it was in the neighborhood of High Point. Mr. Mooney supposed that the Trading Path followed the line of the Southern Railway from the Yadkin to Haw River, which was not the case. The Trading Post ran through the Carraway Mountains a score of miles south of High Point.

The steps to the solution of the mystery were as follows: Lawson's direction given as northwest is misleading.[2] There is no stream of like size five miles west of the Uwharrie. The same distance to the east the Trading Path crossed Carraway Creek. Carraway is by tradition an Indian name, and appears to be the survival of Keyauwee. On Carraway Creek five miles northeast of the crossing of the Uwharrie are extensive bottom lands, or savannas, enclosed by the rocky ridges of the Carraway Mountains. These mountains appear in early spring as Lawson described them, high cliffs with few trees. The soil adjoining the fertile bottom lands is red and yellow clay. On the top of Ridge's or Rich's Mountain a mile west of Carraway Creek is a strange rock formation; great boulders are strewn thickly over many acres, providing numerous caves or rock shelters, which confirm the report of the mountaintop cave. In years past, the village site, located within a stone's throw of the stream, has been revealed by the plow. Arrowheads, stone axes, beads of shell and trade beads, fragments of clay pottery, broken stone pipes, and other objects of Indian origin or usage have been gathered from the fields. Fire pits revealed the bones of animals. Skeletal remains were unearthed by the plow, but few have been preserved. Thus the lost Keyauwee Town was rediscovered on the Carraway. The site has since been partially excavated by the Archaeological Society of North Carolina.

Lawson and the five companions with him at this stage of the journey were assigned by lot to different lodges of the Keyauwee. It was Lawson's privilege to lodge with Keyauwee Jack, the chief, a former Congaree Indian, who had obtained his position of importance by marrying the leading lady of the tribe, royal descent being carried by the female line of inheritance. The "Queen," or chieftainess, had a daughter by a former husband whom Lawson described as "the beautifulest Indian I ever saw, and had an Air of Majesty with her, quite contrary to the general Carriage of the Indians. She was very kind to the English during our abode, as well as her Father and Mother." The description of this Indian maiden, endowed with the charms and graces of gentility, beguiles the imagination. She deserved a kinder fate

[2] Lawson's approach on the Trading Path could account for this error in direction.

than to be consigned to oblivion after brief mention as belle of the village in old Keyauwee. Randolph County can afford to rear a marble shaft in her memory. Among the corn rows that grow on the site of the ancient village have been gathered a handful of beads, a shell hairpin, and a tiny carved stone paint cup. One is led to muse over these trifling remnants of vanished glory and to wonder whether they once were employed in the adornment of the princess of the Royal House of Keyauwee.

Lawson and Keyauwee Jack spent the time agreeably, as the journal notes:

Next day having some occasion to write, the Indian King, who saw me, believed that he could write as well as I. Whereupon I wrote a word and gave it to him to copy, which he did with more exactness than any European could have done, that was illiterate. It was so well that he who could have read mine might have done the same by his. Afterwards he took great delight in making fish-hooks of his own invention which would have been a good Piece for an Antiquary to have puzzled his brains withal, in tracing out the Characters of all the oriental Tongues. He sent for several Indians to his Cabin to look at his handywork and both he and they thought I could read his writing as well as I could my own. I had a Manual in my pocket that had King David's picture in it, and in one of his Private retirements. The Indian asked me who that Indian represented? I told him that it was the picture of a good King that lived according to the rules of Morality, doing all as he would be done by, ordering his life to the service of the Creator of all things; and being now above us in Heaven with God Almighty, who had rewarded him with all the delightful pleasures imaginable in the other World, for his Obedience to him in this. I concluded with telling him that we receive nothing here below, as Food, Raiment, etc., but what came from the Omnipotent Being. They listened to my Discourse with profound Silence, assuring me that they believed what I said to be true.

Concerning the customs of the tribe, Lawson recorded:

All the Indians hereabouts carefully preserve the bones of the Flesh they eat, and burn them, as being of opinion that if they Omitted that Custom, the Game would leave their country, and they would not be able to Maintain themselves by Hunting. Most of these Indians wear Mustaches, or Whiskers, which is rare; by reason the Indians are a people that commonly pull the Hair of their Faces, and other parts up by the Roots and suffer None to grow.

Charred remains of animal bones found in fire pits along many streams of the Piedmont bear witness to the former custom.

Most of Lawson's company decided to go directly to Virginia from Keyauwee Town. There are evidences of an old trail that ran north through the present Randolph and Forsyth counties, crossing the Dan River into Virginia. With one companion Lawson set out, resolved to see more of North Carolina.

The Indian guide secured from the Keyauwee, who led the way, had once been a prisoner among the Seneca, but had outrun them and made his escape, although they had previously cut away his toes and half of his feet. This treatment of prisoners, said to be a common practice among the Seneca, was first to raise the skin, and then to cut away half of the feet. The loose skin was wrapped back over the stumps and left to heal. This method of chiropody prevented prisoners from easily making an escape, since they were not so good travelers as before, and the impressions of their half-feet made a trail easy to follow. Although this poor Keyauwee contrived to escape, he had little heart to venture far from home, and always carried a case of pistols in his girdle, besides a cutlass and a gun.

The first day's travel of twenty miles led across "two pretty Rivers, something bigger than Heighwaree," streams known today as Deep River and Polecat Creek. The crossing was a little north of the present town of Randleman.

The trail was followed across "three Great Rivers," identified as Little and Big Alamance rivers and Haw River. Lawson described the Haw River ford

as having large Stones, about the bigness of an ordinary House, lying up and down the River. As the wind blew cold at the N. W. and we were very weary and hungry, the Swiftness of the Current gave us some cause to fear; but at last we concluded to venture over that night. Accordingly we stripped, and with great difficulty (by God's assistance) got safe to the north side of the famous Hau River. . . . It is called Hau River from the Sissipahau Indians, who dwell upon this Stream.

The ford crossed the river in the neighborhood of the present village of Swepsonville, and bordered the fertile lands of the Haw Fields. Lawson observed that "the Land is extraordinary Rich."

The distance to the Occaneechee town was estimated to be about twenty miles. Along the way next day the travelers saw "great Gangs of Turkies." When about halfway to their destination they met a trading caravan. Several horsemen were leading thirty horses loaded with merchandise to trade with the Indians. The man in charge was named Massey, a native of Leeds in Yorkshire, working out of Virginia. He warned Lawson not to venture into Virginia on account of the dreaded Seneca, and advised him to secure Eno-Will, a faithful Indian guide, who was to be found at one of the villages in the Occaneechee neighborhood. The Virginia traders were impressed with the Haw Fields, stating "that they had never seen twenty Miles of such extraordinary rich Land, lying all together, like that betwixt Hau River and the Achonechy Town."

About three o'clock they reached the Indian town, situated not far from the present Hillsboro.[3] The name "Occaneechee Hills" still remains to designate the eminences south of the Eno. The Indians provided a feast of good fat bear and venison. Their cabins, or lodges, were festooned with dried bear and deer meat, "a good sort of tapestry," which caused the travelers to comment on the bountiful provision of this region, declaring that the Indians possessed "the Flower of Carolina; the English enjoying only the Fag-end of that country."

Within two hours after their arrival Eno-Will came to the Occaneechee chief's lodge where the travelers were quartered. He was a Shoccoree Indian. His people had joined the Eno tribe and another nation known by the name Adshusheer. These three tribes had combined their greatly reduced forces under the authority of Eno-Will, their chief. When he was asked if he would conduct the party to the English settlements, and what pay he would expect for his trouble, he replied that he would go along and that what he was to receive would be left to the discretion of the travelers.

The next morning the party set out with their new guide,

[3] The Archaeological Society of North Carolina has discovered abundant evidence of Indian occupation in this area.

accompanied by several Indians of Eno-Will's tribe. They left the Trading Path and traveled eastward. At Occaneechee Town they crossed Eno River, and proceeded about fourteen miles, crossing several small streams and traveling over stony land. Lawson reported: "The Stony Way made me quite Lame, so that I was an hour or two behind the rest, but Honest Will would not leave me, but bid me welcome when we came to his House, feasting us with Hot Bread and Bear's Oil; which is wholesome Food for Travellers."

The Indian town, situated along a "Pretty Rivulet," was northwest of the present city of Durham. Two roosters were brought in and their larger feathers plucked while the fowls were yet alive, preparatory to singeing away the smaller feathers. Lawson took one of the roosters, desiring to clean the chicken before cooking, a preparation which the Indians habitually overlooked. The Indians laughingly told him that Eno-Will had taken the fowl from the stock of an Indian not at home, and that it was designed for another use. Lawson conjectured that the rooster had been kept for sacrificial purposes, and stated that "notwithstanding all this, we cooked him and eat him, and if he was designed for him, cheated the Devil."

Lawson here added another favorable sketch of the friendly, noble Indian who ruled the country now embraced in Durham and Orange counties, and whose name deserves to be commemorated: "Our guide and Landlord, Enoe-Will, was of the best and most agreeable Temper I ever met with in an Indian, being always ready to serve the English, not out of Gain, but real Affection; which makes him apprehensive of being poisoned by some wicked Indians, and was therefore very earnest with me, to promise him to revenge his death should it so happen. He brought some of his chief Men into his Cabin, and two of them having a Drum and a Rattle, sung by us as we laid in bed, and struck up their music to serenade and welcome us to their Town. And tho' at last we fell asleep, yet they continued their Consert until morning."

This village was fortified. Here the surviving Eno tribesmen and their confederates had not forgotten their ball play with stones, a game already commented upon by Lederer. They were "much addicted to a sport they call Chenco, which is carried on with a

Staff and Bowl made of stone, which they trundle upon a smooth place, like a Bowling Green, made for that purpose." This game probably accounts for numerous biscuit-shaped stones found in the region.

The next morning the party was again on the march, accompanied by several Indians, who intended to go to the English to buy rum. The distance to the next station, called Lower Quarter, was estimated at forty miles. On the second day they passed a large stone "about the size of a large Oven, and Hollow. This the Indians took great notice of, putting some Tobacco into the concavity, and spitting after it."

This day they reached the town, "which was parcel of nasty, smoaky holes, much like the Watterees." The land was swampy, and the decline from the Piedmont tableland was noted. Most of the Indians had but one eye, Lawson commented, "but what Mischance or quarrel has bereaved them of the other I could not learn." Food was scarce, though a sufficiency was found for the travelers. Lawson saw among these Indians "very long Arrows, headed with pieces of Glass, which they had broken from bottles. They had shaped them neatly like the head of a dart." These arrowheads may have been made from fragments of glass, but it is quite likely that they were chipped from pure quartz. The skill of the Indian in such stone work shows considerable merit. (Enterprising counterfeiters of "Indian relics" have also excelled in this art.)

After a rainy day spent in the Indian town, the travelers proceeded another ten miles. The swollen water of the river caused a halt until the water had fallen. The guide called the stream the Eno, and said that it emptied into Eno Bay, near his old home; whereby Lawson supposed that Eno-Will may have been a Coree Indian by birth.

A mare belonging to one of the travelers ran away, and Eno-Will went back as far as Lower Quarter to secure her. Meanwhile two Tuscarora Indians appeared on the opposite bank of the stream, which they had been prevented from crossing by high water. The travelers could hear them, but could not understand their language. When the guide returned, he interpreted their speech and said they told him that the English were very wicked people and threatened the Indians for hunting near their plantations. These Tuscarora Indians were on their way to the Shoccoree and Occaneechee to sell wooden bowls and ladles in exchange for raw skins. Their stories frightened an old Indian and his son from going any farther, but Eno-Will said that "nothing they should say would frighten him, he believing them to be a couple of Hog-Stealers; and that the English only sought restitution of their losses by them." A servant of the guide, a Saxapahaw Indian, killed several wild turkeys, which provided a feast during the delay of the crossing.

When the travelers forded the river, they found the stream about breast high. They landed on the north shore and proceeded about ten miles to the falls of "a large creek, where lay mighty Rocks, the Water making a strange Noise as if a great many Water-Mills were going at once." Lawson supposed this to be the falls of the Neuse, called by the Indians Wee quo Whom. It is thought that these are the falls not far distant from Wake Forest.

Here by the light of the campfire is given another picture of Eno-Will:

My guide Will desiring to see the book that I had about me, I lent it to him; and as soon as he saw the picture of King David, he asked me several questions concerning the book, and picture, which I resolv'd him, and invited him to become a Christian. He made me a very sharp reply, assuring me that he loved the English extraordinarily well, and did believe their ways to be very good for those that had always practised them, and had been brought up therein, but that for himself, he was too much in years to think of a change, esteeming it not proper for old people to admit such an Alteration. However, he told me that if I would take his son Jack, who was then about fourteen years of age, and teach him to talk in that Book, and make paper speak, which they call our Way of Writing, he would wholly resign him to my tuition; telling me he was of opinion, I was very well affected to the Indians.

Two days later the travelers reached a hunting quarter of five hundred Tuscarora Indians. The hunters had made streets of lodges built of pine bark, not with round tops as was the common use, but ridge fashion. Only some corn was obtained for food, as the large number of Indians accounted for scarcity of game. The same day a town of the Indians was reached where only a few old women were at home, all the men being at the hunting quarter. The following day a Tuscarora received the travelers and promised to go with them to the white settlement if they would stay two days with him, he expecting to journey then to buy rum. Here the travelers saw a medicine man give treatment to a patient, scarifying the body with rattlesnake teeth and sucking out quantities of blood. The Indian host provided for his guests a choice dish of beaver tail. Accompanied by the Tuscarora, the party traveled through country thickly settled with Indian towns and arrived at the Pamlico settlement. Eno-Will, faithful to the end of the trail, delivered his patron in safety to the English habitation. Perhaps we shall meet this worthy chief again in these pages after vices of the white man's civilization have robbed him of some of his heathen virtues.

REFERENCES

Lawson, John. *History of North Carolina.* London, 1714.

Mooney, James. *Siouan Tribes of the East.* Bulletin No. 22, Bureau of American Ethnology. Washington, 1894.

Rights, Douglas L. "The Trading Path to the Indians," *North Carolina Historical Review,* VIII (1931), 403-426.

Speck, Frank G. *Gourds of the Southeastern Indians.* The New England Gourd Society. Boston, 1941.

CHAPTER IX

The Dividing Line

COLONEL WILLIAM BYRD's history of the survey of the dividing line between North Carolina and Virginia comes next in review. Commissioners from both states started at Currituck Inlet in March, 1728. They proceeded west and carried the line through Dismal Swamp. On April 2 they crossed the Chowan River and encamped in an Indian field. Clearings such as this camp ground afforded were noted by the early explorers and settlers, and when the name "Old Field" appears on an early map, there is good reason to believe that the location was once the site of a former Indian village or planting ground.

Three Meherrin Indians made a visit to the camp. According to the surveyor's journal:

They told us that the Small Remains of their Nation had deserted their Ancient Town, situated near the Mouth of Meherrin River, for fear of the Catawbas, who had kill'd 14 of their People the Year before; and the few that Survived that Calamity, had taken refuge amongst the English, on the East side of Chowan. Tho', if the complaint of these Indians were true, they are hardly used by our Carolina Friends. But they are the less to be pitied, because they have ever been reputed the most false and treacherous to the English of all the Indians of the Neighbourhood.

This tribe was of Iroquoian stock, with whom fugitive Susquehanna, or Conestoga, had united. They were kinsmen of the Nottoway Indians, who were met on the seventh of March by the surveyors. The name of this latter tribe signified "snakes" or "enemies" in their language, and the name applied to them by the coastal tribes, Mangoac, was the general name for the Iroquois, meaning "stealthy ones," frequently written "Mingo."[1]

[1] For *Mingo*, see F. W. Hodge, *Handbook of American Indians North of Mexico*, Part 1, p. 867.

A runner was dispatched to the Nottoway Town, on the river of that name, to announce the visit of the surveyors. The women of the village had been posted on a hill to watch for the visitors, and greeted them with vociferous whoops. At this signal the chief men of the place came out and escorted the party into the fort, a palisade about ten feet high, leaning outwards slightly to make scaling difficult. Each side of the square was about one hundred feet long; loopholes were set at intervals. Within the enclosure were huts made of saplings covered with bark. Furniture consisted of frames covered with mats or deer skins.

The young men, who had painted themselves in hideous manner, entertained with war dances. Music was furnished for the dancing by means of an Indian drum fashioned out of a gourd with a skin stretched across the mouth. The women were dressed in red and blue coats made of cloth bought from traders, and their hair was beaded with white and blue shell beads. However, the charm of their attire was nullified because "the whole Winter's Dirt was so crusted on their Skins, that it requir'd a strong appetite to accost them." Firearms were in general use, only the small boys handling bows and arrows. The population of the town was about two hundred, and they were said to be the only Indians of any consequence then living in Virginia. Their rapid decline was attributed chiefly to disease and rum.

Colonel Byrd mentioned the efforts of William and Mary College and of several individuals to educate Indian children. Little seems to have been accomplished, as the educated Indians relapsed into their former manner of living. Governor Spottswood was praised for his attempt to assemble the straggling remnants of the Carolina and Virginia tribes and to improve their condition. He had established a refuge for them at Fort Christanna, where Saponi, Tutelo, Keyauwee, Eno and other survivors of the central North Carolina tribes had been summoned for their protection.

The Indians provided corn for the surveyors' horses and received in turn what rum was left over from the night's sojourn. The exchange was evidently satisfactory to the Nottoway, as we are told that they loved rum "better than they do their wives and children." Baskets made of silk-grass were offered by the women, such offerings being looked upon with suspicion by their visitors, who regarded an Indian present as "a Liberality put out to Interest, and a bribe placed to the greatest Advantage." At the departure of the guests, the braves of the village fired a salute in their honor.

After an interval of some months the surveyors assembled in September to continue the line. On the twenty-ninth Colonel Byrd sent to Fort Christanna to secure Saponi Indian hunters to join the party in order to provide game to feed the company on the long march. Of the five Indians responding, two were chosen. One of these was Bearskin, a Saponi who has left us most that we know of the language and customs of his people. He has given us a favorable impression of the ancient inhabitants of the Dan and Yadkin valleys.

The Indians joined the surveyors at a camp not far from the Roanoke River crossing of the famous Trading Path. The ford was called Moniseep by the Indians, which in the Saponi language signified Shallow Water. On October 2 they crossed a large creek called by the Indians Massamoni, meaning Paint Creek, on account of the red soil along the bank that tinged the stream with red color. Three miles beyond they came to Yapatsco, or Beaver Creek. The beavers had dammed the creek and had raised the waters considerably. Three and one-half miles farther on they reached Ohimpa-moni, or Jumping Creek, so named on account of the frequent jumping of fish during the spring season. On the third they crossed Tewahominy, or Tuscarora Creek, given this name because the body of a Tuscarora warrior slain near by had been thrown into the creek. Buffalo tracks were found in the vicinity. Blewing, or Blue Wing Creek, and Sugar Tree Creek were crossed next. On the fifth they came to Hico-ott-mony, or Turkey Buzzard River, the well-known Hyco Creek of today. The stream acquired its name from the buzzard roosts in the trees along the banks. On the seventh, signs of the buffalo[2] were found near a stream called Buffalo Creek. The same day one of the men of the party killed a fat buck and several turkeys, which were

[2] For further information about the buffalo, see Douglas L. Rights, "The Buffalo in North Carolina," *North Carolina Historical Review*, IX (1932), 242-249.

boiled together in a pot with rice and barley, making a savory soup. Byrd's narrative states that Ned Bearskin, the Indian hunter, "was very superstitious in this Matter, and told us, with a face full of concern, that if we continued to boil Venison and Turkey together, we Shou'd for the future kill nothing, because the Spirit that presided over the Woods would drive all the Game out of our Sight."

Several touches of humor on the part of the affable Indian hunter reveal that the Piedmont Indians were a jovial people. The thick bushes tore the bags in which the bread of the expedition was packed. Several times a day a halt was made in order to mend them. "The Carolina Men pleas'd themselves with the Joke of one of the Indians, who said we shou'd soon be forced to cut up our House (meaning the Tent) to keep our Baggs in Repair." The jest proved near earnest, and the travelers ordered that skins of deer that were killed be made use of in covering the tattered bread bags.

On the tenth a stream was crossed called Cocquade Creek, thus named for the reason that here the travelers began to wear the beards of the wild turkeys in their hats for a cockade. A mile to the west they crossed the Dan River[3] for the first time, and pitched their camp for the night two and one-half miles beyond at Cane Creek. The following day they crossed the Dan again and encamped two miles beyond. A fat buck furnished a tasty dish for the evening meal. Bearskin shot a turkey also, but confessed that he did not bring it to camp for fear that it might be cooked in the same pot with the venison and thus spoil the hunter's luck. In spite of his superstitions, or, as he may have believed, on account of them, the Indian furnished a great plenty of meat for the hungry surveyors.

On Sunday, October 13, campfire talk was as follows:

In the evening we examin'd our Friend Bearskin, concerning the Religion of his Country and he explained it to us, without any of that Reserve to which his Nation is Subject.

He told us he believ'd there was one Supreme God, who had Sev-

---

[3] The origin of the name of the Dan River is unknown. There are some fanciful legends that have little foundation. It seems likely that it is derived from the Siouan language.

eral Subaltern Deities under Him. And that this Master-God made the World a long time ago. That he told the Sun, the Moon, and Stars, their Business in the Beginning, which they, with good looking after, have faithfully perform'd ever Since.

That the same Power that made all things at first has taken care to keep them in the same Method and Motion ever since.

He believ'd God had form'd many Worlds before he form'd this, that those Worlds either grew old and ruinous, or were destroyed for the Dishonesty of the Inhabitants.

That God is very just and very good—ever well pleas'd with those men who possess those God-like Qualities. That he takes good People into his safe Protection, makes them very rich, fills their Bellies plentifully, preserves them from sickness, and from being surpris'd or Overcome by their Enemies.

But all such as tell Lies, and Cheat those they have Dealings with, he never fails to punish with Sickness, Poverty and Hunger, and, after all that, Suffers them to be knockt on the Head and Scalpt by those that fight against them.

He believ'd that after Death, both good and bad People are conducted by a strong Guard into a great Road, in which departed Souls travel together for some time, till at a certain Distance this Road forks into two Paths, the one extremely Levil, and the other Stony and Mountainous.

Here the good are parted from the Bad by a flash of Ligtening, the first being hurry'd away to the Right, the other to the Left. The Right hand road leads to a charming warm Country, where the Spring is everlasting, and every Month is May; and as the year is always in its Youth, so are the People, and particularly the Women are bright as Stars, and never Scold.

That in this happy Climate there are Deer, Turkeys, Elks, Buffaloes innumerable, perpetually fat and gentle, while the Trees are loaded with delicious Fruit quite throughout the four Seasons.

That the Soil brings forth Corn Spontaneously, without the Curse of Labour, and so very wholesome, that None who have the happiness to eat of it are ever Sick, grow old, or dy.

Near the Entrance to this Blessed Land Sits a Venerable Old Man on a Mat richly woven, who examins Strictly all that are brought before Him, and if they have behav'd well, the Guards are order'd to open the Crystal Gate, and let them enter into the Land of Delights.

The left Hand Path is very rugged and uneven, leading to a dark and barren Country, where it is always Winter. The Ground is the whole year round cover'd with Snow, and nothing is to be seen upon the Trees but Icicles.

All the People are hungry, yet have not a Morsel of anything to eat, except a bitter kind of Potato, that gives them the Dry-Gripes, and fills their whole Body with loathsome Ulcers, that Stink, and are unsupportably painful.

Here all the Women are old and ugly, having Claws like a Panther, with which they fly upon the Men that Slight their Passion. For it seems these haggard old Furies are intolerably fond, and expect a vast deal of Cherishing. They talk much and exceedingly Shrill, giving exquisite pain to the Drum of the Ear, which in that Place of the Torment is so tender, that every Sharp Note wounds it to the Quick.

At the End of this Path sits a dreadful old Woman on a monstrous Toad-Stool, whose head is cover'd with Rattle-Snakes instead of Tresses, with glaring white Eyes, that strike a Terror unspeakable into all that behold her.

This Hag pronounces Sentence of Woe upon all the miserable Wretches that hold up their hands at her Tribunal. After this they are deliver'd over to huge Turkey-Buzzards, like harpys, that fly away with them to the Place above mentioned.

Here, after they have been tormented a certain Number of years, according to their several Degrees of Guilt, they are again driven back into this World, to try if they will mend their Manners, and merit a Place the next time in the Regions of Bliss.

This was the Substances of Bearskin's Religion. . . . It contain'd . . . the three Great Articles of Natural Religion: The Belief of a God; The Moral Distinction betwixt Good and Evil; and the Expectation of Rewards and Punishments in Another World.

The thoughts of the party turned to more worldly things next day as they lingered in camp on account of rain. Since game was plentiful, there was much feasting and "the Frying Pan was not cool til next Morning." We are told that

in such a Glut of Provisions, a true Woodsman, when he has nothing else to do, like our honest countrymen the Indians, keeps eating on, to avoid the imputations of Idleness; Though, in a Scarcity, the Indian will fast with a much better Grace than they. They can Subsist Several days upon a little Rocahominy, which is parch'd Indian Corn reduc'd to powder. This they moisten in the hollow of their Hands with a little water, and 'tis hardly credible how small a Quantity of it will

Support them. Tis true they grow a little lank upon it, but to make themselves feel full, they gird up their Loins very tight with a Belt, taking up a Hole every day. With this Slender Subsistence they are able to travel very long Journeys; but then, to make themselves Amends, when they do meet with better Chear, they eat without ceasing, till they have raven'd themselves into another Famine.

On the fifteenth the surveyors crossed Sable Creek, now known as Wolf Island Creek. Wild geese, called "Cohunks" by the Indians, were seen in the neighborhood. On the following day, about three miles farther on they came to Lowland Creek, the present Whiteoak Creek. Within the next two miles near the river they found several Indian fields and encamped near one of them. They supposed that these fields had been previously occupied by the Saura Indians. On the seventeenth they halted on the banks of Cascade Creek, noting the falls which gave a name to the stream, and examining the rock formation which underlies this Triassic area. The next day they reached Irvin River, which they named after one of the members of the surveying party, the present Smith River. Bearskin here killed a very fat doe and came across a bear which had been killed and half devoured by a panther.

About four miles beyond Smith River they reached Matrimony Creek, "call'd so by an unfortunate marry'd man, because it was exceedingly noisy and impetuous." (Colonel Byrd perpetrated a pun in naming this creek with a play on the Siouan word *moni*.) An immense flock of wild pigeons appeared flying southward. Not far from Mayo River they found the atmosphere smoky because of the firing of the woods by the Indians. Some of the men found a camp near by, where not long before Indians had been dressing skins. They were now near the war trail of the Northern Indians on their way to attack the Catawba and other Southern Indians. The trail followed closely the present Norfolk and Western Railway line. Colonel Byrd commented on the Indian campaigns:

And now I mention the Northern Indians, it may not be improper to take Notice of their implacable Hatred to those of the South. Their Wars are everlasting, without any Peace, Enmity being the only Inheritance among them that descends from Father to Son, and either Party will march a thousand Miles to take their Revenge upon such Hereditary Enemies.

These long Expeditions are Commonly carry'd on in the following Manner, Some Indian, remarkable for his Prowess, that has rais'd himself to the Reputation of a War-Captain, declares his Intention of paying a Visit to some Southern Nation; hereupon as many of the Young Fellows as have either a Strong Thirst of Blood or Glory, list themselves under his command.

With these Volunteers he goes from One Confederate Town to another, listing all the Rabble he can, til he has gather'd together a competent Number for Mischief.

Their Arms are a Gun and Tomahawk, and all the Provision they carry from Home is a Pouch of Rockahominy. Thus provided and accoutr'd, they march towards their Enemy's Country, not in a Body, or by Certain Path, but Straggling in Small Numbers, for the greater convenience of Hunting and passing along undiscover'd.

So soon as they approach the Grounds on which the Enemy is used to hunt, they never kindle any Fire themselves, for fear of being found out by the smoak, nor will they Shoot at any kind of Game, tho' they shou'd be half famisht, lest they might alarm their Foes, and put them upon their Guard.

Sometimes indeed, while they are still at some distance, they roast either Venison or Bear, till it is very dry, and then having Strung it on their Belts, wear it round their Middle, eating very Sparingly of it, because they know not when they shall meet a fresh Supply. But coming nearer, they begin to look all round the Hemisphere, to watch if any smoke ascends, and listen continually for the Report of Guns, in order to make some happy Discovery for their own advantage.

It is amazing to see their Sagacity in discerning the Track of a Human Foot, even amongst dry leaves, which to our Shorter Sight is quite undiscoverable.

If by one or more of those Signs they be able to find out the Camp of any Southern Indians, they Squat down in some Thicket, and keep themselves hush and Snug till it is dark; Then creeping up Softly, they approach near enough to observe all the Motions of the Enemy. And about two a clock in the Morning, when they conceive them to be in a Profound Sleep, for they never keep Watch and Ward, pour in a Volley upon them, each Singling out his Man. The Moment they have discharg'd their Pieces, they rush in with their Tomahawks, and make sure work of all that are disabled.

Sometimes, when they find the Enemy Asleep around their little Fire, they first Pelt them with little Stones to wake them, and when they get up, fire in upon them, being in that posture a better Mark than when prostrate on the Ground.

Those that are kill'd of the Enemy, or disabled, they Scalp, that is, they cut the Skin all around the Head just below the hair, and then clapping their Feet to the poor Mortal's shoulders, pull the Scalp off clean, and carry it home in Triumph. . . .

The Prisoners they happen to take alive in these expeditions generally pass their time very Scurvily. They put them to all the Tortures that ingenious Malice and cruelty can invent. And (what shews the baseness of the Indian Temper in Perfection) they never fail to treat those with the greatest inhumanity that have distinguish'd themselves most by their Bravery. . . .

They are very cunning in finding out new ways to torment their unhappy Captives, tho', like those of Hell, their usual Method is by Fire. Sometimes they Barbecue them over live-Coals, taking them off every now and then, to prolong their Misery; at other times they will Stick Sharp Pieces of Lightwood all over their Body's, and setting them afire, let them burn down into the Flesh to the very Bone. And when they take a Stout Fellow, that they believe able to endure a great deal, they will tear all the Flesh off his Bones with red hot Pincers.

While these and such like Barbarities are practising, the Victors are so far from being touch'd with Tenderness and Compassion, that they dance and Sing round these wretched Mortals, shewing all the Marks of Pleasure and Jollity. And if such cruelties happen to be executed in their Towns, they employ their Children in tormenting the Prisoners, in order to extinguish in them betimes all Sentiments of Humanity.

In the mean time, while these poor Wretches are under the Anguish of all this inhuman Treatment, they disdain so much as to groan, Sigh, or shew the least Sign of Dismay or concern, so much as in their Looks; on the Contrary, they make it a Point of Honour all the time to Soften their Features, and look as pleas'd as if they were in the Actual Enjoyment of Some Delight; and if they never sang before in their Lives, they will be sure to be Melodious on this sad and dismal Occasion.

So prodigious a Degree of Passive Valour in the Indians is the more to be wonder'd at, because in all Articles of Danger they are apt to behave like Cowards. And what is still more Surprizeing, the very Women discover, on such Occasions, as great Fortitude and Contempt, both of Pain and Death, as the Gallantest of their Men can do.

In the region of Mayo River bears were plentiful. Three were killed along the way in one day. Bearskin shot one bear that was so fat that the only way of bringing him down was to shoot through the ear. Colonel Byrd explained: "The fore part of the Skull of that Animal being guarded by a double Bone, is hardly penetrable, and when it is very fat, a Bullet aim'd at his Body is apt to lose its force, before it reaches the Vitals. This Animal is of the Dog kind, and our Indians, as well as Woodsmen, are as fond of its Flesh as the Chinese can be of the Common Hound."

The surveyors were now within sight of the mountains. To the north were the Blue Ridge, and to the south was the small range including the Pilot and Saura Town mountains. Some of the party, former traders among the Indians, supposed the Pilot to be "Kiawan mountain" (Keyauwee-Carraway), which they had seen on their trading expeditions over the southern route to the Cherokee. Colonel Byrd was of the opinion that a continuation of the survey would soon reach the Cherokee, then "a considerable Nation of Indians, which have 62 Towns, and more than 4000 Fighting Men." The survey ended on October 26 in the neighborhood of Peters Creek, Surry County, 241 miles from the Carolina coast.

Members of the party were fatigued by the hard travel and were quite ready to return. Their leader noted that

the Indians, who have no way of travelling but on the Hoof, make nothing of going 25 miles a day, and carrying their little Necessaries at their backs, and sometimes a Stout Pack of Skins into the Bargain. And very often they laugh at the English, who can't stir to Next Neighbor without a Horse, and say that 2 Legs are too much for such lazy people, who cannot visit their next neighbour without six.

Bearskin was given the skins of all the deer he killed; the other men received a like share. At night they dried the skins around the fire. The Indians used deer's brains for dressing skins.

As the party neared Hyco Creek, they tried fire hunting in the manner of the Indians. The dry leaves were fired in a ring of five miles' circumference, which, burning inwards, drove the game to the center. Three deer were slain. This method of hunting did not appeal to Colonel Byrd, who was touched by the pitiful sight of the deer surrounded by the fire, that "weep and Groan like a Human Creature, yet can't move and compassion of those hard-hearted People, who are about to murder them." He was well pleased, however, when one of the men killed a buffalo near Sugar Tree Creek, and "the Men were so delighted with this new dyet, that the Gridiron and Frying-Pan had no more rest all night, than a poor Husband Subject to Curtain Lectures."

At Tewaw-hommini (Tuscarora) Creek Colonel Byrd was reminded of the disaster that befell the Tuscarora Nation. In his account of their warfare and defeat he included the following legend:

These Indians have a very odd Tradition amongst them, that many years ago, their Nation was grown so dishonest, that no man cou'd keep any goods, or so much as his loving Wife to himself. That, however, their God, being unwilling to root them out for their crimes, did them the honour to send a Messenger from Heaven to instruct them, and set Them a perfect Example of Integrity and kind Behaviour towards one another.

But this holy Person, with all his Eloquence and Sanctity of Life, was able to make very little Reformation amongst them. Some few of the Old Men did listen a little to his Wholesome Advice, but all the Young fellows were quite incorrigible. They not only Neglected his Precepts, but derided and Evil Entreated his Person. At last, taking upon Him to reprove some Young Rakes of the Conechta Clan very sharply for their impiety, they were so provok'd at the Freedom of his Rebukes, that they tied him to a Tree, and shot him with Arrows through the Heart. But their God took Lightning from Heaven, & has ever since visited their Nation with a continued Train of Calamities, nor will he ever leave off punishing, and wasting their People, till he shall have blotted every living Soul of them out of the World.

Bearskin was responsible for the following squirrel story:

One of our People Shot a large Gray Squirrel with a very Bushy Tail, a singular use of which our merry Indian discover'd to us. He said whenever this little Animal has occasion to cross a run of Water, he launches a Chip or Piece of Bark into the Water, on which he embarks, and, holding up his Tail to the wind, he Sails over very Safely.

At the Trading Path crossing Colonel Byrd recalled the former glory of this ancient trail:

About three Miles from our Camp we passed GREAT CREEK, and then, after traversing very barren grounds for 5 Miles together, we crost the Tradeing Path, and soon after had the pleasure of reaching the uppermost Inhabitant. . . .

The Trading Path above-mention'd receives its Name from being the Route the Traders take with their Caravans, when they go to traffick with the Catawbas and other Southern Indians. The Catawbas live about 250 Miles beyond Roanoke River, and yet our Traders find their Account in transporting Goods from Virginia to trade with them at their own Towne.

The Common Method of carrying on this Indian Commerce is as follows: Gentlemen send for Goods proper for such a Trade from England, and then either Venture them out at their own Risk to the Indian Towns, or else credit some Traders with them of Substance and Reputation, to be paid in Skins at a certain Price agreed betwixt them.

The Goods for the Indian Trade consist chiefly in Guns, Powder, Shot, Hatchets, (which the Indians call Tomahawks,) Kettles, red & blue Planes, Duffelds, Stroudwater blankets, and some Cutlary Wares, Brass Rings and other Trinkets.

These Wares are made up into Packs and Carry'd upon Horses, each Load being from 150 to 200 Pounds, and which they are able to travel about 20 Miles a day, if Forage happen to be plentiful.

Formerly a Hundred Horses have been employ'd in one of these Indian Caravans, under the Conduct of 15 or 16 persons only, but now the Trade is much impair'd, insomuch that they seldom go with half that Number.

The Course from Roanoke to the Catawbas is laid down nearest Southwest, and lies thro' a fine Country, that is Water'd by Several beautiful Rivers.

Those of greatest Note are, first Tar river, which is the upper Part of Pamptico, Flat river, Little river and Eno river, all three Branches of Neuse.

Between Eno and Saxpahaw rivers are the Haw old fields, which have the reputation of containing the most fertile high land in this part of the World, lying in a Body of about 50,000 acres.

This Saxpahaw is the upper Part of Cape Fair River, the falls of which lye many Miles below the Trading Path.

Some Mountains overlook this Rich Spot of Land, from whence all the soil washes down into the Plane, and is the cause of its exceeding Fertility. Not far from thence the Path crosses ARAMANCHY [Alamance] River, a branch of Saxpahaw, and about 40 miles beyond that, the Path intersects the Yadkin, which is there half a Mile over, and is supposed to be the South Branch of the same Pedee.

The Soil is exceedingly rich on both sides of the Yadkin, abounding in rank Grass and prodigiously large Trees;[4] and for plenty of Fish, Fowel and Venison, is inferior to No Part of the Northern Continent. There the Traders commonly lie Still for some days, to recruit their Horses' Flesh as well as to recover their own Spirits. Six Miles further is Crane Creek, so nam'd from its being the Rendezvous of great Armies of Cranes, which wage a more cruel War at this day, with the Frogs and the Fish, than they us'd to do with the Pigmies of the Days of Homer.[5]

About three-score Miles more bring you to the first Town of the Catawbas, call'd Nauvasa, situated on the banks of Santee [Catawba] river. Besides this Town there are five Others belonging to the same Nation, lying all on the same Stream, within the Distance of 20 Miles.

These Indians were all call'd formerly by the general Name of the Usherees, and were a very Numerous and Powerful People. But the frequent Slaughters made upon them by the Northern Indians, and, what has been still more destructive by far, the Intemperance and Foul Distempers introduc'd amongst them by the Carolina Traders, have now reduc'd their Numbers to a little More than 400 Fighting Men, besides Women & Children. It is a charming Place where they live, the Air very Wholesome, the Soil fertile, and the Winters ever mild and Serene.

So Soon as the Catawba Indians are inform'd of the Approach of the Virginia Caravans, they send a Detachment of their Warriors to bid them Welcome, and escort them Safe to their Town, where they are receiv'd with great Marks of Distinction. And their Courtesys to the VIRGINIA Traders, I dare say, are very Sincere, because they sell them better Goods and better Pennyworths than the Traders of Carolina. They commonly reside among the Indians till they have barter'd their Goods away for Skins, with which they load their Horses and come back by the Same Path they went.

There are generally some Carolina Traders that constantly live among the Catawbas, and pretend to Exercise dictatorial Authority over them. These petty Rulers don't only teach the honester Savages all sorts of Debauchery, but are unfair in their dealings, and use them with all kinds of Oppression.

This indignant arraignment of the Carolina traders may have been justified for the most part. It must be remembered that the

[4] This seems to verify the name "Yadkin" as derived from a Siouan term referring to large trees.

[5] Many white herons are still sighted on Crane Creek.

Catawba were then located in South Carolina territory and were subject to authority from that direction. Colonel Byrd had little praise for the Carolinians anyway. It is to be suspected that his Virginia traders, too, were not angels disguised as merchants.

The Trading Path, like many other Indian trails, had a prominent part in determining the course of immigration taken by white settlers. It was the main highway of the pioneers, and for a time was the only road worthy of mention in the Piedmont.[6] When Bishop Spangenberg reached the Catawba River west of Salisbury in 1752, he commented that he had been hitherto on the Trading Path where he could find at least one house in a day's travel, but that beyond it he turned into the pathless wilderness. The family of Daniel Boone settled on the Yadkin a score of miles north of Trading Ford. The ancestors of four presidents of the United States, Andrew Jackson, Andrew Johnson, James K. Polk, and Herbert Hoover, were settlers either along the trail or near it. The older settlements, such as Charlotte, Salisbury and Hillsboro, sprang up along the Path, and the Winston-Salem and Greensboro communities developed not far from the famous road. The first railroad in the Piedmont followed the trail from Hillsboro to the Haw River, whence it was deflected, later to strike directly upon the trail again from Salisbury to Charlotte. With this deflection, the former Indian trail is still the Great Trading Path of North Carolina, hard-surfaced from Virginia to South Carolina, embracing within a half-hour drive from its line one-fifth of the population, nine-tenths of the industrial development, and nine-tenths of the institutions of higher learning in the State.

As the party had now reached the settlements, Bearskin was discharged with the following benediction:

I also dismiss our honest Indian Bearskin, after presenting him with a note of £3 on Majr. Mumford, a Pound of Powder with Shot in proportion. He had besides the Skins of all the Deer he had kill'd in the whole Journey, and had them carry'd for him into the Bargain. Nothing cou'd be happier than this honest Fellow was with all these Riches, besides the Great Knowledge he had gain'd of the Country.

[6] For further information about the Trading Path, see Douglas L. Rights, "The Trading Path to the Indians," *North Carolina Historical Review*, VIII (1931), 403-426.

He kill'd a Fat Buck, great part of which he left us by way of a Legacy, the rest he cut into pieces, toasted them before the Fire, & then strung them upon his Girdle, to serve him for his Provisions on his way to Christanna-Fort, where his Nation liv'd.

In another version of Colonel Byrd's diary the faithful Indian is called "our Worthy Friend and Fellow Travellaur, Mr. Bearskin, who had so plentifully Supplyed us with Provisions during our long Expedition."

This was not the last to be seen of Friend Bearskin, however, for he appeared two days later, as the Colonel's narrative relates:

All the Grandees of the Sappony Nation did us the Honour to repair hither to meet us, and our worthy Friend and Fellow Traveller, Bearskin, appear'd among the gravest of them in his Robes of ceremony. Four Young Ladies of the first Quality came with them, who had more the Air of cleanliness than any copper-colour'd Beauties I had ever seen. . . .

The Men had something great and Venerable in their countenances, beyond the common Mien of Savages; and indeed they ever had the Reputation of being the Honestest, as well as the bravest Indians we have ever been acquainted with.

This People is now made up of the Remnant of Several other Nations, of which the most considerable are the Sapponys, the Occaneches, and Steukenhocks [probably Conestoga], who not finding themselves Separately Numerous, enough for their Defence, have agreed to unite into one Body, and all of them now go under the Name of Sapponys.

Each of these was formerly a distinct Nation, or rather a Several clan or Canton of the same Nation, Speaking the Same Language, and using the same Customs. But their perpetual Wars against all other Indians, in time, reduc'd them so lo as to make it Necessary to join their Forces together.

They dwelt formerly not far below the Mountains, upon Yadkin River, about 200 Miles West and by South from the Falls of the Roanoak. But about 25 years ago they took Refuge in Virginia, being no longer in condition to make Head not only against the Northern Indians, who are their Implacable enemies, but also against most of those to the South. All the Nations round about, bearing in mind the Havock these Indians us'd formerly to make among their Ancestors in the Insolence of their Power, did at length avenge it Home upon them, and made them glad to apply to this Government for protection.

Colo Spotswood, our then Lieut. governor, having a good Opinion of their Fidelity & Courage, Settled them at Christanna, ten Miles north of Roanoak, upon the belief that they wou'd be a good Barrier on that Side of the Country, against the Incursion of all Foreign Indians. And in Earnest they wou'd have served well enough for that Purpose, if the White People in the Neighbourhood had not debauch'd their Morals, and ruin'd their Health with Rum, which was the Cause of many disorders, and ended at last in a barbarous Murder committed by one of these Indians when he was drunk, for which the poor Wretch was executed when he was sober.

It was a matter of great Concern to them, however, that one of their Grandees should be put to so ignominious a Death. . . .   The Sapponys took this Execution so much to Heart, that they soon after quitted their Settlement and remov'd in a Body to the Cataubas.

The Daughter of the TETERO [Tutelo] King went away with the Sapponys, but being the last of her Nation, and fearing she Shou'd not be treated according to her Rank, poison'd herself, like an Old Roman, with the Root of the Trumpet-Plant.   Her Father dy'd 2 Years before, who was the most intrepid Indian we have been acquainted with.   He had made himself terrible to all other Indians by his Exploits, and had escaped so many Dangers that he was esteemed invulnerable.   But at last he dy'd of a Pleurisy, the last Man of his Race and Nation, leaving only that unhappy Daughter behind, who could not long survive Him.

The most uncommon Circumstance in this Indian visit Was, that they all came on Horse-back, which was certainly intended for a Piece of State, because the Distance was but 3 Miles, and 'tis likely they had walk't a foot twice as far to catch their Horses.   The Men rode more awkwardly than any Dutch Sailor, and the Ladies bestrode their Palfreys a la mode de France, but were so bashful about it, that there was no persuading them to Mount till they were quite out of our Sight.

This description of the pitiful remnants of the Saponi is complimentary, and furnishes a picture, though touched with the pathos of tribal degradation by contact with their neighbors, yet truly praiseworthy of the former proud and virile possessors of the Piedmont.

At a little stream thirteen miles beyond Meherrin River the

homeward-bound party was reminded of another Indian story, the last recorded in this memorable survey:

We came to STURGEON-Creek, so call'd from the Dexterity an OCCAANECHY Indian shewed there in Catching one of those Royal Fish, which was perform'd after the following Manner.

In the Summer time 'tis no unusual thing for Sturgeons to Sleep on the Surface of the Water and one of them having wander'd up into this Creek in the Spring, was floating in that drowsy condition.

The Indian, above mention'd, ran up to the Neck into the Creek a little below the Place where he discover'd the Fish, expecting the Stream wou'd soon bring his Game down to Him.

He judg'd the Matter right, and as Soon as it came within his Reach, he whip't a running Noose over his Jole. This waked the Sturgeon, which being Strong in its own Element darted immediately under Water and dragg'd the Indian after Him. The Man made it a Point of Honour to keep his Hold, which he did to the Apparent Danger of being drown'd. Sometimes both the Indian and the Fish disappear'd for a Quarter of a Minute, & then rose at some Distance above, and sometimes under Water, for a considerable time, till at last the Hero Suffocated his Adversary, and haled his Body ashore in Triumph.

REFERENCES

Byrd, William. *Dividing Line Histories.* Edited by William K. Boyd. Raleigh, 1929. (Quotations from this edition are reprinted by permission of the North Carolina Department of Archives and History, Dr. C. C. Crittenden, secretary.)

Mooney, James. *Siouan Tribes of the East.* Bulletin No. 22, Bureau of American Ethnology. Washington, 1894.

Rights, Douglas L. "The Trading Path to the Indians," *North Carolina Historical Review,* VIII, (1931), 403-426.

CHAPTER X

The Land of Eden

Colonel William Byrd was so favorably impressed with the land he had seen on the survey of the dividing line that he purchased from the North Carolina commissioners twenty thousand acres in the region of the junction of Dan and Smith rivers, to which he later added six thousand acres adjacent. In the fall of the year 1733, he set out to survey his recently acquired tract, called the Land of Eden, which lay mostly within the confines of the present county of Rockingham. The journey began on September 11, and as he went along through the settlements he recruited the other members of the expedition, making occasional short trips aside to inspect mining property.

He recorded that on the twelfth

we sent for an old Indian called Shacco-Will, living about seven miles off, who reckoned himself seventy-eight years old. This fellow pretended he could conduct us to a silver mine, that lies either upon Eno river, or a creek of it, not far from where the Tuscaroras once lived. But by some circumstances in his story, it seemed to be rather a lead than a silver mine. However, such as it is, he promised to go and show it to me whenever I pleased. To comfort his heart, I gave him a bottle of rum, with which he made himself very happy, and all the family very miserable by the horrible noise he made all night.

Who could this be other than our old friend, the noble Indian Eno-Will? It is recalled that he was a Shoccoree, or Shakori; that the remnants of his tribe fled to Virginia near where Colonel Byrd found him; that the thirty-two years elapsed from the time of Lawson's visit, when he was a chieftain in his prime of life, would have added age corresponding to the estimate he made to Colonel Byrd; that he was familiar with the Eno and its vicinity, where mines have been developed in the Occaneechee Hills, not of silver, but of talc; that he was friendly to the English—these points of evidence lead to the conclusion that he may be identified as our old friend. Only the degradation in character which marked him as a victim of the white man's firewater appears to differentiate him from the former noble lord of the Eno.

On the fifteenth the Colonel inspected the land in the vicinity of the junction of the Dan and Staunton rivers, and gave the following description:

My land there in all extends ten miles upon the river; and three charming islands, namely, Sapponi, Occaneeche, and Totero, run along the whole length of it. The lowest of these islands is three miles long, the next four, and the uppermost three, divided from each other by only a narrow strait. The soil is rich in all of them, the timber large, and a kind of pea, very grateful to cattle and horses, holds green all the winter. Roanoke River is divided by these islands; that part which runs on the north side is about eighty yards, and that on the south more than one hundred. A large fresh will overflow the lower part of these islands, but never covers all, so that the cattle may always recover a place of security. The middlemost island, called Occaneeche island, has several fields in it where Occaneeche Indians formerly lived, and there are still some remains of the peach trees they planted.

This middle island was the former home of the Occaneechee to which we traced Lederer and Needham and Arthur. On the uppermost island the Saponi had dwelt. The Tutelo had settled on the lowest island, described thus by the Colonel's narrative:

We met with old fields where the Indians had formerly lived, and the grass grew as high as a horse and his rider. . . . There is a cave in this island, in which the last Totero king, with only two of his men, defended himself against a great host of northern Indians, and at last obliged them to retire.

Three Tuscarora Indians were recruited for the journey. Colonel Byrd understood that they had been kept on his land to serve as hunters for his overseer, Harry Morris. After considerable persuasion they consented to go along. Two days later they had not yet joined him, according to their promise, and he began to doubt the veracity of the Tuscarora. However, on the following day, September 19, the lagging Indians showed up, resolved to serve as hunters on condition that they be supplied with powder and shot and that they be allowed to have the skins of all the deer they killed. On the following day the expedition was under way, there having assembled with the Colonel "4 gentlemen, 5 woodsmen, 4 negroes, the 3 Tuscarora Indians, 20 horses, and 4 dogs."

The hunters did not come up to the excellent standard set by Bearskin on the former expedition. On the day of departure they killed three deer, but were so lazy that they did not bring the game to camp, pretending that the animals were too lean. On the following day they were so fearful of falling into the hands of the Catawba that they did not venture out of sight of their patrons; hence they killed nothing, and the party was forced "to make a temperate supper of bread and cheese." They improved, however, as they journeyed along, for on Sunday, the twenty-third, according to the Colonel:

Our Indians having no notion of the sabbath, went out to hunt for something for dinner, and brought a young doe back along with them. They laughed at the English for losing one day in seven, if idleness and doing nothing to the purpose may be called loss of time. These gentiles have no distinction of days, but make every day a sabbath, except when they go out to war or a hunting, and then they will undergo incredible fatigues. Of other work the men do none, thinking it below the dignity of their sex, but make the poor women do all the drudgery. They have a blind tradition amongst them, that work was first laid upon mankind by the fault of a female, and therefore it is but just that that sex should do the greatest part of it. This they plead in their excuse; but the true reason is, that the weakest must always go to the wall, and superiority has from the beginning ungenerously imposed slavery on those who are not able to resist it.

Most of the travelers were fearful of an attack by hostile Indians. There was great alarm when one of the woodsmen brought in the news that he had found a deserted camp of ten huts, the poles of which still had fresh green leaves upon them. The Colonel sought courageously to allay the fears of his companions.

On the twenty-sixth they reached Sable Creek (Wolf Island), and a survey of the Land of Eden began. On the twenty-ninth they crossed the Irvin (Smith) River and came to the end of the line. The next day being Sunday a halt was made. Although the weather was chilly, several of the party went swimming in the river. According to the narrative: "One of our Indians went in along with us, and taught us their way of swimming. They strike not out both hands together, but alternately one after the other, whereby they are able to swim both farther and faster than we do." The surveying party turned south of the Land of Eden and crossed the Dan about one and one-half miles west of its junction with the Smith River. They turned then to the east and rode three miles downstream along the south bank over the rough highground. In the Colonel's words:

But then on a sudden the scene changed, and we were surprised with an opening of large extent, where the Sauro Indians once lived, who had been a considerable nation. But the frequent inroads of the Senecas annoyed them incessantly, and obliged them to remove from this fine situation about thirty years ago. They then retired more southerly, as far as Pee Dee River, and incorporated with the Kewawees, where a remnant of them is still surviving. It must have been a great misfortune to them to be obliged to abandon so beautiful a dwelling, where the air is wholesome, and the soil equal in fertility to any in the world. The river is about eighty yards wide, always confined within its lofty banks, and rolling down its waters, as sweet as milk, and as clear as crystal. There runs a charming level, of more than a mile square, that will bring forth like the lands of Egypt, without being overflowed once a year. There is scarce a shrub in view to intercept your prospect, but grass as high as a man on horseback. Towards the woods there is a gentle eminence, that overlooks the whole landscape. This sweet place is bounded to the east by a fine stream, called Sauro creek, which running out of the Dan, and tending westerly, makes the whole a peninsula. I could not quit this pleasant situation without regret, but often faced about to take a parting look at it as far as I could see, and so indeed did all the rest of the company. But at last we left it quite out of sight, and continued our course down the river, till where it intersects my back line, which was about five miles below Sauro Town.

This paradise so generously described by the possessor of the Land of Eden is situated a few miles east of the present town of Leaksville. It became many years ago the property of the Broadnax family, and was the ancestral home of the late Governor Robert Broadnax Glenn. Old maps show another settlement designated Upper Sauratown, located on Dan River northeast of Walnut Cove. Both sites show ample signs of Indian occupation.

By November 3 the surveyors were out of the Land of Eden and began measuring the land of Major Mayo, a member of the party. They crossed Cliff Creek (Hogan's Creek) and Hixe's Creek (Moon Creek). The next stream they met on their course east they called Hatcher's Creek (Rattlesnake Creek), according to the narrative,

from two Indian traders of that name, who used formerly to carry goods to the Sauro Indians. Near the banks of this creek I found a large beech tree, with the following inscription cut upon the bark of it, J.H., H.H., B.B., lay here the 24th day of May, 1673. It was not difficult to fill up these initials with the following names, Joseph Hatcher, Henry Hatcher and Benjamin Bullington, three Indian traders, who had lodged near that place sixty years before, in their way to the Sauro Town. But the strangest part of the story was this, that these letters, cut in the bark, should remain perfectly legible so long, Nay, if no accident befalls the tree, which appears to be still in a flourishing condition, I doubt not but this piece of antiquity may be read many years hence. We may learn from it, that the beech is a very long-lived tree, of which there are many exceedingly large in these woods.

It will be recalled that Henry Hatcher, whose initials were cut on the tree, was the trader who in 1674 confirmed the news of the murder of James Needham at Trading Ford. Perhaps the old tree is still standing at the mouth of Rattlesnake Creek in Caswell County.

References

Byrd, William. *A Journey to the Land of Eden.* Edited by Mark Van Doren. New York, 1928. (Quotations from this edition are reprinted by permission of the Vanguard Press.)

CHAPTER XI

Last Chronicles of the Piedmont Tribes

SAPONI AND TUTELO

WHEN LAWSON was at Trading Ford, the Saponi offered to sell him their land on the Yadkin as they were preparing to move eastward to be under protection of the government. Soon after 1701 this migration began. The Saponi and Tutelo combined their reduced forces and set out together seeking a new home. The name Sapony Creek in Nash County may indicate a halting place on their trail. They crossed the Roanoke, probably before the Tuscarora War in 1711, and made a settlement called Sapona Town about fifteen miles west of Windsor in Bertie County in the region of the friendly Tuscarora. In 1712 they were invited by the government of North Carolina to join in the campaign against the hostile Tuscarora. They were asked to make their own terms, and were promised provision for their families if they would remove to the settlements in the Albemarle region. This invitation was probably accepted. These tribes, as well as others of Siouan stock, had little love for the Iroquoian—Tuscarora, Nottoway, and Meherrin—of the east.[1]

In 1709 the Saponi chief complained that the Nottoway and Tuscarora had killed two of his people. The Nottoway replied that the Saponi had killed three of theirs and had wounded two others not long before, and that they thought it reasonable that they as well as the Saponi should have satisfaction. The Saponi then proposed, according to Indian custom, that the Nottoway should pay for the two murdered Saponi, which the Nottoway agreed to do provided the Saponi would pay for the three Nottoway. The judge to whom they had come, disgusted at the procedure, told them that if they would make such bargains among

[1] The Nottoway and Meherrin were located in eastern Virginia near the North Carolina boundary.

themselves, he would have nothing to say, but it was not the white people's law to sell men's lives for money. The Saponi then tried to shift the blame upon the Tutelo, but the Nottoway answered that they were both as one people, and further stated that some time before they had paid the Saponi a quantity of wampum to enlist their aid in exterminating the Tutelo; but that the false Saponi, after taking the wampum, had broken their promise and had privately warned the Tutelo of the plot. To settle the whole matter the Nottoway proposed that if the Saponi would fulfil their agreement and join them against the Tutelo, the Nottoway would not only let them keep the wampum, but would also pay them for the two men killed. The Saponi chief promised to take the matter under consideration and returned home, whereupon the judge wrote to the Virginia government that if a Tuscarora were delivered up to be killed by the Saponi, some English lives would certainly pay for it.

Through the persuasion of Governor Spottswood of Virginia these two tribes moved to Fort Christanna, ten miles north of Roanoke River in the present Brunswick County, Virginia, probably soon after the outbreak of the Tuscarora War. The benevolent Governor exerted himself to provide well for the Indian refugees. He sought to bring the children of the chiefs to the college established at Williamsburg, which had been chartered in 1691 with provisions for training Indian youths. He sent a schoolmaster to the Saponi, Charles Griffin, described as "a man of good family, who, by the innocence of his life, and the sweetness of his temper, was perfectly well qualify'd for the pious undertaking. Besides, he had so much the secret of mixing pleasure with instruction, that he had not a scholar, who did not love him affectionately." Unfortunately, he was called back to the college before he could accomplish much, and the Saponi were bereft of their amiable instructor.

Even under the supervision of the authorities at Fort Christanna the straggling remnants of the Carolina tribes were a prey to the debauching influences of the white man's civilization. Nor were they free from the depredations of their enemy tribesmen. In 1717 a party of Catawba and others of the smaller tribes of South Carolina came to the fort to make a treaty of peace and to leave some of their children to be educated as a pledge of their good faith. While encamped outside the fort, having delivered up their arms to the commander, they were attacked during the night by a party of Iroquois who killed five of their number and carried off several prisoners, including a chief of the Catawba. When the English at a council in Albany, New York, called the Iroquois to account for this crime, these warriors replied that three years before, the Catawba had treacherously killed five of their men asleep during the night, after a treaty of peace had been made. In the year 1722, at an Albany conference, a lasting treaty of peace was finally declared, which brought to an end the long years of strife between the Iroquois confederacy and the southern tribes.

This treaty, however, did not end the troubles at the Virginia fort. A report of the year 1728 stated that a delegation of Saponi went to the Catawba to enlist a hundred warriors to aid them in demanding satisfaction of the English for imprisoning one of their men. They also threatened that if one of their men, Captain Tom, were hanged, they would move their women and children across the Roanoke and would drive the white settlers beyond the James. The white men were told that they had no business to come to the fort to concern themselves about the Indians' killing one another.

To free themselves from this unhappy state of affairs they decided to move, this time to join their former enemies, the Iroquois in the North. By 1740 this migration was under way, and it continued for a number of years. In 1748 the famous missionary to the Indians, David Zeisberger, found some of them living on the north branch of the Susquehanna River in a settlement which he described as "the only town on the continent inhabited by Tuteloes, a degenerate remnant of thieves and drunkards." In 1753 the Cayuga adopted the Saponi and Tutelo, who thus became part of the Iroquois confederacy, although Governor Dobbs reported in 1755 that fourteen men and fourteen women of the Saponi were in Granville County.[2] The Cayuga, after the destruction of their settlement during the Revolution, fled with their incorporated southern Indians to Canada. The Tutelo who went

[2] A remnant of Indians remains in Person County, once a part of Granville. Investigation has shown that they are a branch of, or have mixed with, the Indians of Robeson County. There is a possibility that a few Saponi remained here.

with them established their village at what is now known as Tutelo Heights, a suburb of Brantford. The last surviving Tutelo, known as Nikonha, stated in 1870, a year before his death, that when his people fled to Canada they parted with the Saponi at Niagara, and what afterward became of the Saponi he did not know. This last full-blood of the Tutelo believed himself to be more than one hundred years old and was a pensioner of the War of 1812. He was described as a man of marked intelligence and lively humor. His memory, which ran back to days before the Revolution, recalled that the tribes with whom the Tutelo had been most often at war were the Tuscarora, the Seneca, and the Cayuga. A handful of mixed Tutelo-Cayuga still exists, and as late as the year 1932 Dr. Frank G. Speck collected a number of Tutelo legends from them on the reservation in New York State.

Thus has come to an end a race once described as the "honestest and bravest Indians" Virginia ever knew.

The Occaneechee

The warlike Occaneechee, it is thought, followed their old neighbors, the Saponi and Tutelo, on the northward migration. They disappeared so quickly and so completely from the scene of their former dominion that they left scarcely a trace of information as to their fate.

Saura, Keyauwee, and Eno

According to Colonel Byrd, the Saura left their pleasant home on the Dan River to unite with the Keyauwee and to move eastward. The name of the former tribe is preserved in the Saura Town Mountains near the Dan River, and the Keyauwee name seems to have lingered in the Carraway Mountains of Randolph County.

At the same time the Eno, Shoccoree, and Adshusheer combined their forces under the tribal name Eno. In 1716 Governor Spottswood attempted to settle these tribes at Eno Town on the upper Neuse River, to serve as a protection against the hostile Tuscarora and their northern allies, and the Yamassee. The Governments of North and South Carolina protested that the Saura were then engaged in the war against South Carolina, and that the Eno and Keyauwee were probably aiding them. At the same time North Carolina raised a force of Indians and colonists to attack the Saura. Complaints were made that the Indians were supplied with arms and ammunition from the Virginians in return for skins, slaves, and goods plundered from South Carolina settlers; that the Saura were responsible for most of the mischief done north of Santee River, and that they were endeavoring to draw the Winyaw and Waccamaw into the same alliance; that Virginia encouraged these depredations in order to monopolize the Indian trade. A South Carolinian declared: "I heartily wish Virginia had all our Indians, so we were but secured from them."

At the close of the Yamassee War the Saura were located on the Peedee River, and were known as the Cheraw. Their village was across the river from the town in South Carolina which today bears their name. A report of 1715 gives the population as 510, seemingly too high. Under pressure of attacks from Northern Indians they were forced to combine with the Catawba, among whom they retained their name and dialect for some time.

The *South Carolina Gazette* reported a visit to Charleston of eleven chiefs of the Catawba and Cheraw in July, 1739. The Cheraw, however, did not altogether favor their residence among the Catawba, and scattered bands of the former remained eastward near the settlements. The *Gazette* carried the news on June 2, 1746, that Governor Glen of South Carolina had in April met a delegation of Catawba Indians on the Santee River near the Congaree. There a trader among the Catawba, named Brown, informed the Governor that some of the "Pedees and Cheraws (two small tribes who have long been incorporated with the Catawbas), intended to leave them, which might prove of dangerous consequence at a time when they were so closely attacked by their enemies, the Northern Indians." The Governor's conference proceeded in the following manner:

The governor ordered the rammers of all the pistols which he had delivered to the Indians to be laid upon the table, desiring that such as were Pedees and Charaws might advance, and they, being in a body near him, he spoke to them in these words: "It gives me great concern, my friends, to hear that you entertain the least thought of leaving the Catawbas, with whom you have been so long and so closely united. This union makes you strong, and enables you to defend yourselves and annoy your enemies; but should you ever separate, you would thereby weaken yourselves, and be exposed to every danger. Consider that if you were single and divided, you may be broke as easily as I break this stick" (at the same time breaking one of the rammers); "but if you continue united together, and stand by one another, it will be as impossible to hurt or break you, as it is impossible for me to break these," (his excellency then taking up a handful of rammers).

After this they all promised to continue together in their camp.

The Governor of South Carolina wrote to Governor Clinton of New York, on May 24, 1751, pleading for assistance in reconciling the differences between the Northern and Southern Indians. He mentioned several Southern tribes, including the Cherokee and the Catawba, and also "all tribes in friendship with these nations, or that live amongst our settlements, such as Charraws, Uchees, Pedees, Notches, Cape Fears, or other Indians." From this we gather that there were straggling bands of the Cheraw who were not living with the Catawba, but preferred to linger in eastern Carolina. That a part of the tribe at least was still among the Catawba and possessed of considerable strength at the time may be judged by the report in the *Gazette* published in June, 1759:

On Tuesday last, 45 Charraws, part of a nation of Indians incorporated with the Catawbas, arrived in town, headed by King Johnny, who brought to the governor the scalp of a French Indian, which he had taken near Loyal-Henning. He and several others that are with him here, were with Gen. Forbes during the whole expedition against Fort Du Quesne. Their chief business seems to be, to see his excellency and receive presents.

In 1759 smallpox ravaged the Catawba Nation and appeared also among the white settlements. The Cheraw, or Saura, must have suffered also.

As late as 1768 remnants of the Saura were reported as still living among the Catawba, reduced by wars and disease to fifty or sixty people. After the Revolution smallpox again swept through the Catawba country, and it is asserted that the wasted tribe was advised to invite the Cheraw to unite with them, an indication that some of the Cheraw were still holding out for themselves at that date. Fifty years later, inhabitants of the Cheraw neighborhood on the Peedee remembered visits of the

Saura-Cheraw to their old home in the vicinity. Nothing further is known definitely of them. Their name survives in Saura Town Mountains of Stokes County in North Carolina, in the town of Cheraw in South Carolina, and possibly in the Uwharrie River and Mountains of the middle Piedmont area of the former state.

The Keyauwee probably followed the trail of the Saura, as did most of the confederated Eno. A few of the Eno-Shoccoree found their way to Virginia, as we have previously noted. Eno River and Shocco Creek still recall their names.

The Saxapahaw

The Saxapahaw received favorable mention from the colonists, whom they aided in the Tuscarora War. It has been stated that they joined with the Yamassee against South Carolina in 1715. Further than this no one knows what became of the tribe that gave the name to Haw River and Haw Fields. This tribe has been identified with the Shoccoree, or Shakori.

Cape Fear Indians

The Cape Fear Indians were represented in Colonel Barnwell's expedition. They are supposed to have been of Siouan stock. Like most of their neighbors, it is probable that they joined in the Yamassee uprising. They do not seem to have been incorporated with the Catawba. They were last noticed in 1715 as one of the small friendly tribes living near the settlements with whom the South Carolina government desired the Iroquois to be at peace.

Catawba Confederates

The Waxhaw, Wateree, Congaree, Santee, Sugaree, and other neighboring tribes located near the Catawba Nation, merged, as would be expected, with their stronger Catawba kinsmen.

Lost Tribes

Several tribes of northeastern South Carolina whose territory extended upstream above the state line, including Waccamaw, Peedee, Winyaw, Sewee, and other small groups, thought to be of Siouan stock, continued to live near the settlements during the early years of the eighteenth century. Occasional references in colonial records tell of their troubles, of poverty, pestilence, and strife. The government sought to maintain peace, but in vain, for the scattered tribes in their weak condition were a prey to straggling war parties seeking revenge or endeavoring to secure slaves. The Peedee, who have given their name to the lower Yadkin, were settled on the lower portion of the stream. In 1743 the governor of South Carolina signed an order

to provide for the Pedee Indians now in town the following particulars, viz: *Presents.*—To the three head men, each of them, a gun and knife; to the others, each of them, a knife. For the three women, each of them, a looking-glass, twenty bullets, half a pound of vermilion to be divided among them. Also, an order on Col. Brewton for ten pounds of gunpowder for use of the said Indians.

In 1744 Catawba Indians were seeking revenge for the loss of several of their warriors, and Governor Glen reported that the Peedee and another tribe, implicated in the affair, had been forced to come down near the settlements for protection. Two years later the Governor tried to persuade the Saura and Peedee who were then among the Catawba to continue to remain there. A considerable number of the Peedee, however, were evidently not living among the Catawba at the time, as indicated by the following letter to the Governor, written by Chief Haiglar:

There are a great many Pedee Indians living in the settlements that we want to come and settle among us. We desire for you to send them, and advise them to this, and give them this string of wampum in token that we want them to settle here, and will always live like brothers with them. The Northern Indians want them all to settle with us; for, as they are now at peace, they may be hunting in the woods or straggling about, killed by some of them, except they join us, and make but one nation, which will be a great addition of strength to us.

CATAWBAS, 21st November, 1752

THE (his x mark) KING

The journal of John Evans, who was sent by Governor Glen to the Catawba in 1755, contains references to Indians still lingering on the outskirts of the settlements:

October 17th—Met a Catawba man and woman, and informed by them, that in the summer, the Cherrackees and Notchees had killed some Pedees and Waccamaws in the white people's settlements.

October 18th—I got into the Catawbas. King Hazler was gone a hunting the day before; the next morning they sent for him, and he came in that night. . . .

21st—The king and head man met, and desired to know what I was come for. I told them that there was two Pedee women killed and scalped, and two boys carried away from out the settlements, and that it was done by some of their nation; and one Notchee, which was called the Notchee Doctor, and his excellency, the governor, desired that they would not come into the settlements without they were sent for. The white people might mistake them, and do them mischief, believing them to be enemy Indians. I further said that it was his excellency, the governor's pleasure, that the Catawba people should not attempt to carry away any of the Indians now living in the settlements up to their nation on any pretence whatsoever without his permission first. Their answer was, that old men should always speak truth; and the most of them were grey-headed and they, for their parts, did not hurt the Pedees, and did not know or believe the mischief was done by any belonging to that nation; and further said, that when the North-ward Indians were in their nation, they bound the same three women and two men; and the Catawbas released the three women, but the Northward Indians carried the men away.

These casual references show that during the first half of the eighteenth century scattered remnants of the eastern South Carolina tribes struggled along near the settlements and refused to unite with the Catawba, and that their position was precarious, since they were exposed to attacks by their enemies and were neither prepared to defend themselves, nor sufficiently protected by their neighbors. The natural retreat for these tribes would be found in the isolated regions of the headwaters of the streams near which they resided, away from the main roads of travel and distant from the settlements where they might be mistaken for enemy Indians or exposed to slave hunters. The swampy region of Robeson County afforded such a retreat. There with united forces they could offer stronger resistance. This uninviting territory was not quickly claimed by white settlers.

It is reported that in 1740 a Mr. Vaughn appropriated a large tract of land in Duplin County, together with a hundred slaves, for the purpose of Christianizing five Indian tribes in that vicinity. These Indians, not named, disappeared as the settlements encroached. The Bladen County report to a circular of Governor Dobbs stated in 1754 that on Drowning Creek at the head of Little Peedee River there was a "mixed crew" of lawless people possessing the land without patent or paying quit rents. Thus it appears that the lost tribes that disappeared from the neighborhood of the settlements to the south, together with mixed-bloods and white refugees, may have made their last stand in the secluded swamplands of Robeson County and adjoining territory, where they were found later by the settlers who slowly penetrated the region. This solution is offered to the problem connected with the origin of the eight thousand or more inhabitants of this county who have been called Croatan Indians by their neighbors.

Siouan Tribes of the East

In the latter part of the nineteenth century it was found through language study that the Indian tribes discovered by the early explorers in Piedmont Virginia and the Carolinas were related linguistically to the populous Siouan tribes of the West. Further study revealed that the Siouan tribes of the East were grouped in two divisions, northern and southern. It appears that the southern group, composed of the Catawba, Wateree, Congaree, and other tribes of the lower area, had come much earlier to the South than the upper tribes. There is indication that they may have migrated from the North around the western fringes of the Appalachians, as there have been found remnants of this stock also in the lower Mississippi Valley. The affinities noted in the grouping of the Siouan tribes in the Carolinas tends to confirm this view. The upper group, Saponi, Tutelo, and others, were latecomers in the Piedmont, and had evidently migrated into Virginia territory long after the Catawba and kindred tribes established themselves in their southern home. The location of their former habitations in Virginia gives indication that these Indians migrated across the Blue Ridge from Midwestern territory.

The researches of Dr. John R. Swanton, which conform with the views of Dr. Frank G. Speck, have led to interesting explanations of the presence of the Eno, Saxapahaw, Keyauwee, and possibly the Catawba, Wateree, and Waxhaw, in the locations where they were discovered by the English explorers. Evidence shows that these tribes were probably located farther south at an earlier date and were met by Spanish explorers, whose disturbing incursions may have caused the removal northward. Investigation shows also a close connection in language, customs, etc., of the southern group with the Muskhogean stock, which merits further study.

REFERENCES

Byrd, William. *Dividing Line Histories.* Edited by William K. Boyd. Raleigh, 1929.

The Colonial Records of North Carolina. Edited by William L. Saunders. Vols. I-V. Raleigh, 1886.

Gregg, Alexander. *History of the Old Cheraws.* New York, 1867.

Hale, Horatio. "The Tutelo Tribes and Language," *Proceedings of the American Philosophical Society,* Vol. XXI (1883), No. 114.

Hodge, F. W. *Handbook of American Indians North of Mexico.* Bulletin No. 30, Bureau of American Ethnology, Parts 1 and 2. Washington, 1907, 1910.

Lawson, John. *History of North Carolina.* London, 1714.

Mooney, James. *Siouan Tribes of the East.* Bulletin No. 22, Bureau of American Ethnology. Washington, 1894.

Rivers, W. J. *A Sketch of the History of South Carolina.* Charleston, 1856.

Speck, Frank G. "Tutelo Rituals: Aboriginal Carolina History Revealed in Canadian Research," *Bulletin of the Archaeological Society of North Carolina,* II (Sept., 1935), 1-7.

————. *The Tutelo Spirit Adoption Ceremony.* Harrisburg, 1942.

Swanton, John R. "Early History of the Eastern Siouan Tribes," in *Essays in Anthropology in Honor of Alfred Louis Kroeber,* Berkeley, Calif., 1936, pp. 271-282.

————. *The Indians of the Southeastern United States.* Bulletin 137, Bureau of American Ethnology. Washington, 1946.

Virginia State Papers. Edited by William Plummer. Vol. I. Richmond, 1875.

CHAPTER XII

The Catawba

SIOUAN SURVIVORS

THE LARGEST and most important tribe of Siouan stock in the Piedmont was the Catawba. The name *Catawba* is probably derived from a Choctaw word meaning "divided" or "separated," possibly signifying the southern branch of the great stock. In their own language they called themselves Nieye, "real people," using the same term that most other aboriginal tribes employed in referring to themselves. From earliest contacts they have been known as the "river people," their word *iswa*, meaning "river," furnishing the basis for derivations such as Esaw, Ushery, Issa, etc., of the early explorers.

According to a tradition of the tribe, they migrated from the North, and as the Siouan tribes were noted as buffalo hunters, it is thought that the southern branch of this stock came from the Midwest on their hunting expeditions and settled in the Piedmont country. They were first mentioned in the account of the expedition of Juan Pardo, and the next reference to them was made nearly one hundred years later by Lederer. Since the time of Lederer's visit the Catawba have lived along the river called by their name.

They were a sedentary, agricultural people. The women were described by Lawson as being "reasonably handsome," delighting in feather ornaments and industrious in domestic pursuits. They were skilful in making pottery and weaving baskets and still practice the arts with great proficiency. The Catawba women are the only pottery-makers of the tribes in the eastern United States who carry on this profession in the manner of their ancestors by using cylindrical strips of clay. The men were described as being trustworthy, courageous, and friendly, though regarded by some as being more easygoing and lacking in energy than Indians generally. Perhaps the mild southern climate and pleasant surroundings of the Piedmont country contributed to make them so. They were skilful hunters. Certainly they were brave and gave their enemies many a telling blow, but they were no match for their inveterate enemies, the Five Nations. Against the Cherokee and the Tuscarora, Iroquoian of the South, they held their own and kept both tribes at respectful distance.

The Catawba were hereditary enemies of the Cherokee. When the Cherokee joined with the colonists in the war against the Tuscarora, this was the only instance in which Cherokee and Catawba operated together. The Cherokee claimed that they held the country about the headwaters of the Catawba River to below the present town of Morganton until game became scarce; then they retired west of the Blue Ridge, and afterward "loaned" the eastern territory to the Catawba.

A tradition recorded by Schoolcraft, which incorrectly represents the Catawba as latecomers from the north, stated that on arriving at the Catawba River they found their progress disputed by the Cherokee. A battle was fought with no decisive result, although the advantage was on the side of the Catawba, who had guns, while their opponents had only the cruder weapons of Indian warfare. This allusion places the conflict near the close of the seventeenth century. Preparations were made to renew the fight when the Cherokee offered to recognize the river as the boundary. The agreement was made that the Catawba be allowed to occupy the country east of that river and that the Cherokee hold the country west of Broad River, with the region between as neutral territory. Stone piles were heaped upon the battlefield to commemorate the treaty, and Broad River was henceforth called Eswau Huppeday (Line River) by the Catawba.

Relations with the colonists, except during the Yamassee War of 1715, were uniformly friendly. With the exception of this one brief outbreak of hostility they have maintained a meritorious record for friendliness toward their white neighbors. They aided in the campaign against the Tuscarora in the east and served as a barrier against tribes of the west. The flood of immigration that poured into the Piedmont area after 1700 was little opposed by the friendly Catawba. Although constant encroachment on their hunting territory called forth repeated protests, there was no serious outbreak except the minor defection already noted.

They aided in expeditions against the French and their Indian allies at Fort DuQuesne and elsewhere during the French and Indian War, and in the same struggle they helped to protect the Piedmont Carolina settlers from invasions of the Cherokee. In 1756 Governor Dobbs stated that no attacks had been made on the frontier, owing principally to the frontier guardsmen and "the Neighbourhood of the Catawba Indians, our friends." A single mention from the colonial records of the same year, which tells of their aid in pursuit of a roving band of Cherokee marauders, of the recovery of goods stolen from settlers, and of the return of the goods to Salisbury for distribution to rightful owners, indicates the Catawba good will and protection which have made the people of the Carolinas ever indebted to them. If in this time of danger the Catawba Nation had made alliance with enemy Indians and had taken up arms against the settlers instead of fighting valiantly for them, there is no doubt that many a family of the Piedmont, whose descendants dwell happily in the region today, would have been massacred.

In 1763 it was proposed to use them and the Cherokee against the lake tribes under Pontiac. During the Revolution they assisted the colonists against the British, and were forced to leave their homes, with their families, and to seek refuge in Virginia until peace was restored. Catawba scouts led the way for General Greene to the battle of Guilford Court House. Their warriors were prominent in Williamson's expedition against the Cherokee. Catawbans served with valor in the Confederate Army. In the First World War several of their young men were enlisted out of a total surviving population of less than two hundred, and made an honorable record in the United States Army. In the Second World War their response was no less praiseworthy. This is a notable record, hardly surpassed by any other tribe of the American continent.

This once populous tribe, like others of the Carolinas, suffered a rapid decline. Diseases introduced by the whites, especially smallpox, swept away great numbers. Liquor furnished its share of destruction. The Northern Indians repeatedly made inroads over the long war trail and constantly claimed their victims. After the Iroquois declared peace the Shawnee continued depredations. In 1762 a small party of the latter killed the noted Catawba chief, King Haiglar, as he was returning from Waxhaw attended by a single servant, and from that time the tribe ceased to be of importance except in conjunction with their white neighbors. As President George Washington journeyed over the Trading Path toward Charlotte in 1791, he was met at the Catawba River by the chief of the sadly reduced tribe, who came to greet the Great White Father and to plead the cause of the unfortunate Catawba Nation.

It has been estimated that in the early seventeenth century the population of the tribe was over five thousand. In 1701 Lawson referred to them as a "powerful tribe" and commented on their numerous villages. Adair mentioned that one of their cleared fields extended seven miles, besides which they had several smaller village sites. In 1721 they were reported to have had a population of about twelve hundred, described by the English as "brave fellows as any on the continent of America, and our firm friends." In 1728 Colonel Byrd stated that they had six villages on the Catawba River within twenty miles. By 1784 only about 250 members of the tribe were to be found; in 1826 the population was listed as 110. Notwithstanding the incorporation of the remnants of neighboring tribes, the Catawba narrowly escaped total extermination.

In 1840 about one hundred Catawbans, nearly all who were left of the tribe, being dissatisfied with their condition in South Carolina, moved up in a body and took up their residence with the Cherokee in western North Carolina. Latent tribal jealousies broke out, however, and at their own request, negotiations were begun in 1848, through Colonel Thomas, their agent, and others, for their removal to Indian Territory. An act of Congress approved on July 29, 1848, granted an appropriation of $5,000 to defray expenses of removal of the Catawba Indians to the country west of the Mississippi, provided that the Catawba would give their consent and that a home could be found near some friendly tribe without additional cost to the government. Officials of the government, seeking to carry out this proposal, entered into correspondence with Cherokee authorities. As the Cherokee, however, were unwilling to give up without full compensation any portion of their lands to be occupied by another tribe, the subject was dropped. The effort having been without result, the Catawba soon after began to drift back to their own homes, until, in 1852, there were only about a dozen remaining among the Cherokee. In 1890 only one was left, an old woman, the widow of a Cherokee husband. She and her daughter, both of whom spoke the language, were expert potters according to the Catawba method, which differed markedly from that of the Cherokee. At the close of the past century, two Catawba women, married to Cherokee husbands, lived within the tribe and still practiced their art of making pottery. While residing among the Cherokee, the Catawba acquired a reputation as doctors and leaders of the dance.

In 1934 the tribe numbered 199 members, 220 in 1937, 240 in 1941, and 280 in 1944, most of them living on the reservation along the Catawba River not far from the mouth of Sugar Creek, where the ancient center of the Catawba Nation was located.

About the year 1884 missionaries of the Church of the Latter Day Saints began work among the Catawba. Some of the converts went west to make their home. Nearly all of the remaining members of the tribe are now affiliated with this religious body.

With decrease in population there was commensurate shrinkage of property holdings. The territory once claimed by the Catawba extended over the broad area drained by the Catawba River between Broad River and the Yadkin, and from the headwaters of the Catawba far down into South Carolina. In 1763 they had confirmed to them a reservation, assigned a few years before, of fifteen square miles, on both sides of the Catawba River within the present York and Lancaster counties in South Carolina. The triangular indentation in the boundary line between the Carolinas marks the former northern limits of the reservation. In 1826 nearly the whole of their reservation was leased to white neighbors for a few thousand dollars. In 1840 the state of South Carolina acquired all but a single square mile, on which they now reside. The treaty with the state was signed by the chief, Colonel Samuel Scott, a grandson of Chief Haiglar. Here the surviving members of the tribe, with the exception of a few who migrated west, still cling to their ancestral home on the banks of the Iswa Tavora—the Catawba River.

For more than two centuries this friendly and courageous people, despite the ravages of disease, the devastation of war, the surrender of territory, and the accursed evils of the new civilization, have, with only one almost negligible exception, ever stood loyally by their neighbors and fought their battles. As their light has failed, it has left an afterglow of fidelity and honor.

———

For a long time the state of South Carolina made a grant to the Indians of $35 each per year. In 1944 recognition long delayed was given when the Federal Government assumed charge of the affairs of the Catawba Indians, assuring them the protection and guidance which they had hitherto lacked and sorely needed. The state of South Carolina purchased about two thousand acres of land to add to the reservation. Thus the Catawba Nation has been given a well-deserved place in the family of wards of the United States Government.

King Haiglar

Chief Haiglar deserves more than a word of passing comment. He became leader of the tribe about 1748. His friendly attitude toward the governments of North and South Carolina and his faithful conduct made him respected and trusted throughout the colonies. The political boundaries of Catawba territory during his administration were confined to South Carolina, but he was often called upon by the northern colony to aid in its protection. Though disposed to peace, he offered his services to the governor of South Carolina when the Cherokee took up arms against the settlers in 1759. As a member of Colonel Grant's forces he was actively engaged in the severe battle of Etchoe, and assisted materially in gaining the victory. He is described as a "man of sterling character, just in his dealings, and true to his word, acting the part of a father to his people, by whom he was greatly beloved."

Reports of conferences between Chief Haiglar and commissioners of the North Carolina government are very informing as to relations between the Catawba Nation and the colonial government, as to Indian logic, and as to the character of the chief.[1] Following is a partial account of a treaty held on August 29, 1754, in Salisbury:

The Commission which was sent by his Honr the President to the above Commissioners, being Read in the presence of King Hagler and sundry of his headmen and Warriors, after which it was interpreted by Mr. Matthew Tool, Together with the letter which was also sent by his Honr to Capt. McCleachan Andw Perkins Esqr and Others, as Concerning said Indians.

After Each sentence was Distinctly Interpreted by Mr. Tool, who was Sworn for that purpose the King made the following Speech**

BROTHERS AND WARRIORS

I am Exceeding glad to meet you here this day, and to have the opportunity of haveing a talk one with an Other in a Brotherly and Loveing manner, and to Brighten, and Strengthen, that Chain of Friendship which has so long remained between us and the people of those three Provinces, and I am very Sorry to hear those Complaints that are Laid to our People's Charge, But now will Open our Ears to here those Grievances & Complaints that shall be made by you against our Young men and Others, and we do Heartily Thank our Good Brother the President of North Carolina for his good Talk in his Letter to us, and also for his appointing You to meet us here, to have this Discourse.

Then William Morrison Appeared, to support the Complaint that was by him Made to the Officers at a late Court martial held in Rowan County, Concerning the Indian Insults to him at his own house, sometimes before, when they Came to him at his mill and Attempted to Frow a pail of Water into his Meal Trough, and when he would prevent them they made many attempts to streik him with their guns over his head.

To which some of the Indians said what they Intended to do with the water was only to put a handful or Two of the meal into it to make a kind of Drink which is their way and Custom.

The King also Said that it was well that one of them had killed him, for said he had they killed You or anybody Else we would surely have killed him for they would not let him Live above the ground, but would put him under the ground, as Lately we have Done to one

---

[1] If these reports from *The Colonial Records of North Carolina* prove dull reading, the reader can skip them. He may find it worth while, however, to return to them at leisure and read them in their entirety to get the atmosphere of official negotiations with the Indians.

of our Young Fellows who got Drunk and in his Liquor met with a
little girl on his way below the Waxhaw Settlement and kill'd her we
were Immediately aprized of it by one of our own People, and we soon
Discovered who, it was that Committed the fact whereupon we Directly Caused an Other young man the fellows own Cousin to kill
him, which he readily did in the presence of some of our Brothers,
the white people in Order to shew our Willingness to punish such
offenders.

Then Came James Armstrong William Young and William Mc-
Night who Laid sundry things to the Indians Charge, (to wit)
Concerning their taking Bread meat meal and Cloaths and also for
attempting to Take away a child, and attempting to stab men and
women if opposed by them from Committing those Crimes, To which
the King & some of the Headmen, Answered

Brothers as You are Warriors Yourselves, You well know that we
oftentimes goe to War against our Enemies or in pursuit of them,
which prevents us from hunting for meat to Eat when we are in Danger, least our Enemy should Discover us; and as this is our Case many
times we are forced to go to Your houses when Hungry, and no sooner
we do appear but your Dogs bark and as soon as You Discover Our
Coming You Imediately hide Your Bread Meal and Meat or any
Other thing that is fit to Eat about your houses, and we being sensible
that this is the Case, it is True we serch, and if we finde any Eatables
in the house we Take some, and Especially from those who behave so
Churlish and ungreatfull to us, as they are very well assured, of our
great need many times for the Reasons we now give, If we ask a little
Victuals you Refuse them & then You Complain and say those are
Transgressions, it is True there are many in those Settlements that are
very kind and Courtious to us when or as often as we come they give
us Bread and milk meat or Butter very freely if they have any ready
and never Do refuse whether we ask or no, and if it should happen
that they have nothing we goe away Contented with them, for we will
know that if they had anything ready we would have it freely & not
Refused by them. One of the Captains named James Bullin Owned
that not Long agoe he and his men were in pursuit of the Enemy and
then on their Track he Came to James Armstrong's house, the above
Complainant, who gave him a small Cake of Bread, and being very
hungry he asked more for himself and his men, and being Told by sd
Armstrong that there was no more ready in the house One of the
Indians Lifted up a bag that lay in the house Under which they Discovered Some Bread which they had Suspected was hid from them,

and taking some of it the woman struck one of them Over the head, which is the Cause of our Taking, Those things without law that we would not do to those who are kind to us in our Necessity when we apply to them.

KING—You I Remember Brothers accuse our People with attempting To take away a Child from one of Your People, but I hope you will not harbour this Thought of us so as to Imagine it was done in Earnest, for I am informed it was Only done by way of a joke by one of our wild Young men in order to Surprize the People, that were the parents of the Child, to have a Laugh at the Joke.

But as to their Takeing other things such as knives Cloaths or such Things we own it is not right to do but there are some of our young fellows will do those tricks altho' by us they are oftentimes Cautioned from such ill Doings altho' to no purpose for we Cannot be present at all times to Look after them, and when they goe to war or hunting Among the Inhabitants we generally warn them from being any ways offencive to any white person upon any Consideration whatever,

KING—Brothers here is One thing You Yourselves are to Blame very much in, That is You Rot Your grain in Tubs, out of which you take and make Strong Spirits You sell it to our young men and give it to them, many times; they get very Drunk with it this is the Very Cause that they oftentimes Commit those Crimes that is offencive to You and us and all thro' the Effect of that Drink it is also very bad for our people, for it Rots their guts and causes our men to get very sick and many of our people has Lately Died by the Effects of that strong Drink, and I heartily wish you would do something to prevent Your People from being accused of those Crimes that is committed by our young men and will prevent many of the abuses that is done by them thro' the Effects of that Strong Drink.

[An accusation of horse-stealing followed.]

KING—Brothers and Warriors You Talk very well, and as to your talk about our people takeing your Horses and Mares, it is very True there are a great many of our Creatures that Runs amongst the white peoples and there are also many stole from us by these people for it is not long since we caught a white man with some of our Horses and sent him to Justice, but was not punished as Represented to us while agoe.

COMMISSRS—Who was that Justice you Carried him before?

INDIANS—Before Mr. McGirt in South Carolina below the Waxhaw settlement.

COMMRS—This offence was not in our power to punish for we

have no authority in another Government so that we are Excusable in this Case.

KING—As to our Liveing on those Lands we Expect to live on those Lands we now possess During our Time here for when the Great man above made us he also made this Island he also made our forefathers and of this Colour and Hue (Showing his hands & Breast) he also fixed our forefathers and us here to inherit this Land and Ever since we Lived after our manner and fashion we in those Days, had no instruments To support our living but Bows which we Completed with stones, knives we had none, and as it was our Custom in those days to Cut our hair, which we Did by Burning it of our heads and Bodies with Coals of Fire, our Axes we made of stone we bled ourselves with fish teeth our Cloathing were Skins and Furr, instead of which we Enjoy those Cloaths which we got from the white people and Ever since they first Came among us we have enjoyed all those things that we were then destitute of for which we thank the white people, and to this Day we have lived in Brotherly Love & peace with them and more Especially with these Three Governments and it is our Earnest Desire that Love and Friendship which has so Long remain'd should Ever Continue.

[Further declaration of friendship.]

KING—We Never had the pleasure of seeing our Good Brother the President of North Carolina as yet, but this Let our Brother know that we want to be brothers and Friends, with him & all his people, and with the great king over the water, and all his Children, and to Confirm the same I shall as soon as get home I will Call all our nation together and charge the young men and Warriors Not to Misbehave on any Consideration whatever to the white people and as we do Expect an Everlasting Friendship between you and us, we Expect your kinds to us for ever as you many depend upon our Friendship and kindness to you.

And tell our Brother the President of North Carolina that if this war Continues between the white people and the french that I and my people are ready and Willing to Obey his Orders in giveing all possible assistance in my power to him when called by him or the Governor of Virginia and as a pledge of the same Take our Brother this letter as a token of Everlasting Friendship and return him Thanks for our good Talk this, Day with Each other.

Then they shook hands all round.

KING HAGLAR

The following incident recorded in the Moravian Records

under date of May 18, 1756, describing a Moravian Brother's adventure with a marauding band of Indians on the Virginia trail not far from the present town of Germanton, furnishes a commentary on one of the subjects debated in another conference of the Catawba with their white friends:

Br. Jacob Loesch, who had ridden out early in the morning to get oil, came home in the evening and reported that he had met 11 Indians, who had a white woman with them. They wanted to take his horse and repeatedly ordered him to dismount, but he refused to do it. They asked him if he had rum in the keg which he had taken for the oil,— he said no, and struck the keg to show that it was empty. Then they again told him to dismount, he refused and said he needed the horse, that he could not travel afoot. They looked surly, and he then asked them whether they were hungry, and told them to come to his farm, twelve miles away, and he would fill them full of food. The white woman said he was a fool to tell them where he lived, that they would come and take everything he had. Then they went on their way and he on his, filled his keg, fed his horse, and set out on his return. On the way back he heard that the Indians had been to a farm and seized the horses and saddles, that they had taken Mr. Haltem's horse from him after he left us, and that Mr. Benner and all his family had fled, whereupon he came home at a gallop.

SALISBURY Thursday 26 May 1756

At two o'Clock this afternoon King Hagler of the Catawba Nation of Indians with 15 of his principal Warriors and about 30 of his young Men painted and armed in the manner that they are when going to War and in great Order and regularity marched through this Town, and encamped a small distance from it, about an hour after he waited upon Peter Henly Esqre Chief Justice at the House of Edward Cusick, and by an Interpreter expressed himself as follows.

I and my people are Brothers and fast friends to the English and intend always to be so: Having heard of some Injuries lately done to my Brethren it has given me great concern, and being told that you and many more of them were to be here at this time I am come to talk with you about these Matters, and to endeavour to make all things streight.

To which the Chief Justice answered: King Hagler I have a sensible pleasure in seeing you and my other Brothers the Catawbas here. As I dont know the particular Articles upon which you desire this Conference when you please to communicate yourself on that subject, I will hear you with the greatest attention.

To which the King replied, I thank you, but as it is now late I will defer doing it to 9 o'Clock tomorrow morning if that time be agreable to you, which being answered by the Chief Justice in the Affirmative on Friday May 27th the Chief Justice and principal Gentlemen in Town with King Haglar 15 of his Warriors and the rest of his people went to the House of Peter Arran and being seated round a Table, the King spoke as follows—

The Cherokees We and the White people have been Brothers, and I desired that the path between us might be kept clear but the Cherokees have been playing the Rogue at which I am extremely concerned.

All the White People from South to North as far as New York nay beyond the great Waters under the great King are our Brothers, should the French come we will stand by our Brethren the English or go down into the Grave with them.

The Cherokees have told me that they would enter into a Friendship with the French but be assured that the White People shall still be my Brothers and I will assist them, these men I have brought here (pointing to his Warriors) are all come freely and voluntarily to acquaint the English that they will stand by them as long as they live, Mine is a small Nation yet they are brave men, and will be fast friends to their Brothers the White people as long as the sun endures.

I always advise my Men to be kind and obliging to the White People, as they are their Brothers and I shall continue to do so and remain their Brother 'till a sharp thing pierces my Breast so that I die, when that happens they must do as they please.

As I suppose there will soon be a War, I desire the Governour of North Carolina as this Land belongs to Him to send us some Ammunition as soon as possible, and that he will build us a fort for securing our old men and women and children when we turn out to fight the Enemy on their coming and as we love to wear silver plates on our Breasts and Arms I should be glad he would send us some of them and some Wampum.

Colo Alexander Colo Harris and Capt Berry told me they would make my Warriors a small present for assisting the White People in retaking their Goods Horses &c: from the Cherokees which they had plundered them of.

I go very much among the White People and have often my Belly filled by them and am very sorry they should at any time be distracted.

I return the Governour thanks for his care in purchasing Corn for my people which has saved the lives of many of our old men women and children.

As my people and the White people are Brethren I desire that when they go to their houses they may give them victuals to eat, some of the White People are very bad and quarrelsome and whip my people about the head, beat and abuse them but others are very good.

I desire a stop may be put to the selling strong Liquors by the White people to my people especially near the Indian Nation. If the White people make strong drink let them sell it to one another or drink it in their own Families. This will avoid a great deal of mischief which otherwise will happen from my people getting drunk and quarreling with the White people. Should any of my people do any mischief to the White people I have no strong prisons like you to confine them for it, Our only way is to put them under the ground and all these men (pointing to his Warriors again) will be ready to do that to those who shall deserve it.

I desire to know what is to be done with the White Woman I took from the Cherokees: I hope she will not be put to death, she is but a Woman and can do no great harm and I think she was compelled by the Cherokees to do what she did.

To which the Chief Justice answered, Nothing has hitherto appeared against her that will effect her life. I am informed she is an indented servant to a man in Virginia, if that be the case and she should not be charged with any offence I shall direct her to be conveyed to her proper owner.

To which King Hagler replied, I am glad of it. I am always sorry to lose a Woman. The loss of one Woman may be the loss of many lives because one Woman may be mother of many children. At which the audience smiling, he added I believe I have spoken nothing but Truth.

. . . .

After this the King informed the Chief Justice he had nothing more to say to him but had something to observe to his Warriors and thereupon addressed himself to them and then to his young men and desired them to declare whether in what he had said to his Brethren the English he had expressed their sentiments as well as his own to which they unanimously answered that he had. Then he added, That should his Brethren of Carolina be engaged in a War as he feared they soon would be would have his Men all ready on the first notice to march to their assistance. He desired them to fight on such an occasion as became Catawbas and do nothing that might lessen the great

Character they had obtained by their Military achievements. He added they were under the greatest obligations to do this for two reasons. First because the English had cloathed them naked and fed them when hungry. Secondly because the White people were seated now all round them and by that means had them entirely in their power.

To which the Warriors and young men all answered they would remember what he had given them in charge.

On this the King presented the pipe of Peace to the Chief Justice who as well as the rest of the company accepted it in the usual manner. The King was then informed that the Chief Justice would Answer his Speech the next morning and they met accordingly, as before, when he spoke as follows:

KING HAGLER, BRETHREN AND FRIENDS SACHEMS AND WARRIORS OF THE BRAVE CATAWBA NATION

It can't help giving me vast satisfaction to see here so many great Indian Warriors who are as remarkable for their conduct and Intrepidity in Battle as their brotherly affection for the English. I look upon your coming here upon this occasion as a fresh instance of the inviolable friendship you have for our common Father and Benefactor the King of Great Britain as well as for us his children and your brothers.

Your expressions of concern in regard to the Behaviour of the Cherokees your determined resolution to stand by and assist us against the French or go down into the Grave with us and the Willingness with which your Warriors have embraced the same resolution require the particular acknowledgement of us all.

Let the Cherokees behave as they will I hope We and our Brethren the brave Catawbas shall stand together like a large mountain which cannot be moved.

The Station our Great King has been pleased to place me in will in many Instances enable me to be assisting in the Preservation of that Peace and Harmony which subsists between us and if any Injuries or offenses should again be committed against you by the White People I will take care upon a proper Application to me that they shall not go unpunished.

You have our Thanks for the resolution you have taken of punishing such of your young people as shall commit any Injuries upon us as your Brethren, but we hope you will not have occasion to make any Examples of that kind.

Your observation in respect to the White peoples selling Liquor to the Indians is very just as there is no Law at present to prevent it. I will mention to the Governor the necessity of making one to restrain these pernicious practices for the future.

I will also take the first opportunity of representing to him in the strongest manner I can the singular services you have done in compelling the Cherokees to deliver up the White Woman and in obtaining restitution of the Goods they had unjustly taken from us.

The application of the publick money, belongs to the Governor and Assembly with the advice of the Council, over that I have no power but I will use all the Interest I have to obtain a present from them as a small acknowledgement of the Obligations we think ourselves under to you upon that account.

I shall also faithfully represent the request you have made by me to your Brother the Governor to have a speedy supply of Ammunition to have a fort built as soon as possible for the pretection of your old men your wives and children and some silver plates for your Breasts and arms with some Wampum.

In the mean time as a Testimony of the great regard we have for our brave friends and Brethren the Catawbas we have procured at our own Expence such a supply of powder and lead as we could get to supply your present necessities which we now present you with.

. . . .

To which the King answered, I look upon you as my elder Brother and what you told me to day I shall not forget tomorrow but remember as long as I live. If any of the English shall at any time be attacked by the Enemy let me know it as soon as possible by any hand and I and my people will immediately come to your assistance.

The Chief Justice observed to him that their Brethren the White people of Virginia and the Nottaway Indians were now fighting to the Northward against the French and their Indians and had long expected their joining them and were surprised they had not yet done it.

The King replied that when the Gentlemen of Virginia were in their parts, his Warriors were all willing and desirous to go with them, but when they were gone Governor Glenn sent an express to him and forbad him to let them go unless he should order it, and that he had sent the said Govr for answer that he would wait till he had further considered of the matter but that he had taken up the Hatchet against the French and could not lay it down without useing it.

N.B.   There were two Interpreters sworn Mr. Giles and Mr. Tool.

Letter from Governor Dobbs to the Board of Trade:

NEWBERN 14th June 1756

MY LORDS

There having been a conference with the Cataubas held at Salisbury by their King Hagler and some of his Warriors with Chief Justice Henley which has been sent down to me I thought proper to send you a Copy of it, it was occasioned by some of the Cherokees who were returning from Virginia after their disappointment of attacking the Shawanese, who carried off a White woman from Virginia and 'tis supposed at her Instigation they carried off some horses saddles and Plunder from the Back Settlers as they passed thro the Province, but I suppose would not supply them with provisions, and our Mad settlers want to repel force with force but I have sent up strict orders at their peril to make any opposition but to save their lives. . . . I shall order 100 weight of Gunpowder and 400 weight of Lead to the Cataubas our friends altho we have not 1000 Weight in the Province and none can be got unless the Government supplies us from England in case of War. . . .

ARTHUR DOBBS

A CATAWBA LEGEND

The bravery of the Catawba in their encounters with their northern enemies is reflected in the following legend recorded by James Adair. We may well believe that this legend was the substance of one of the ceremonial songs which old men of the tribe chanted for the entertainment and inspiration of their audiences:

A party of Senekah [Seneca] Indians came to war against the Katahba [Catawba], bitter enemies to each other. In the woods, the former discovered a sprightly warrior belonging to the latter, hunting in their usual light dress; on his perceiving them, he sprung off for a hollow rock, four or five miles distant, as they intercepted him from running homeward. He was so extremely swift, and skilful with the gun, as to kill seven of them in the running fight, before they were able to surround and take him. They carried him to their country in sad triumph: but, though he had filled them with uncommon grief and shame, for the loss of so many of their kindred, yet the love of martial virtue induced them to treat him, during their long journey, with a great deal more civility, than if he had acted the part of a coward. The women and children, when they met him at their several towns, beat and whipped him in as severe a manner as the occasion required, according to their law of justice, and at last he was formally condemned to die by the fiery tortures. It might reasonably be imagined that what he had for some time gone through, by being fed with a scanty hand, a tedious march, lying at night on the bare ground, exposed to the changes of the weather, with his arms and legs extended in a pair of rough stocks, and suffering such punishments on his entering into their towns, as a prelude for those sharp torments for which he was destined, would have so impaired his health, and affected his imagination, as to have sent him to his long sleep out of the way of any more sufferings. Probably, this would have been the case with the major part of white people, under similar circumstances: but I never knew this with any of the Indians: and this cool-headed brave warrior did not deviate from their rough lessons of martial virtue, but acted his part so well, as to surprise and sorely vex his numerous enemies. For, when they were taking him unpinioned, in their wild parade, to the place of torture, which lay near to a river, he suddenly dashed down those who stood in his way, sprung off, and plunged into the water, swimming underneath like an otter, only rising to take breath till he had made the opposite shore. He now ascended the steep bank; but though he had good reason to be in a hurry, as many of the enemy were in the water, and others running every way, like blood-hounds, in pursuit of him, and the bullets flying around him, from the time he took to the river, yet his heart did not allow him to leave them abruptly, without taking leave in a formal manner, in return for the extraordinary favors they had done, and intended to do him. He first turned his backside toward them, and slapped it with his hand; then moving round, he put up the shrill war whoop, as his last salute, till some more convenient opportunity offered, and darted off in the manner of a beast broke loose from its torturing enemies. He continued his speed so as to run about midnight of the same day, as far as his eager pursuers were two days in reaching. There he rested, till he happily discovered five of those Indians, who had pursued him—he lay hid a little way off their camp, till they were sound asleep. Every circumstance of his situation occurred to him, and inspired him with heroism. He was naked, torn, hungry, and his enraged enemies were come up with him. But there was now everything to relieve his wants, and a fair opportunity to save his life, and get great honour, and sweet revenge, by cutting them off. Resolution, a covenient spot, and sudden surprize, would effect the main object of all his wishes and hopes. He accordingly creeped towards them, took one of their tomohawks, and killed them all on the spot.

Plate 33

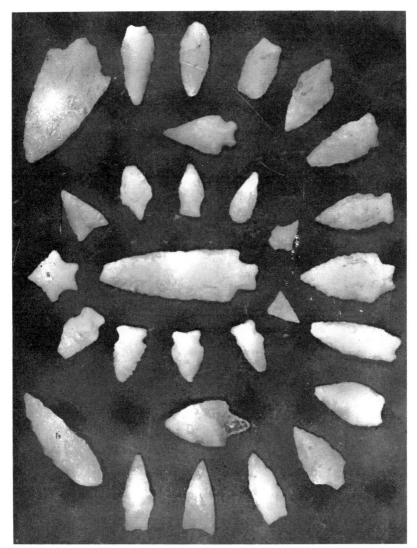

Arrowheads of White Flint

(This stone is found in abundant outcrops.)

Plate 34

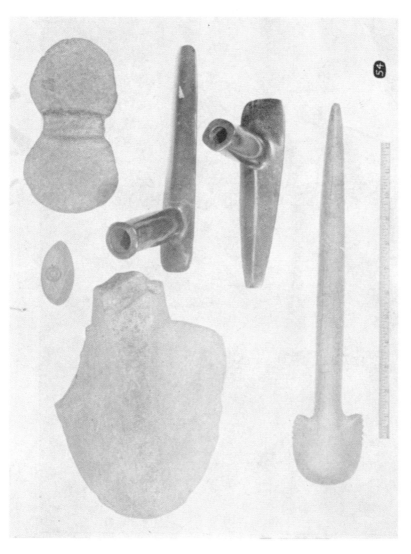

Above: Three Unfinished Stone Artifacts. *Right center:* Platform Pipes, the Upper from Surry County, the Lower from Yadkin County. *Below:* Stone Spatulate Form Associated with a Burial along Town Fork Creek, Stokes County

Photograph by Roy J. Spearman

Plate 35

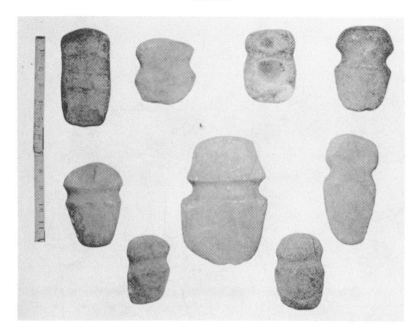

Stone Axes

Photograph by Roy J. Spearman

Artifacts from the Major Winston Plantation in Stokes County,
along Town Fork Creek, Gathered by John R. Shipley

Plate 36

Stone Axes

Photograph by Roy J. Spearman

Plate 37

The arrow points to Mrs. Sally Gordon, one of the few members of the Catawba who can speak their language

Catawba Pottery-Makers

Plate 38

Bird Pipe, Yadkin River

Pottery Vessels—the Larger an Effigy Bowl with Bird or Beaver
Head on One Side and Tail on the Other, the Smaller the First
Water Bottle Found in North Carolina

(Restored from fragments gathered on Yadkin River in Caldwell County by a farmer
who had plowed into Indian burials.)

Photograph by Roy J. Spearman

Plate 39

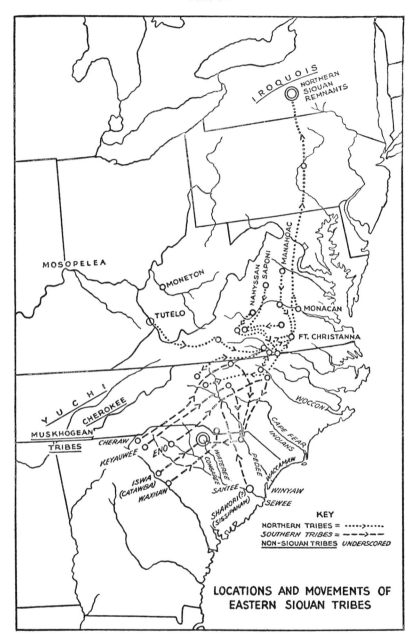

LOCATIONS AND MOVEMENTS OF
EASTERN SIOUAN TRIBES

By courtesy of Dr. John R. Swanton, of the Bureau of American Ethnology and the
University of California Press

Plate 40

A Robeson County Indian Youth

Photograph by Bill Baker, by courtesy of the North Carolina Department of Conservation and Development

Plate 41

"Old Main" Auditorium, Pembroke State University

Sampson Hall, Administration Building, Pembroke State University

Photographs by courtesy of Pembroke State University

Plate 42

Spearhead from Sauratown Mountains, Stokes County, and
Arrowheads from Forsyth and Davidson Counties

Triangular-shaped Arrow Points from Donnaha Village Site

Photograph by Roy J. Spearman

Plate 43

Pottery Vessels from the Yadkin River

(The smallest is one inch in height. In the largest, unearthed near Badin by the
great flood of 1916, the skeleton of an infant was found.)

Photograph by Roy J. Spearman

Plate 44

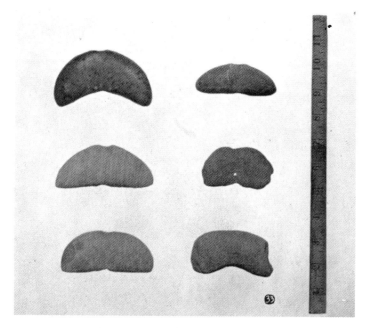

Lunar-shaped Banner Stones

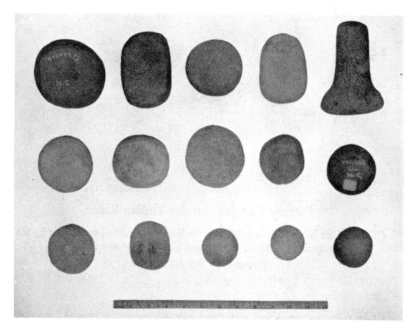

Hammer Stones, Bell-shaped Pestle, and Three Stone Spheres

Photograph by Roy J. Spearman

Plate 45

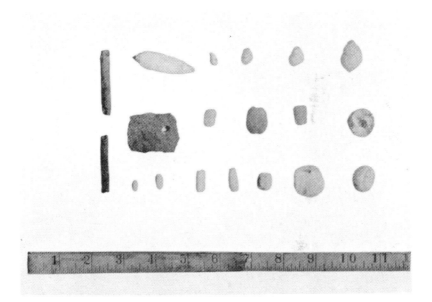

Beads of Shell, Bone, Clay, Antler, and Copper; Perforated Oliva
Shell, and Pottery Fragment—All Found on One Village Site

Photograph by Roy J. Spearman

Shell Beads and Oliva Shells Pierced for Stringing

Photograph by Herman Dezern

Plate 46

Series of Soapstone Vessels

Photograph by Roy J. Spearman

Plate 47

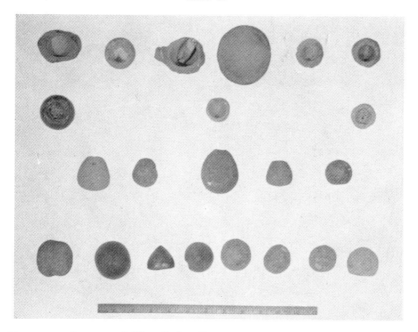

First row: Stone and Clay Paint Cups (Bear's Tooth Found in Third Cup). *Second row:* Problematical Stone with Four Perforations, Two Stone Paint Cups. *Third row:* Plummet Shapes—One Stone, Four Hematite. *Fourth row:* Ground Stone, Iron Hemisphere, Three Iron and Two Stone Cones, Unfinished Perforated Quartz.

Photograph by Roy J. Spearman

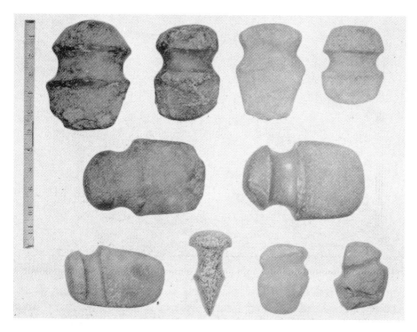

Stone Axes

Photograph by Roy J. Spearman

Plate 48

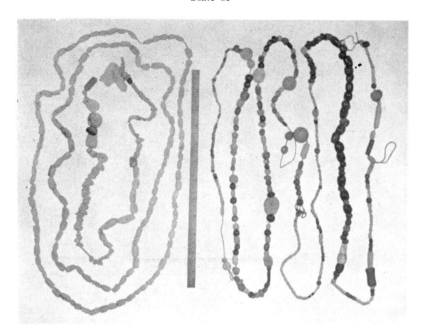

Left: Indian Shell Beads. *Right:* Trade Beads

Photograph by Roy J. Spearman

Shell Beads; Marine Shells Pierced for Stringing; Bone Tubes;
Antler Arrowhead; Animal Teeth; Pair of Antler Ear Plugs; Green,
Blue, and White Trade Beads; Shell Bangle; Shell Pin

Photograph by Herman Dezern

He then chopped them to pieces, in as horrid a manner, as savage fury could excite, both through national and personal resentment—he stripped off their scalps, clothed himself, took a choice gun, and as much ammunition and provisions as he could well carry in a running march. He set off afresh with a light heart, and did not sleep for several successive nights, only when he reclined as usual a little before day, with his back to a tree. As it were by instinct, when he found he was free from the pursuing enemy, he made directly to the very place where he had killed seven of his enemies, and was taken by them for the fiery torture. He digged them up, scalped them, burned their bodies to ashes, and went home with singular triumph. Other pursuing enemies came on the evening of the second day to the camp of their dead people, when the sight gave them a greater shock, than they had ever known before. In their chilled war council, they concluded, that, as he had done such surprising things in his defence, before he was captivated, and since that, in his naked condition, and was now well armed, if they continued the pursuit, he would spoil them all, for he surely was an enemy wizard. And therefore they returned home.

CATAWBA TEXTS

Dr. Frank G. Speck, long interested in the Catawba, succeeded in obtaining narrations in their native tongue from some of the old people of the tribe. The results of his painstaking work were published in 1934 in his volume *Catawba Texts*. This is an exceedingly valuable contribution to language study and to the ethnology of the Siouan tribes. It is fortunate that Dr. Speck completed his task before the language, perilously near extinction, had entirely vanished from the realm of the spoken word. The aged narrators who contributed this linguistic material were Mrs. Samson Owl, formerly Susan Harris, aged 83, wife of a Cherokee chief; Mrs. Margaret Wiley Brown, aged 85; Mrs. Sally Gordon, formerly Sally Brown, and Sam Brown, daughter and son of Mrs. Brown. The texts, "a last feeble voice from the grave of a defunct native culture of the southeast," cannot be expected to reveal the fulness and color of myths and folklore obtained by students from some of the other Indian tribes, the Cherokee for instance, whose language is still spoken by large numbers. There is much, however, that repays interest in these survivals. A selection from them is herewith given:[2]

UGNI, THE COMET

(Original) Himbariwe meutcere wariwe hapmore mahotcire himbari monamurere. Kuriwa ninuhaprare napre korere ninuhaprare wiyarup hukaihare. Ume Ugne huktugere wiya kithere. "Huktuksere naciatcore," kauhatcore, "hopo!". . . .

(Translation) All the people in the world want to go up above to Heaven where God alone is. A woman and her son went up and left a rope hanging down from the sky. Ugni (an old woman—the comet) took hold of the rope and tried to go up alone (to steal the boy) and the rope broke. She cried out "Hopo! I am falling down, I am frightened."

HOW THE OPOSSUM LOST HIS BUSHY TAIL

The opossum said, "I alone have a tail with a pretty top. It is like a squirrel's tail." He went in a hole and came out saying, "The snail has eaten off my tail hair. Then my body, my back I turned and my tail hair was not there." He was very much ashamed and did not come out for one year. His head was low and "He-who-slobbers-fluid-much" (opossum) turned away ashamed.

RABBIT AND SNAIL GO FOR A DOCTOR

A rabbit and a snail went for a doctor. The rabbit went straight on. When he returned he found the snail sitting on the door step. When the snail came back he asked, "Did the doctor come?" "Yes, he did! The doctor came. The sick person has been dead for two months," was the answer.

HAWK AND BUZZARD

The hawk steals things. He said to the buzzard, "How do you make your living?" The buzzard said, "I wait for God to take care of me." Then said the hawk, "Oh! you will always be hungry. Me, see what I do." He flew off to catch a chicken, and was killed. The buzzard ate him up completely. "If one waits for God, one will wait for the better."

ORIGIN OF THE HUMMING BIRD

The humming bird was created by man, an Indian man. He took —plant down (dandelion) in his hand and blew upon it and, verily— the bird flew off. He was a smart man.

[2] Frank G. Speck, *Catawba Texts* (New York: Columbia University Press, 1934), reprinted by permission of the Columbia University Press.

FOLK BELIEFS

Rabbit foot around neck will make anyone love another.

If the groundhog sees his shadow, he will go back in the ground and the weather will be bad.

A falling star means trouble.

It is not good to mix both the deer meat and the turkey meat in one pot.

REFERENCES

Adair, James. *History of the American Indians.* London, 1775.

Byrd, William. *Divding Line Histories.* Edited by William K. Boyd. Raleigh, 1929.

The Colonial Records of North Carolina. Edited by William L. Saunders. Vols. V-VI. Raleigh, 1886.

Fries, Adelaide L. (ed.). *Records of the Moravians in North Carolina.* Vol. I. Raleigh, 1922.

Henderson, Archibald. *Washington's Southern Tour.* Boston, 1923.

Hodge, F. W. *Handbook of American Indians North of Mexico.* Bulletin No. 30, Bureau of American Ethnology. Part 1. Washington, 1907.

Lawson, John. *History of North Carolina.* London, 1714.

Mooney, James. *Siouan Tribes of the East.* Bulletin No. 22, Bureau of American Ethnology. Washington, 1894.

Speck, Frank G. "The Cane Blowgun in Catawba and Southeastern Ethnology," *American Anthropologist,* n.s. XL (1938), 198-204.

———. "Catawba Games and Amusements," *Primitive Man,* XVII (1944), 19-28.

———. "Catawba Medicines and Curative Practices," *Twenty-fifth Anniversary Studies: Philadelphia Anthropological Society,* Philadelphia, 1937, pp. 179-197.

———. *Catawba Texts.* New York, 1934.

Swanton, John R. *The Indians of the Southeastern United States.* Bulletin 137, Bureau of American Ethnology. Washington, 1946.

CHAPTER XIII

The Indians of Robeson County

THE FATE OF THE Lost Colony of Sir Walter Raleigh's expedition has remained a mystery.

In the latter part of the nineteenth century the belief was expressed by several interested citizens that the Indians residing in Robeson County were descendants of the ancient people among whom the lost colonists found refuge. North Carolinians generally would like to hold this belief and to see it established beyond question, but the thread of evidence of a connection between these Indians and the Lost Colony is so slender that it will not hold together. Like the search for the Lost Tribes of Israel, the quest for the Lost Colony would be expected to fall upon any likely prospect. It so happens that the Robeson County Indians and their affiliates are the only existing group in North Carolina hitherto unidentified. Why should they not be the long-sought survivors of the friendly Indians who received John White's colonists? In support of the affirmative side of the proposition, it has been advanced that a large percentage of the English names of the colony is found among these Indians. Against this it may be said that the names have been long familiar in Carolina, and intermarriage with white settlers would be expected to extend such names among mixed-bloods; a goodly percentage of the same names has survived among the Catawba. Survival of the pronunciations and idioms of early English has been noted; but this has been found also in other isolated regions of the state, in the mountains and along the coast, and would be expected in this community long sequestered. Some of the pronunciations noted are distinctly Scotch, to be expected in a neighborhood which had a large population of Highland settlers. These people had early adopted the manners and customs of the English settlers; they built houses, cultivated crops, etc. In this respect, however, they did not differ from the Cherokee and Catawba, and as from early times they have been known as a mixed-blood people, the adoption of manners and customs of the whites would be expected. The question hinges upon whether or not the friendly Indians of Manteo's tribe, usually identified as the Hatteras, in some way migrated from Algonquian territory on the sandbanks of the Atlantic to the swamp regions of upper Little Peedee River in the present county of Robeson.

The fate of the Lost Colony has brought forth occasional references for three centuries.[1]

The report of the Virginia Council of the Virginia Company of London, in 1609, referred to an Indian town "pecarecamicke where you shall find foure of the englishe alive, left by Sir Walter Rawley which escaped from the slaughter of Powhatan of Roanoke, uppon the first arrivall of our Colonie, and live under the proteccon of a wiroane [chief] called Cepanocon enemy to Powhaton." This location has been identified as a settlement somewhere along Dan River near Oconahoen, or Occaneechee, at the confluence of the Dan and Staunton rivers. A reference by Strachey mentions the same village, where Spaniards are said to have been in 1611, five days' journey south of Jamestown. Lawson commented on the appearance of mixed-bloods among the Hatteras on the sandbanks of North Carolina and believed them to have been survivors of the Lost Colony. As has already been noted, the Hatteras dwindled away in the coastal region along with neighboring tribes, and there is no record that any of them passed over to the territory occupied by the Siouan people.

The presence of a considerable body of Siouan survivors in the neighborhood of the Peedee and Waccamaw rivers has suggested a retreat of these people to the territory in question. Unfortunately, the ancient language of the Robeson County Indians has disappeared. If in any way their former speech can be resurrected, there will be a clue to their identity which would go a long way

---

[1] The finding of the so-called Virginia Dare Stones in the 1930's aroused considerable interest and speculation. The first stone was found near the coast, where there is no native stone. This cast suspicion from the start, for it is not likely that the survivors would have carried about with them stone writing material, even though they might have had available some imported ballast rock at Roanoke Island.

toward settling the matter. If Algonquian, there will be a score in favor of the Croatan theory; if Siouan, or other language, the count will be against it. Perhaps there still survive some place names, traditional terms, designations of plants, animals, games, etc., or other linguistic evidence that will help to clear the mystery. For instance, the name Shoe Heel, designation of a small creek and settlement not far from Scuffletown, the traditional center of the Indians, bears some resemblance to Suali, Xualla, and other variations of the Saura tribe. A post office was established at Shoe Heel in 1866, and in 1886 the name was changed to Maxton.

The theory of the Lost Colony was brought forward by Hamilton McMillan, an eminent lawyer of the county, who befriended the Indians and was first to designate them as Croatan. He was honest in his belief. Arnold A. McKay, of Maxton, says of him, "Mr. McMillan, or Mr. Hamilton, as everybody called him, was a very high-minded man. He may not have been a scientist, but he was an honest scholar; no trader."

Local tradition indicates that there was gradual accretion from various directions: James Lowrie settled in Robeson about 1769. He came with Silas Atkins from Bute County, now Franklin and Warren counties. Other families, Thompsons, Kitchens, Coles, Drakes, Moores, Humphreys, and Bridgerses, came from Franklin, Nash, Warren, and Edgecombe counties. James Lowrie married Sarah Kearsey, said to be a half-breed Tuscarora woman. James Lowrie's son, William, married Bettie Locklaer, a half-breed Tuscarora Indian woman, the name Locklaer meaning "hold fast." Allen Lowrie, son of William, married Polly Cumba, or Cumbo, said to be of Portuguese extraction. The name Cumbo was also attributed to a half-breed Tuscarora. Woodes came from Sampson County; Ransoms, Oxendines, Cummingses, Goinses, and Braboys, from Halifax. At any rate, the survivors are there, estimated at from five to thirty thousand, in Robeson and adjacent counties, and scattered in small groups in other parts of the country.

Land grants date from 1732 and even earlier. In response to Governor Dobbs's circular of 1754, Bladen County reported, "Drowning Creek on the head of Little Peedee, 50 families, a mixt Crew, a lawless People, possess the Lands without patent or paying quit rents; shot a surveyor for coming to view vacant lands being enclosed in swamps." The report listed no Indians in the county, although the reference indicates the presence of mixed-bloods. Mr. McMillan stated, "They occupied the country as far west as the Pee Dee, but their principal seat was on the Lumber, extending along that river for twenty miles. They held their lands in common and land titles only became known on the approach of the white man." About the year 1735 neighboring settlers began to appear and took up land on every side.

The Indians have a well-fixed tradition that they participated with Colonel Barnwell in his campaign against the Tuscarora. It is even told that several Mattamuskeet prisoners were brought back as slaves and were later incorporated into the tribe. A number of the Indians served in the Continental Army during the Revolution, and in the War of 1812 a company was mustered into the United States Army. They were represented also in the armies of the Confederate States. In both World Wars they have furnished their full share of men.

During the Civil War some of the Indians were executed, two on false charges of desertion and two others on charges of robbery. Resentment and determination for revenge developed. A band of outlaws, led by Henry Berry Lowrie, committed many robberies and killed thirty men. For nine years Robeson County was terrorized. Deserters from the Federal Army, a white native of the county, and one or two Negroes were included in the band; the others were Robeson Indians. After the death of its ablest members the outlaws fled. McKay says of Lowrie:

Like Robin Hood and all other heroes of the common people, Henry Berry Lowrie has become something of a legendary hero among the Croatans. Some say Henry Berry (reported slain) went West and grew rich, and that he came back once or twice. They all seem agreed that he was really kind to all his people, never harmed anyone who let him and his band alone, never took from those who had little, and that his word could be relied upon. The white folks tell a different story. They say that he and his band were the incarnation of all that is insufferably bad in savage nature; that the uprising caused the death of many useful citizens, which unfortunate circumstances could have been averted had the state taken firm measures to punish the outlaws soon after they started in their wild career.

According to Stephen B. Weeks:

From 1783 to 1835 they had the right to vote, performed military duties, encouraged schools, and built churches; but by the constituent convention of 1835 the franchise was denied to all "free persons of color," and to effect a political purpose it was contended by both parties that the Croatans came under that category. The convention of 1868 removed this ban; but as they had long been classed as mulattoes they were obligated to patronize negro schools. This they refused to do as a rule, preferring that their children should grow up in ignorance. . . . Finally, in 1885, through the efforts of Mr. Hamilton McMillan, who has lived near them and knows their history, justice long delayed was granted to them by the General Assembly of North Carolina. They were officially recognized as Croatan Indians;[2] separate schools were provided and intermarriages with the negroes forbidden. Since this action by the State they have become better citizens. . . . They are almost universally landowners, occupying about sixty thousand acres in Robeson County. They are industrious and frugal, and anxious to improve their condition. . . . In religious inclinations they are Methodists and Baptists, and own sixteen churches. The State has provided them with a normal school for the training of teachers and this action will go very far toward their mental and moral elevation. Their school houses[3] have been built entirely by private means. . . . They are quick-witted, and are capable of development. Mr. John S. Leary, a prominent politician of Raleigh, and professor of law in Shaw University, was a member of the tribe, and one of their members has reached the Senate of the United States . . . Hon. Hiram R. Revels.

Anyone who visits Robeson County will agree that Mr. Weeks's favorable opinion is justified.

REFERENCES

The Colonial Records of North Carolina. Edited by William L. Saunders. Vols. III-IV. Raleigh, 1886.

Lawson, John. *History of North Carolina.* London, 1714.

[2] Doubt and dissatisfaction over the name "Croatan" led the Robeson County Indians to seek another designation by the state, and they have been referred to as Cherokee, much to the displeasure of the Cherokee of western North Carolina.

[3] The schools are now provided by the state. The Indian State Normal College is located at Pembroke.

McKay, Arnold A. "Nobody Knows Anything about the Croatans," *The State* (Raleigh, N. C.), Feb. 24, 1934.

McLean, A. W. "Historical Sketch of the Indians of Robeson County." *See* McPherson, *Indians of North Carolina.*

McMillan, Hamilton. "Sir Walter Raleigh's Lost Colony." *See* Mc-Pherson, *Indians of North Carolina.*

McPherson, O. M. *Indians of North Carolina.* Washington, 1915.

Norment, Mary C. *The Lowrie History.* Wilmington, N. C., 1875.

Rights, Douglas L. "The Lost Colony Legend," *Bulletin of the Archaeological Society of North Carolina,* Vol. I, No. 2 (Sept., 1934), pp. 3-7.

Strachey, William. *The historie of travelle into Virginia Britannia.* Hakluyt Society Publications, Vol. VI. London, 1849.

Swanton, John R. *Probable Identity of the "Croatan" Indians.* Bulletin, Office of Indian Affairs, Washington, 1933.

Virginia Council of the Virginia Company. *Report.* London, 1609.

Weeks, Stephen B. "The Lost Colony of Roanoke: Its Fate and Survival," American Historical Association *Papers,* V (1891), 441-480.

CHAPTER XIV

The Cherokee

PART I

IROQUOIAN STOCK OF THE SOUTHERN MOUNTAINS

ACCORDING to Charles C. Royce:

The Cherokee Nation has probably occupied a more prominent place in the affairs and history of what is now the United States of America, since the date of the early European settlements, than any other tribe, nation, or confederacy of Indians, unless it be possible to except the powerful and warlike league of Iroquois or Six Nations of New York.

James Mooney wrote that "the Cherokees are probably the largest and most important tribe in the United States, having their own national government and numbering at any time in their history from 20,000 to 25,000 persons."[1] (They are outnumbered by the Navaho and possibly other tribes.)

Unlike other tribes of the Carolinas, they afford abundant material for historical consideration. They have concluded more treaties with the government than any other tribe; eminent scholars have had opportunity to study them in intimate association; missionaries have worked among them for more than a century; a member of the tribe, through the invention of an alphabet, preserved their language; the tribe, or nation, now probably outnumbers the population existent when first contact with the colonists was made.

The tribal name is derived from "Tsalagi," or "Tsaragi," by which they commonly called themselves, denoting "cave people,"

---

[1] Charles C. Royce and James Mooney are the leading authorities in a study of the Cherokee. Their contributions afford the groundwork of this chapter. See Charles C. Royce, "The Cherokee Nation of Indians," *Fifth Annual Report of the Bureau of American Ethnology* (Washington, 1887), pp. 121-378; and James Mooney, "Myths of the Cherokee," *Nineteenth Annual Report of the Bureau of American Ethnology* (Washington, 1900), Part 1, pp. 3-548.

probably another way of saying "mountaineers." Like other tribes they originally called themselves "real people," in their tongue, "Ani-Yunwiwa."[2] Within the tribe are still seven clans: Wolf, Deer, Bird, and Paint, and three designated by John P. Brown in *Old Frontiers* as Blue People, Kituwah People, and Long Hair People, the last two being designated as Wild Potato and Twisters by William H. Gilbert, Jr., in *The Eastern Cherokees*.[3]

They were truly a mountain folk, and like the mountains they were strong and rugged. For a long time they possessed or controlled all the region of the Alleghenies in southwest Virginia, western North Carolina, northwestern South Carolina, eastern Tennessee, and northern Georgia and Alabama. Their settlements overflowed into the pleasant, fruitful valleys of the foothills. An estimate of their population in the seventeenth century is given by Mooney and Swanton as 22,000. They controlled 40,000 miles of territory and claimed much more.

The ancient capital town was Echota, situated near the mouth of Little Tennessee River. This was a town of refuge, or peace town, affording much protection, as was offered by the cities of refuge among the ancient Hebrews. Adair told of how a trader who had killed an Indian in order to protect his own property took refuge in Echota, and after being there for some months prepared to return to his trading post a short distance away, but was assured by the chiefs that he would be killed if he ventured outside the town. He was accordingly obliged to stay longer until the tears of the bereaved relatives had been wiped away with presents.

There were three dialects spoken according to the following divisions of habitation: Lower, in the foothill settlements of South Carolina and Georgia; Middle, in the area centering on the Tuckasegee River in western North Carolina; Upper, in the region of North Georgia, East Tennessee, and extreme Western North Carolina, the dialect spoken by the survivors who at present dwell

[2] See F. W. Hodge, *Handbook of American Indians North of Mexico.* Bulletin No. 30, Bureau of American Ethnology, Part 1 (Washington, 1907).

[3] John P. Brown, *Old Frontiers* (Kingsport, Tenn., 1938) and William Harlen Gilbert, Jr., *The Eastern Cherokees*, Bulletin No. 133, Bureau of American Ethnology (Washington, 1943). The latter volume presents a comprehensive study of the social life of the Cherokee survivors in western North Carolina.

in this state. It may be noted that only the Lower dialect included the sound of the letter *r*, possibly obtained through oral association with Siouan or other near-by tribes who used that pronunciation.[4] These divisions of speech corresponded with geographical areas separated by mighty barriers of mountain ranges. There were, in fact, four such natural divisions described by Hammerer as "separated from one another by such craggy mountains and bad roads that it will ever be impracticable to make any communication by wagon-roads from one to another." These divisions following the mountain walls were located cross fashion:

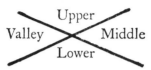

Like the Swiss cantons, the divisions developed local distinctiveness. For instance, the Lower Cherokee called the Upper "pipemakers" and "frog eaters."

William Bartram listed the towns and villages of the Cherokee Nation in 1776 as follows:

No.		
1	Echoe	On the Tanase East of the Jore mountains
2	Nucasse	
3	Whatoga	
4	Cowe	
5	Ticolossa	Inland on the branches of the Tanase
6	Jore	
7	Conisca	
8	Nowe	
9	Tomothle	On the Tanase over the Jore mountains
10	Noewe	
11	Tellico	
12	Clennuse	
13	Ocunnolufte	
14	Chewe	
15	Quanuse	
16	Tellowe	
17	Tellico	Inland towns on the branches of the Tanase and other waters over the Jore mountains

[4] This pronunciation is open to dispute.

18 Chatuga
19 Hiwasse
20 Chewase
21 Nuanha

22 Tallase   Overhill towns on the Tanase or Cherokee river

23 Chelowe
24 Sette
25 Chote great
26 Joco
27 Tahasse

28 Tamahle   Overhill towns on the Tanase or Cherokee river

29 Tuskege
30 — — Big Island
31 Nilaque
32 Niowe   Lower towns East of the mountains
1 Sinica   On the the Savanna or Keowe river
2 Keowe
3 Kulsage

4 Tugilo   On Tugilo river
5 Estotowe

6 Qualatche   On Flint river
7 Chote

Towns on the waters of other rivers
Estotowe great. Allagae. Jore. Nae oche.
In all forty-three towns.

Although strongly entrenched in their mountain home, the Cherokee were comparative latecomers into this territory. They succeeded another stock that had dwelt there earlier and had left numerous mounds as memorials of their occupancy. The Cherokee were a detached branch of Iroquoian stock, as were their kinsmen, the Tuscarora of eastern North Carolina.

On his northward course De Soto came to a province called Chelaque, "the poorest country of maize that was seen in Florida." Of the Indians it was recorded that they "feed upon roots and herbs, which they seek in the fields, and upon wild beasts, which they kill with their bows and arrows, and are a very gentle people. All of them go naked and are very lean." One version of the De Soto narrative states that the "Chelaques" deserted their towns on the approach of the white men and fled to the mountains, leaving only the old men and women and some who were nearly blind. The country abounded in "gallinas," evidently wild turkeys, and one town made the soldiers a present of seven hundred fowls, according to the figure of the narrator. A chief presented De Soto with two deer skins.

It is improbable that these Indians were Cherokee, although they were long thought to have been of that tribe. The word "Chelaque" was used in describing the wilder tribes of the interior, but it came to be associated with the name Cherokee, a designation of the Iroquoian tribe of the Southern Mountains. The narratives of De Soto's journey give varying accounts concerning the location of the "Chelaque." Ranjel states that "Chalaque" was two days' journey from Cofitachequi. He also mentions Xalaque a day's journey from Xualla. The Elvas narrative gives seven days from Cofitachequi to Chelaque, and thence five days to Xualla. Certainly the Cherokee penetrated this region at a later date.

Nearly one hundred and fifty years elapsed after the De Soto expedition before friendly relations with the colonists began. It is reported that in 1684 an agreement was made between the South Carolina government and eight chiefs of the Cherokee, who signed the document in picture-writing. If the report is true, this is doubtless the oldest Cherokee treaty on record.

In 1690 James Moore, secretary of the South Carolina colony, traveled northwest to the mountains, and reached a point at which, according to his Indian guides, he was within twenty miles of where the Spaniards were engaged in mining and smelting with bellows and furnaces.

In 1693 a delegation of twenty Cherokee chiefs visited Charleston with proposals of friendship and at the same time asked the Governor to assist them in operations against the Esaw (Catawba) and Cossaw (Coosa) tribes, who had captured and carried off a number of the Cherokee. The Savannah (Shawnee) Indians also had been active against them and had captured Cherokees and sold them to colonial authorities as slaves. The Governor gave his promise of protection, but could do nothing for the captive Indians, as they had been carried in slavery to the West Indies. At this time the Cherokee territorial limits in South Carolina were understood to be bounded by Broad River. The region between this river and the Catawba River was neutral hunting ground of both the Cherokee and the Catawba.[5]

About the year 1700 the first guns were introduced among the Cherokee, the event being fixed traditionally as having occurred in the girlhood of an old woman of the tribe who died about 1775.

Though generally friendly to the English, the Cherokee were allied against them in the Yamassee War of 1715.

In 1721 Governor Nicholson of South Carolina, fearing French encroachments, invited the Cherokee to a general congress. With the delegates from thirty-seven of their towns who attended, the Governor smoked the pipe of peace and, after distributing presents, agreed to define boundaries and to appoint an agent for them. This definition of boundaries marked the first cession of land, the beginning of the long series of decreases in Cherokee territory which did not end until all of their ancestral lands were gone.

North Carolina followed with a treaty in 1730. Sir Alexander Cuming was commissioned to make an alliance with the Cherokee and met chiefs and warriors of the nation at Nequasse.[6] The Cherokee acknowledged King George as their sovereign and sent a delegation of six warriors to carry the crown of the nation (consisting of five eagle tails and four scalps) to England and to do homage to the King. By the terms of the treaty of peace and commerce they concluded at Dover on June 30 of that year they agreed:

1. To submit to the sovereignty of the King and his successors.

2. Not to trade with any nation other than England.

3. Not to permit any but Englishmen to build forts or cabins or plant corn among them.

4. To apprehend and deliver runaway Negroes.

5. To surrender any Indian killing an Englishman.

[5] The opinion of Royce that "Keowee Old Town" on Bowen's map of 1752, located near Asheboro, N. C., is evidence of Cherokee occupation is erroneous, as this was the site of the Keyauwee Town of the Siouan Indians visited by Lawson.

[6] At Franklin, in Macon County, where a mound marks the site of the village.

In 1736 Christian Priber, supposed to be acting in the French interest, was among the Cherokee. He learned their language, adopted their dress and customs, and quickly acquired a commanding position among them. Under strong suspicion of designs against the colonists, he was imprisoned by colonial officers and died in confinement.

A brief travel-picture of the Carolina frontier of this period may be found in the notes of Bishop A. G. Spangenberg, who made a survey of the western Piedmont region seeking a location for a Moravian settlement. In 1752 he crossed the state with a few companions, including William Churton, surveyor of the colony. When he reached the Catawba River west of the present Statesville, he wrote, "Hitherto we have been on the Trading Path, where we could find at least one house a day where food could be bought; but from here we were to turn into the pathless forest." Upon reaching the Catawba River, near the present town of Catawba, he halted at the home of a well-known Scotch settler, Andrew Lambert. Forty miles upstream from this place he had occasion to note concerning the country:

Our land lies in a region much frequented by the Catawbas and Cherokees, especially for hunting.[7] The Senecas, too, come here almost every year, especially when they are at war with the Catawbas. The Indians in North Carolina behave quite differently from those in Pennsylvania. There no one fears an Indian, unless indeed he is drunk. Here the whites must needs fear them. If they come to a house and find the men away they are insolent, and the settler's wife must do whatever they bid. Sometimes they come in such large companies that a man who meets them is in real danger. Now and then a man can do as Andrew Lambert did: A company of Senecas came on his land, injured his corn, killed his cattle, etc. Lambert called in his bear hounds of which he had eight or nine, and with his dogs and his loaded gun drove the Indians from his place.[8]

In this wilderness region a hunter was employed to help carry the surveyor's chain and to furnish game. He was John Perkin,

---

[7] This reference indicates that the region of the upper Catawba River was neutral territory for Cherokee and Catawba hunters. The land mentioned by Spangenberg lies between the Catawba and Yadkin rivers.

[8] Lambert's descendants may be traced among families in Iredell County near Buffalo Ford on the Catawba River.

described as being intelligent, well acquainted with the forest, industrious, and a successful hunter. Descendants of this frontiersman are to be found in that region today.

The surveying party met six Cherokee Indians, who conducted themselves quite friendlily. Sprangenberg commented that "the woods are full of Cherokees, and we see their signs wherever we go. They are out hunting." The sites of former Indian settlements were noted from time to time. It was observed that the forest had been ruined by the Indians, who were accustomed to set fire to large tracts to drive out the deer.

After the harrowing experience of crossing the Blue Ridge at Blowing Rock in winter weather the explorers traveled down the headwaters of New River, mistaken for the Yadkin, cutting their way through the laurel thickets, and camped near the present town of Boone.[9] After a few days' wandering in error they descended the Blue Ridge and reached the Yadkin near its confluence with Lewis Fork. Here they met a settler named Owens,[10] the progenitor of the Owens family in Wilkes County, whose home was said to be sixty miles from that of his nearest neighbor. The wide bottom lands in the neighborhood of the present town of Wilkesboro were called "Mulberry Fields" and described as old Indian fields on which the Cherokee probably had once lived.[11] Spangenberg finished his survey by selecting the Wachovia tract, in the center of which has developed the city of Winston-Salem.

THE FRENCH AND INDIAN WAR

The disturbance of the French and Indian War gradually penetrated southward. Friendly dealings with the Cherokee continued in the Carolinas, but ill reports increased like threatening rumblings of an approaching storm. As early as 1753 Matthew Rowan wrote:

Last June three French and five Northward Indians came down to kill some of the Catawbas but were met by thirteen of the Catawba Indians who killed two french & three of the Noward Indians the

[9] A town named for Daniel Boone, who passed this way on his journeys to Kentucky.

[10] An eminence south of the Yadkin River in this vicinity is known as Owens' Knob.

[11] A superficial survey shows remains of an Indian settlement in the Yadkin River valley near North Wilkesboro.

other three made thr escape the five were killed dead so that no information could be had from them this action was within less than two miles of Rowan County Court House dureing the sitting of the Court.

In 1754, Governor Dobbs of North Carolina, who had received large grants of land between the Yadkin and Catawba rivers, persuaded the assembly to provide for equipping a company of 150 men to protect the western frontier and to assist in building a fort. In the month of August the Catawba Indians met with the commission in Salisbury, as previously noted, and declared their readiness to aid the settlers against the French and Northern Indians. In September of the same year a raiding party of Indians supposed to be Cherokee attacked the homes of John Gutrey and James Anshers north of Broad River on Buffalo Creek. It was reported that seventeen people were killed and ten were missing. A messenger from Colonel Clark carried this information to Matthew Rowan, president of the Council, who sent supplies of powder and lead, and ordered Colonel Smith, commanding officer in Rowan County, to assist Colonel Clark. He mentioned that "when Col. Clark's express came away a party of the Cataba Indians were on the track of the Indians that committed the murder. I expect every hour to have an Account of them."

An incident of the Moravian settlement affords a picture of these troublous times. The records of July, 1755, yield the following account:

During our evening service Mr. Benner [Banner] and one of his neighbors arrived; they had been out several days looking for strayed horses. We gave them something to eat, and they went home. About four o'clock in the morning the Brethren were awakened by a terrible crying, and when they investigated they found it was Mr. Benner, who was almost frantic. When he reached home he found his wife and four children gone, and that his house had been robbed; he had searched the near-by woods in vain, and then knew nothing else to do but to come back to us. We did our best to comfort the poor man, but in vain. As we were all up now we held our morning prayers, kneeling before our dear Heavenly Father, and beseeching His care and protection. The Texts for the day suited our circumstances wonderfully. This was the first time that at morning prayer we have used the trumpets, which the last company brought with them from Pennsylvania.

At the close of the service Br. Loesch ordered the gun to be fired twice, and that the blowing of the trumpets be continued, so that if any one was near it would be known that we were not asleep. As the trumpets began again we heard a call, ran thither, and found Mr. Benner's wife and four children; one child she carried on her back, another little one was in the arms of an older child. We were overjoyed, hastily called Mr. Benner, and when he came to his family they fell on each other's neck, and could not speak for weeping. We brought them into our house, full of sympathy for the poor people and their great joy. We gave them food, and when they had somewhat recovered their composure the wife told us what had happened. During the night, as she waited for her husband, the dogs had become very restless, and running towards the woods had returned howling. She went to see who was there, and stones flew by her; then running into the house she took the children and hastened away. As she fled she saw three persons spring into the house, but did not know whether they were whites or Indians. So she and the children fled into the woods, and fortunately found their way hither, though they had never been here before [a distance of five miles through the forest]. . . . About eight o'clock Mr. Benner set out, accompanied by Br. Loesch and Lischer, partly to see how things were at the Benner home, and partly to warn the neighbors.

The Banner home, situated on the Virginia trail near the present town of Germanton, was plundered fourteen times during the French and Indian War. Descendants of the family still live near the old home place in Forsyth County.

In this same year, 1755, the North Carolina Assembly "recommended the erection of a fort between Third and Fourth Creeks, near the South Yadkin." The fort was completed the following year and was described as "a good and substantial building, 53 feet long by 40 feet wide, the opposite angles 24 feet by 22. In height 24½ feet. It contains three floors, and there can be discharged from each floor at one and the same time about one hundred muskets." It was called Fort Dobbs.[12] Captain Hugh Waddell, in charge of the fort, met with representatives of the Cherokee and Catawba and concluded a treaty.

[12] See Rosamond Clark, "A Sketch of Fort Dobbs," *North Carolina Booklet,* Vol. XIX, No. 4 (Raleigh, 1920). The site of the fort is five miles north of Statesville.

About the same time another fort was built on the upper Catawba River, both for the protection of the scattered families of settlers in that region and for the defense of the Catawba Indians against their enemies. The site is known today as Old Fort. Other fortifications were erected on the frontiers of recent purchases from the Cherokee: Fort Prince George and Fort Moore on the Savannah River, and Fort Loudon on the Tennessee.

Ill feeling among the Indians was aggravated by several unfortunate episodes in this critical time. A detachment of Cherokee accompanied Major Andrew Lewis on an expedition against the Shawnee in 1754. The attempt was unsuccessful. Provisions were exhausted and the weather was severe. Horses were killed for food. The weary, hungry Indians started home afoot. They found horses running loose and appropriated them on the theory that, as they had lost their own animals, they deserved this restitution. The frontiersmen, however, considered the warriors only horse-stealers, attacked them, and killed a number of their party. While the women were still bewailing the loss of their braves, an outrage was committed by some lawless officers of Fort Prince George at a neighboring Indian town while most of the men were away hunting. The warriors could no longer be restrained. In spite of efforts of leading chiefs of the nation, other outbreaks followed, provoked by harsh measures on the part of colonial officers.

In 1760 Fort Loudon was besieged by the Indians, and most of the garrison and refugees were massacred. Captain Stuart, who escaped the tomahawk, was escorted to Virginia by the friendly Attakullakulla, famous chief of the Cherokee, who purchased him from his Indian captor, giving to the latter, as ransom, his rifle, clothes, and everything he had with him.

The Cherokee were already on the warpath in Carolina. In the western Piedmont the alarmed settlers fled from their homes in the forest clearings and sought refuge. The men who remained to work the fields were in constant danger and carried arms with them. One of these parties was attacked at the home of Moses Potts, about four miles north of the present town of Statesville, and seven of their number were killed.

On the night of February 27, 1760, Fort Dobbs was attacked. Captain Waddell's account states:

For several Days I observed That a small party of Indians were constantly about the fort, I sent out several small parties after them to no purpose, the Evening before last between 8 & 9 o'clock I found by the Dogs making an uncommon Noise there must be a party nigh a Spring which we sometimes use. As my Garrison is but small, and I was apprehensive it might be a Scheme to draw out the Garrison, I took out Capt Bailie who with myself and party made up ten; We had not marched 300 yds from the fort when we were attacked by at least 60 or 70 Indians I had given my party Orders not to fire until I gave the word which they punctually observed. We recd the Indian's fire: When I perceived they had almost all fired, I ordered my party to fire which We did not further than 12 steps each loaded with a Bullet and 7 Buck shot, they had nothing to cover as they were advancing either to tomahawk or to make us Prisoners: They found the fire very hot from so small a Number which a good deal confused them; I then ordered my party to retreat, as I found the Instant our skirmish began another party had attacked the fort, upon our reinforcing the Garrison the Indians were soon repulsed with I am sure a considerable Loss, from what I myself saw as well as those I can confide in they cou'd not have less than 10 or 12 killed and wounded, and I believe they have taken 6 of my horses to carry off their wounded; the next Morning we found a great deal of Blood and one dead, whom I suppose they cou'd not find in the night. On my side I had 2 men wounded one of whom I am afraid will die as he is scalped, the other is in a way of Recovery, and one boy killed near the Fort whom they durst not advance to scalp. I expected they wou'd have paid me another visit last night, as they attack all Fortifications by Night, but find they have not liked their Reception.

An incident of Cherokee heroism is told by Haywood. In 1760, when the Cherokee were pushing east almost to Salisbury, a party of six or eight warriors was discovered, watched, and followed until they were seen to enter a deserted cabin to pass the night. Shortly before daylight the house was surrounded by settlers, who posted themselves behind fodder stack and outbuildings so as to command both the door and the wide chimney top. They began to throw fire upon the roof to drive out the Indians. When the blaze caught the dry shingles, and death by fire or bullet seemed certain, one of the besieged warriors called to his companions that it was better that one should be a sacrifice than that all should die, and that if they would follow his directions he would save them, even though he should die. The door was opened and he suddenly rushed forth, dodging and running in a zigzag course; so that every gun was emptied at him before he fell dead, covered with wounds. While the settlers were reloading, the other warriors ran out and succeeded in reaching the woods before the besiegers could recover from their surprise.

The first settlement of the Moravians in North Carolina, begun in 1753, was located five miles north of the present Winston-Salem and was called Bethabara. The village became an important center of trade, and as it was located near an old trail leading to Virginia, many travelers visited the settlement. Disturbing reports of hostilities gave the Moravians grave concern, and for protection they built a palisade around the village in 1756. During the following year more than one hundred and fifty Indians passed through. The Cherokee were still friendly, but Northern Indians came within thirty miles of the village, spreading alarm on every side. In 1758 Indians to the number of over five hundred were visitors, mostly Cherokee who conducted themselves well. One party carried a trophy of ten scalps. The Indians were generously fed and otherwise entertained at Bethabara, and so kindly were they provided for that they called the place "the Dutch fort where there are good people and much bread." The Northern Indians were still carrying on their depredations, and in April the Shawnee killed several settlers in the region between Mayo and Smith rivers, forty miles away. Some of the Cherokee passing through Bethabara were on the trail of the marauders.

The next year brought increasing alarms. Settlers were killed on the Yadkin and Ararat rivers not far away. Over a hundred refugees were assembled within the stockade in May. In this time of danger the Moravians began a second settlement, called Bethania, three miles west of the first.

In 1760 the terrors of the Indian warfare surrounded the settlements. The Moravian Records state:

This was the year of fierce Indian war. . . . On the 26th of February they [the Cherokee] attacked Fort Dobbs; and March 8th they killed William Fish and his son a few miles from here. Under these circumstances, we doubled the watch. The Texts of Feb. 28th and March 9th became true of us before we came to them in our reading: "Neither Nehemiah nor his brethren put off their clothes, (Neh. IV: 23) but prayed as they watched." "They appointed watches of the inhabitants." (Neh. VII:3). On the 12th of March many Indians were in our neighborhood; eight miles away, on the Yadkin, houses were burned; two men were killed at the bridge over the Wach [Salem Creek]; two persons were killed on the Town Fork. They had one large camp six miles from Bethania, and a smaller one less than three miles. Here, at the mill, and at Bethania, there were Indian spies every night. March 16th, a beautiful snow fell, lying for several days, and then we could see the smoke from their camps. Among our neighbors more than fifteen people were slain. The Indians said later that they had tried to make prisoners here, but had failed; that several times they had been stopped by the sound of the watchman's horn and the ringing of the bell for morning and evening services.

. . . .

On the 9th a man came, pierced through and through with an arrow. He related that 24 hours before William Fish and his son had asked him to go with them to their farm and get provisions for the families gathered at a certain place on the Yadkin. Some miles up the river they happened upon a party of Indians, who fired at them and then shot many arrows. Fish and his son fell, but this man, longing to reach Bethabara, for his soul's sake rode into the river to escape them. On the further side he found more Indians, but they paid no attention to him and he re-crossed the river, plunged into the woods, where in the darkness and rain he soon lost his way, and wounded by two arrows wandered for many hours, but finally reached the Moravian town [thirty miles of wandering] where Dr. Bonn took out the arrow and saved his life. The next day 50 persons, who gathered on the Yadkin, came to the Bethabara fort for protection. On the 11th a military company passed through, going to the Yadkin to bury William Fish and his son. However, they found the Indians out in force, so let the burial go and contented themselves with visiting the families who had thought to hold their ground, and bringing them to the fort. Next day a messenger came from the Town Fork, where another group of settlers was surrounded, and the militia went to bring them in also, but returned on the 13th with the news that two men had been killed and the rest had escaped. The next night Indians were seen in Bethania; the watchman shot at them and drove them off, then there arose a strong wind and on it came the sound as of the howling of a hundred wolves. . . . On the night of the 15th a snow fell, which stopped the activities of the Indians for a few days; otherwise the danger continued. One of the refugees narrowly escaped death on the path between Bethabara and Bethania; two others going out against the advice of Br. Anspach, who was in command at the mill, were attacked and one of them killed. . . . On the 20th word came that John Thomas, a Baptist minister, had been killed between the Wach [Salem Creek] and the Ens [South Fork], on the road to Ebits [Abbotts] Creek; another party was missing, while the third escaped.

How near the settlement came to being massacred was learned the next year, as the following report shows:

William Priest, who had been with the South Carolina Express, Aaron Price, to the Camp in Virginia, told us that the Little Carpenter had brought an interpreter with Capt Stewart [Stuart] to the Camp. The interpreter had told him that last spring a strong party of the overhills Cherokees had been in North Carolina, where they had lost one of their great chiefs. When they came home they said they had been to a great town, where there were a great many people, where a great bell rang often, and during the night time a horn was blown, so that they feared to attack the town, and had taken no prisoners. In the Virginia Camp no one knew what this town was, but thought it must be somewhere in lower Virginia, but Priest told them that the Indians had been on the Yadkin and that it must be Bethabara, the Moravian town, of which they spoke, for there a bell rang often and there was no other bell within 200 miles.

On November 20th Aaron Price of Charlestown passed through on his way north and letters were sent by him. He confirmed the story told by William Priest, and added that the Indians called this neighborhood Dutchi, and that they said the Dutchi were a dreadful people, very large and very smart, they had seen into their forts.[13]

Another account of Indian warfare in this region is found in the *Papers of Archibald D. Murphey*, which give material supplementary to that furnished in the Moravian Records:

They [the Cherokee] crossed the Blue Ridge at the Head of the Yadkin and came down the Valley of that River. They killed William

---

[13] There is a local tradition that a woman, milking a cow, looked up and saw two Indians peering over the stockade.

Fish near the Mouth of Fish's River.[14] One Thompson who was with him was wounded with two Arrows: one in the Hip, the Other in the back, between the Shoulders. He and Fish were riding together through a Canebrake, along a Trace [trail], on which the Indians were lying. Thompson wheeled his Horse, and made his Way down the Yadkin. Parties of Indians were in his Advance, and he found them in every direction he could travel in. He passed up the Little Yadkin, thence along by the Head branches of the Town Fork, and falling into the Road leading from the Upper Saura Town to Bethabara about 3½ miles from the Town, he hastened to the Town and gave the Alarm.

Had not Providence spared his life to give this Alarm many of the Whites would have been killed. The people in the fort sent out expresses to the Inhabitants to hasten in, and all got into the Forts or into a Blockhouse at the place where the late Col. Winston[15] lived on Town Fork. Two men were killed near the Block House on the next Morning. The Indians had spread themselves over the Neighbourhood, and in the Morning Barnett Lashley and one Robison left the Block House to feed their Cattle; and whilst engaged at this Work were killed. Lashley's Daughter aged 13 Years, went to her Father's House to milk the Cows. She saw nine Indians, who discovering her, pursued her. She by a sudden turn got out of their View, and it being a Wet morning, the Indians pursued her Trail. After Winding for some time up and down the Branches in the Neighbourhood and perceiving that the Indians were pursuing her, she made her way to the Town Creek Fork, and plunging in, kept down the Creek, till she came to a steep Bank covered with Cane, some of which had fallen over into the Water. Under this Cane and in the Water near to the steep Bank she stopped, and secreted herself, and determined to await her fate. The Indians pursued her Trail to the Creek, and not being able to discover which way she had gone, they went down the Bank and were for sometime within a few feet of her on the steep Bank above her Head.[16] They retired and after it was Dark, she left her Retreat and went in Search of the Block House. Having found it, she advanced with cautious Steps, not knowing whether it was in Possession of the Whites or the Indians. She came near and was hailed by one of the Guard; And she being alarmed and not knowing what to do, hesitated in giving an Answer; And the Guard was on the Point of discharging

[14] Now called Fisher River, in Surry County.

[15] Major Joseph Winston, whose name is retained in Winston-Salem.

[16] This high creek bank with overhanging vines, the only site that answers the description of the narrative, has been located near the old Winston home by John R. Shipley.

his Rifle at her, when she made herself known. She went in and was informed of the fate of her Father. She had expected it: as she heard the Gun fired at the Stack, where he had gone to feed his Cattle.

Thompson was treated with all possible Kindness. The Barbed Points of the Arrows were taken out; but the Wounds proved mortal. His Death was more regetted on Account of the Safety which he had given to the Inhabitants, by his timely Notice of the Approach of the Indians.

. . . The Indians extended their Depredations even to the Mouth of Smith's River in Rockingham County. It was in 1759 or 1760, probably—(see Joseph Cloud's Statement)—They killed one Greer and one Harry Hicks on Bean Island Creek. The Indians were near to them and looking at them. They perceived that all had fired and had omitted to load their Guns. They rushed on them, and killed one. Hicks shut himself up in his House, and fought valiantly. The Indians however broke in and killed him. They took his Wife and his little Son two years old, and carried them with some other Women and Children to their Towns on the Tenessee. One of the Indians who admired Hicks for his bravery and gallant defence, took his little Son in his Arms and said, because his Father was so brave a Man, he would take him home safe. He carried him on his Back all the way to the Cherokee Towns. This Woman and Child were regained in 1761, when Gen. Waddell marched to the Cherokee Towns.

A Company of Rangers was kept employed by the State in all times of Danger, who traversed the Country in the Neighbourhood of the Forts, and for forty and fifty Miles around, in Search of the Indians. Anthony Hampton (the Father of Genl. Wade Hampton) commanded the Company of Rangers who protected the upper parts of the Dan and Yadkin, and all the Country along the foot of the Blue Ridge, called the *Hollows* [now the region of Mt. Airy] in Surry County. The Company consisted of about 50 Men, all mounted with Rifles and Muskets. They were clad in Hunting Shirts, with Buckskin Leggins. They ranged the Woods in all directions and slept wherever Night came on. They occasionally visited the Forts and got Supplies. They generally made a Tour or Circuit once a Month.

In one of their Tours through the *Hollows,* they were passing along a small Indian Trace, when they were hailed by a Man at a little distance from them. They went up and found him to be one Wm. McAfee, who had left the Fort at Bethabara in Company with one ——————— [Woodman], to hunt in the Hollows. Here they were attacked by some Indians. McAfee was shot through the Thigh, which was broken, and his Horse killed; but his Horse ran off three hundred Yards before he fell dead. Here was McAfee with his thigh broken 33 miles from the Fort or from any House where any White Family lived; in the Woods and unable to move. In the evening of the day, Hampton with his Rangers passed by and discovered him; they placed him on a Horse and brought him to Fort, where he was attended to, and his Wound cured. He lived for many years, and lame as he was, he would follow his favorite Pursuit of killing Deer.

What became of McAfee's Companion, was never known. He probably perished.

There was a Fort called Fort Waddell (after Genl. Waddell). A Company of Rangers was attached to that , and they ranged through the Forks [of the Yadkin], and towards the Catawba, where Fort Dobbs was established. Daniel Boon[17] belonged to this Company of Rangers, and he buried *Fish,* who was killed by the Indians under the little Carpenter.

There was a Fort on Black Water of Smith's River, and Hampton ranged from that Fort quite to the Mulberry Fields near Wilkesborough. . . .

There was a Chain of Forts from Black Water of Smith's River in Rockingham County, near to the Long Island of Holstein.

1. The Fort at Bethabara.
2. Fort Waddell in the Forks of the Yadkin.
3. Fort Dobbs on the Catawba.
4. Fort Chisholm on New River.
5. Fort Stalnecker near the Crab Orchard.

Two men named Linville from the Forks of the Yadkin went to hunt on the Wataga between 1760 and 1770. They employed John Williams a Lad of 16 to go with them, keep Camp and cook for them. They were sleeping in the Camp, when the Indians came on them and killed the Linvilles. They shot Williams through the thigh and fractured the Bone. He ran off and in about fifty yards, the Bone snapped and he fell. The Indians did not go in Search of him: but gathered up their Skins and Guns, and catching their best Horses went off. Williams crawling on his Belly, found an old Horse at the Camp, and

---

[17] Daniel Boone's home at this time was near the confluence of the Yadkin River and the South Yadkin, the site now included in a park reservation in Davidson County. On the steep hill above the river bank is a cave in granitic rock, known as Boone's Cave. Daniel Boone married Rebecca Bryant, daughter of Morgan Bryant, whose home was across the river on a tract of eight hundred acres lying between the forks of the Yadkin. Bryant also had extensive property on the upper Yadkin. The parents of Daniel Boone are buried in the graveyard near Mocksville, the county seat of Davie County.

geting a Piece of Rope, tied it in his Mouth; and then crawling to a log, he got on the Horse, and with his thigh broken rode from near the Mouth of the Wataga to the Hollows in Surry before he came to a House. He was five days in this Travel, without anything to eat except Blackberries. He was nearly exhausted when he reached the House. He was taken care of, got nearly well, had another Alarm, broke the Bone a second Time. Yet he recovered, and lived to an old Age in Surry, where he became very respectable and was made one of the Justices of the County.

. . . .

Indian Traces [trails]—These generally run in the glades near the water courses, when they led in the right direction; thence through glades on the tops of ridges.

In these perilous days of Indian warfare log houses were built in many sections to shelter endangered families. A number of these were along the Yadkin River. One was on the plantation formerly the property of Thomas W. Griffith, later Tanglewood Farm, home of the late Mr. and Mrs. W. N. Reynolds, which they bequeathed to Forsyth County for a park. Mr. Griffith furnished in a letter to the writer the following account of the traditions of Tanglewood:

The plantation on Yadkin River which I owned until 1921, known now as Tanglewood, the property of Mr. and Mrs. Will Reynolds, came into the possession of my grandfather, James Johnson, Jr., in 1819, by a deed from his father, James Johnson, Sr. This would carry the ownership back to near the time when the Indians established a camp on the northwest side of the farm. When I was a very small boy, my Grandfather Johnson told me many things about the Indians, and I was afraid to go about the farm, thinking some of them might yet be lingering around.

He said that the Indians had a large camp near the river, which caused much uneasiness among the few settlers who lived near the Yadkin, and as a protection against an Indian uprising they built a fort on the hill, midway between the house in which Mr. Reynolds now lives and the river. The fort was torn down sometime between 1860 and 1870. I remember the old fort very distinctly. It was built with huge poplar logs hewed to six or eight inches thick, with portholes in every direction. It was said that the settlers were often compelled to resort to the fort for protection.

The colonists began a determined campaign against the Cherokee in 1761. South Carolinians under Colonel Grant marched into
the Indian country and destroyed fifteen of their towns. North
Carolinians to the number of four hundred, Virginia troops, and
fifty Catawba Indians joined the expedition that brought hostilities
to a close. The treaty was signed at Charleston. Boundary lines
agreed upon were to be the sources of the great rivers flowing into
the Atlantic.

In the years immediately following the French and Indian
War there were friendly relations between the Cherokee and the
colonists. Traders continued to visit the Indians and frequently
established trading posts in the back country. The Cherokee were
quick to learn the ways of their neighbors and made rapid use of
the benefits brought to them by association with the white race.

The Cherokee Nation

Lieutenant Henry Timberlake of the British Army visited
towns of the Cherokee on Tellico and Tennessee rivers in 1762,
seeking to promote friendly relations. He persuaded three of their
chiefs: Ostenaco, Collauna (Raven), and Oconostota, to accompany
him to England, where, with becoming dignity, they were presented to King George III. Timberlake has furnished the following description of the tribe:

The Cherokees are of a middle stature, of an olive color, though
generally painted; and their skin stained with gunpowder, pricked into
it in very pretty figures. The hair of their head is shaved, though
many of the old people have it plucked out by the roots, except a patch
on the hinder part of the head, about twice the bigness of a crown-
piece, which is ornamented with beads, feathers, wampum, stained deer's
hair, and such like baubles. The ears are slit and stretched to an
enormous size, putting the person who undergoes the operation to considerable pain, being unable to lie on either side for forty days. So
soon as the patient can bear it, they are wound with wire to expand
them, and are adorned with silver pendants and rings, which they likewise wear at the nose.

They that can afford it wear a collar of wampum, which are beads
cut out of clam shells, a silver breast-plate, and bracelets on their arms
and wrists of the same metal, cloth over their loins, a shirt of the
English make, a sort of cloth-boots, and mockasons, which are shoes

of a make peculiar to the Americans. A matchcoat thrown over all completes their dress at home; but when they go to war they leave their trinkets behind and the mere necessities serve them.

The old people still remember and praise the ancient days, before they were acquainted with the whites, when they had but little dress, except a bit of skin about their middles, mockasons, a mantle of buffalo skin for the winter, and a light one of feathers for the summer. The women are remarkably well-featured, and both men and women are straight and well-built, with small hands and feet.

They are a very gentle and amicable disposition to those they think their friends, but as implacable in their enmity, their revenge being only completed in the entire destruction of their enemies.

They are very hardy, bearing heat, cold, hunger and thirst, in a surprising manner; and yet no people are given to more excess in eating and drinking, when it is conveniently in their power; the follies, nay mischief, they commit when inebriated, are entirely laid to the liquor and no one will revenge an injury, murder excepted, received from one who is no more himself.

They are particularly careful of the superannuated, but are not so till of great age. Ostenaco's mother is an instance. Ostenaco is about 60 years of age, and the youngest of four; yet his mother still continues her laborious tasks, and has yet strength enough to carry two hundred weight of wood on her back near a couple of miles.

They seldom have their eyes on the person they speak of, or address themselves to, and are always suspicious when people's eyes are fixed upon them. They speak so low, except in council, that they are often obliged to repeat what they were saying, yet should a person talk to any of them above their common pitch, they will immediately ask him if he thought they were deaf?

They generally concur in the belief of one superior Being, who made them, and governs all things, and are therefore never discontent at any misfortune, because they say, the Man above would have it so. They believe in a reward and punishment, as may be evinced by their answer to Mr. Martin, who, having preached the Scripture till both his audience and he were heartily tired, was told at last, that they knew very well, that, if they were good, they would go up; if bad, down; that he could tell no more; that he had long plagued them with what they no ways understood, and they desired him to depart the country.

Here is given a translation of the War Song: Caw Waw noo dee, etc.:

> Where'er the earth's enlightened by the sun,
> Moon shines by night, grass grows, or waters run,
> Be't known that we are going, like men, afar,
> In hostile fields to wage destructive war;
> Like men we go to meet our country's foes,
> Who, woman-like, shall fly our dreaded blows;
> Yes, as a woman, who beholds a snake,
> In gaudy horror, glisten through the brake,
> Starts trembling back, and stares in wild surprise,
> Or pale through fear, unconscious, panting, flies,
> Just so these foes, more tim'rous than the hind,
> Shall leave their arms and only cloaths behind,
> Pinched by each blast, by every thicket torn,
> Run back to their own nation, now its scorn;
> Or in the winter, when the barren wood,
> Denies their gnawing entrails nature's food,
> Let them sit down, from friend and country far,
> And wish, with tears, they ne'er had come to war.

BARTRAM'S TRAVELS

An excerpt from the account written by William Bartram of his travels in 1776 in Cherokee territory will give a descriptive sketch of the land and the people of the valley of the Little Tennessee in the region now embraced in Macon County:[18]

I followed the vale to the right hand, and soon began to ascend the hills, riding several miles over very rough, stony land, yielding the like vegetable productions as heretofore; and descending again gradually, by a dubious winding path, leading into a narrow vale and lawn, through which rolled on before me a delightful brook, water of the Tanase. I crossed it and continued a mile or two down the meadows; when the high mountain on each side suddenly receding, discovered the opening of the extensive and fruitful vale of Cowe, through which meanders the head branch of the Tanase, almost from its source, sixty miles, following its course down to Cowe.

I left for a little while, the stream passing swiftly and foaming

[18] The reader is warned that this is a pastoral interlude, idyllic in its description of Indian life in the Cherokee country, and may not appeal to those who are hungry for excitement. It can be passed over if fancy calls for stirring events. It furnishes, however, a true and intimate picture of Indian life in the mountains in times of peace.

over its rocky bed, lashing the steep craggy banks, and then suddenly sunk from my sight, murmuring hollow and deep under the rocky surface of the ground. On my right hand the vale expands, receiving a pretty silvery brook of water which came hastily down from the adjacent hills, and entered the river a little distance before me. I now turn from the heights on my left, the road leading into the level lawns, to avoid the hollow rocky grounds, full of holes and cavities, arching over the river through which the waters are seen gliding along: but the river is soon liberated from these solitary and gloomy recesses, and appears waving through the green plain before me. I continued several miles, pursuing my serpentine path, through and over the meadows and green fields, and crossing the river, which is here incredibly increased in size, by the continual accession of brooks flowing in from the hills on each side, dividing their green turfy beds, forming them into parterres, vistas, and verdant swelling knolls, profusely productive of flowers and fragrant strawberries, their rich juice dying my horses feet and ancles.

These swelling hills, the prolific beds on which the towering mountains repose, seem to have been the common situations of the towns of the ancients, as appears from the remaining ruins of them yet to be seen, and the level rich vale and meadows in front, their planting grounds.

. . . .

I mounted again and followed the trading path about a quarter of a mile through the fields, then gently ascended the green beds of the hills, and entered the forests, being a point of a chain of hills projecting into the green vale or low lands of the rivers. This forest continued about a mile, the surface of the land level but rough, being covered with stones or fragments of rocks, and very large, smooth pebbles of various shapes and sizes, some of ten or fifteen pounds weight: I observed on each side of the road many vast heaps of these stones, Indian graves undoubtedly.

. . . .

Thus was my agreeable progress for about fifteen miles, since I came upon the sources of the Tanase, at the head of this charming sloping green hill beneath lofty forests of the mountains on the left hand, and at the same time observing a man crossing the river from the opposite shore in a canoe and coming towards me, I waited his approach, who hailing me, I answered I was for Cowe; he entreated me very civilly to call at his house, adding, that he would presently come to me.

I was received and entertained here until next day with the most perfect civility. After I had dined, towards evening, a company of Indian girls, inhabitants of a village in the hills at a small distance, called, having baskets of strawberries; and this man, who kept here a trading house, being married to a Cherokee woman of family, was indulged to keep a stock of cattle, and his helpmate being an excellent house-wife, and a very good woman, treated us with cream and strawberries.

. . . .

After riding about four miles mostly through fields and plantations, the soil incredibly fertile, arrived at the town of Echoe, consisting of many good houses well inhabited. I passed through, and continued three miles farther to Nucasse [the present town of Franklin] and three miles more brought me to Whatoga. Riding through this large town, the road carried me winding about through their little planta-tions of Corn, Beans, &c. up to the council-house, which was a very large dome or rotunda, situated on the top of an artificial mount, and here my road terminated. All before me and on evey side, appeared little plantations of young Corn, Beans, &c. divided from each other by narrow strips or borders of grass, which marked the bounds of each one's property, their habitation standing in the midst. Finding no com-mon high road to lead me through the town, I was now at a stand how to proceed farther: when observing an Indian man at the door beckoning to me to come to him, I ventured to ride through their lots, being careful to do no injury to the young plants, the rising hopes of their labour and industry; crossed a little grassy vale watered by a silver stream, which gently undulated through; then ascended a green hill to the house, where I was chearfully welcomed at the door, and led in by the chief, giving the care of my horse to two handsome youths, his sons. During my continuance here, about half an hour, I ex-perienced the most perfect and agreeable hospitality conferred on me by these happy people; I mean happy in their dispositions, in their apprehensions of rectitude with regard to our social and moral conduct. O divine simplicity and truth, friendship without fallacy or guile, hos-pitality disinterested, native, undefiled, unmodifyed by artificial refine-ments!

My venerable host gracefully and with an air of respect, led me into an airy, cool apartment; where being seated on cabins, his women brought in a refreshing repast, consisting of sodden venison, hot corn cakes, &c. with a pleasant cooling liquor made of hominy well boiled, mixed afterwards with milk; this is served up, either before or **after** eating, in a large bowl, with a very large spoon or ladle to sup it with.

After partaking of this simple but healthy and liberal collation, and the dishes cleared off, Tobacco and pipes were brought; and the chief filling one of them, whose stem, about four feet long, was sheathed in a beautiful speckled snake skin, and adorned with feathers and strings of wampum, lights it and smoaks a few whiffs, puffing the smoak first towards the sun, then to the four cardinal points, and lastly over my breast, hands it towards me, which I chearfully received from him and smoaked; when we fell into conversation. He first enquired if I came from Charleston? if I knew John Stewart, Esq., how long since I left Charleston? &c. Having satisfyed him in my answers in the best manner I could, he was greatly pleased; which I was convinced of by his attention to me, his cheerful manners, and his ordering my horse a plentiful bait of corn, which last instance of respect is conferred on those only to whom they manifest the highest esteem, saying that corn was given by the Great Spirit only for food to man.

I acquainted this ancient prince and patriarch with the nature and design of my peregrinations, and that I was now for Cowe, but having lost my road in the town, requested that I might be informed. He cheerfully replied, that he was pleased I was come in their country, where I should meet with friendship and protection, and that he would himself lead me into the right path.

After ordering my horse to the door, we went forth together, he on foot, and I leading my horse by the bridle; thus walking together near two miles, we shook hands and parted, he returning home, and I continuing my journey for Cowe.

This prince is the chief of Whatoga, a man universally beloved, and particularly esteemed by the whites for his pacific and equitable disposition, and revered by all for his exemplary virtues, just, moderate, magnanimous and intrepid.

He was tall and perfectly formed; his countenance cheerful and lofty, and at the same time truly characteristic of the red men, that is, the brow ferocious, and the eye active, piercing or fiery, as an eagle. He appeared to be about sixty years of age, yet upright and muscular, and his limbs active as youth. . . .

I arrived at Cowe[19] about noon. This settlement is esteemed the capital town: it is situated on the bases of the hills on both sides of the river, near to its bank, and here terminates the great vale of Cowe, exhibiting one of the most charming mountainous landscapes perhaps

---

[19] A mound at Cowee on the Little Tennessee marked the site of this village. It is reported that the mound has been leveled.

anywhere to be seen; ridges of hills rising grand and sublimely one above and beyond another, some boldly and majestically advancing into the verdant plain, their feet bathed with the silver flood of the Tanase, whilst others far distant, veiled in blue mists, sublimely mounting aloft with yet greater majesty lift up their pompous crests, and overlook vast regions.

The vale is closed at Cowe by a ridge of mighty hills, called the Jore mountain, said to be the highest land in the Cherokee country, which crosses the Tanase here.

I took up my residence with Mr. Galahan the chief trader here, an ancient respectable man, who had been many years a trader in this country, and is esteemed and beloved by the Indians for his humanity, probity, and equitable dealings with them; which, to be just and candid I am obliged to observe (and blush for my countrymen at the recital) is somewhat of a prodigy; as it is a fact, I am afraid too true, that the white traders in their commerce with the Indians, give great and frequent occasions of complaint of their dishonesty and violence: but yet there are a few exceptions, as in the conduct of this gentleman, who furnishes a living instance of the truth of the old proverb, that "Honesty is the best policy"; for this old honest Hibernian has often been protected by the Indians, when all others round about him have been ruined, their property seized, and themselves driven out of the country or slain by the injured, provoked natives.

Soon after crossing this large branch of the Tanase, I observed descending the heights at some distance, a company of Indians, all well mounted on horse-back; they came rapidly forward: on their near approach, I observed a chief at the head of the caravan, and apprehending him to be the Little Carpenter, emperor or grand chief of the Cherokees, as they came up I turned off from the path to make way, in token of respect, which compliment was accepted, and gratefully and magnanimously returned; for his highness with a gracious and cheerful smile came up to me, and clapping his hand on his breast, offered it to me, saying, I am Ata-cul-culla; and heartily shook hands with me, and asked if I knew it. I answered that the Good Spirit who goes before me spoke to me, and said, that is the great Ata-cul-culla; and added, that I was of the tribe of white men, of Pennsylvania, who esteem themselves brothers and friends to the red men, but particularly so to the Cherokees, and that notwithstanding we dwelt at so great a distance, we were united in love and friendship, and that the name of Ata-cul-culla was dear to his white brothers of Pennsylvania.

After this compliment, which seemed to be acceptable, he inquired if I came lately from Charleston, and if John Stewart was well, saying that he was going to see him. I replied, that I came lately from Charleston on a friendly visit to the Cherokees; that I had the honour of a personal acquaintance with the superintendent, the beloved man, whom I saw well but the day before I set off, and who, by letters to the principal men in the nation, recommended me to the friendship and protection of the Cherokees. To which the great chief was pleased to answer very respectfully, that I was welcome to their country as a friend and brother; and then shaking hands heartily bid me farewell, and his retinue confirmed it by an united voice of assent. After giving my name to the chief, requesting my compliments to the superintendent, the emperor moved, continuing his journey for Charleston; and I, yet persisting in my intention of visiting the Overhill towns, continued on.

References

Adair, James. *History of the American Indians.* London, 1775.

Bartram, William. *Travels through North and South Carolina, Georgia, East and West Florida.* Philadelphia, 1791.

Bourne, Edward Gaylord (ed.). *Narratives of the Career of Hernando de Soto.* Vols. I-II. New York, 1922.

Brown, John P. *Old Frontiers.* Kingsport, Tenn., 1938.

The Colonial Records of North Carolina. Edited by William L. Saunders. Vols. III-IV. Raleigh, 1886.

Fries, Adelaide L. (ed.). *Records of the Moravians in North Carolina.* Vol. I. Raleigh, 1922.

Gilbert, William Harlen, Jr. *The Eastern Cherokee.* Bulletin No. 133, Bureau of American Ethnology. Washington, 1943.

Haywood, John. *Natural and Aboriginal History of Tennessee.* Nashville, 1823.

Hodge, F. W. *Handbook of American Indians North of Mexico.* Bulletin No. 30, Bureau of American Ethnology. Part 1. Washington, 1907.

Martin, F. X. *History of North Carolina.* New Orleans, 1829.

Mooney, James. "Myths of the Cherokee," *Nineteenth Annual Report of Bureau of American Ethnology,* Washington, 1900, Part 1, pp. 3-548.

Murphey, Archibald D. *Papers.* Vol. II. Raleigh, 1914.

Rights, Douglas L. "The Trading Path to the Indians," *North Carolina Historical Review*, III (1931), 403-426.

Royce, Charles C. "The Cherokee Nation of Indians," *Fifth Annual Report of the Bureau of American Ethnology*, Washington, 1887, pp. 121-378.

Schwarze, Edmund. *Moravian Missions among Southern Indian Tribes*. Bethlehem, Pa., 1923.

Timberlake, Henry. *Memoirs*. London, 1765.

THE CHEROKEE

Part II

The Cherokee War

In these years of friendly relations various treaties were made, usually concerned with purchase of land. The most remarkable purchase was effected in 1775, when Richard Henderson and eight associates obtained for £10,000 worth of merchandise a tract of land that comprises now nearly the whole of central and western Kentucky as well as part of north central Tennessee. The Cherokee were bold in their claims, which included a vast territory beyond their settlements, but no one was present to dispute ownership. It may be said of this purchase, however, that such sale of land by Indians to private individuals was not recognized by the government. In this case the states of North Carolina and Virginia, successors to the royal government, claimed the territory, but in consideration to Colonel Henderson and his friends, the legislature of North Carolina in 1783 granted to them a tract of 200,000 acres and the Virginia legislature made a grant of like amount. Daniel Boone made scouting trips from his home on the Yadkin to Kentucky, assisting Colonel Henderson.

Sales of land were often made by one party of Indians to the displeasure of other portions of their tribe. Resentment followed. Before such dealings came into practice, tribal territory was considered common ground. Purchase of land by the colonists was followed by a rapid inflow of settlers, careless about boundaries, who encroached on hunting grounds of the Indians. Diminishing lands and dispute over ownership made trouble.

Adding to the unrest in consequence of such dealings was the influence of British agents among the Cherokee, who sought to enlist them against the colonists during the Revolution. One of these, a Scotsman named Cameron, had long resided among the Indians and exerted great power in the affairs of the Cherokee Nation.

An indication of the plans of the British agents is shown in letters intercepted in 1776, as noted in the diary of the Moravian colonists at Bethabara on May 26:

An express arrived from Transylvania [Kentucky], bringing letters signed by Messrs. Cameron and Stuart. The letters had evidently been written to friends, and as they revealed what was being planned, they were sent to this Congress. The plan was this:—the white people, who were loyal to the King, were to take their wives and children to Florida, where they should have land; then the men should go into the war. He wrote that he already had 2,000 soldiers, nearly 1,000 Indians, and that four or five hundred whites were in the Cherokee Nation.

The Continental Congress sent a commission to the Savannah River to meet with representatives of the Southern Indians, and obtained a promise of neutrality. The British agent, Captain John Stuart, however, did not despair, and succeeded in winning the Indians to his cause. It was agreed that 500 Creeks, 500 Chickasaws, some troops from Pensacola, and the Cherokee Nation should attack the frontiers of Virginia and the Carolinas. In 1776 the movement was averted by the efforts of Nancy Ward, a remarkable Indian woman, who warned the residents of the Tennessee River Valley to flee to the forts for protection. Two persons, a Mrs. Bean and a boy named Moore, were taken. The boy was burned at the stake and Mrs. Bean was bound ready for similar execution when Nancy Ward rescued her. This Cherokee woman was a half-breed, niece of Attakullakulla (Little Carpenter), the famous chief who in earlier years had visited England. He was a friend of the colonists in the struggle now under consideration.

The warriors advanced into North Carolina. Settlers were attacked on Crooked Creek, near the present town of Rutherfordton. On July 14, 1776, General Rutherford wrote to the Council of Safety:

Honourable Gentlemen,

I am Under the Nessety of sending you by Express, the Allerming Condition, this Contry is in, the Indins is making Grate Prograce, in Distroying & Murdering, in the frunteers of this County, 37 I am informed was killed Last Wednesday & Thursday, on the Cuttaba River, I am also Informed that Colo McDowel 10 men more & 120 women & children is Beshaged, in sume kind of a fort, & the Indins Round them, no help to them before yesterday, & they were surrounded on Wednesday . . . pray Gentlemen Consider oure Distress . . . three off oure Captans is kild & one Wounded. This Day I set out with what men I can Raise for the Relefe of the Distrest,

I am Gentelmen in hast

Youre Humble sert

Griffith Rutherford.

Tradition states that a Mrs. Hunter, who lived on Linville River, grandmother of the late Swan Burnett and Mrs. J. Sewell Brown of McDowell County, was scalped by Indians who appeared at her house without warning; that she was left senseless, but recovered, lived many years after, and reared a large family. This was but one of the many sanguinary encounters with the enraged warriors who scoured the foothills country.

In addition to Old Fort, other forts in the region were at Turkey Cove, at Fort Defiance near Lenoir, at Warrior Ford north of Morganton, and at several other places in the exposed settlements.

Plans were soon in operation for a campaign against the Cherokee to be carried into their country. Colonel Williamson of South Carolina, with 1,800 soldiers and a band of Catawba Indians, crossed Rabun Gap to the Little Tennessee, in the present county of Macon. General Rutherford assembled 2,500 men of Western North Carolina. In July he left the main body at Old Fort and with 500 men marched across the Blue Ridge. Reinforced by a regiment of militia from Surry County, while another regiment from Surry crossed the mountains to the north and joined the Virginians, Rutherford proceeded rapidly into the Cherokee country. His route led probably over an ancient trail, seemingly the same that was traversed by Needham and Arthur a century before, which has since become the main highway and line of the railroad in that part of the state. The Indians were put to flight with considerable loss, towns were burned, and crops destroyed. In October General Rutherford returned.

A little side light on Indian warfare is given in the account of Captain Moore's expedition. This officer was left by General Rutherford to "clean up" some of the Indian country. On his return a dispute arose between him and his whole body of officers and men concerning the sale of the prisoners. He reported:

I allowed that it was our Duty to Guard Them to prison, or some place of safe Custody till we got the approbation of the Congress Whether they should be sold Slaves or not, and the Greater part Swore Bloodily that if they were not sold for Slaves upon the spot, they would Kill & Scalp them Immediately. Then the 3 prisoners was sold for £242. The Whole plunder we got including the Prisoners Amounted Above £1,100. Our men was Very spirited & Eager for Action, and is Very Desirous that your Honour would order them upon a second Expedition.

The action of the soldiers is not surprising to those familiar with the following laws of North Carolina, passed in 1760, near the close of the French and Indian War:

13. And for the greater encouragement of such persons as shall enlist voluntarily to serve the said companies, and other inhabitants of this province who shall undertake any expedition against the Cherokees and other Indians in alliance with the French; be it further enacted by the authority aforesaid, that each of the said Indians who shall be taken a captive during the present war by any person as aforesaid, shall, and is hereby declared to be a slave, and the absolute right and property of who shall be the captor of such Indians. . . . And if any person or persons, inhabitant or inhabitants of this province not in actual pay, shall kill an enemy Indian or Indians, he or they shall have and receive ten pounds for each and every Indian he or they shall kill, and any person or persons who shall be in the actual pay of this province, shall have and receive five pounds for every enemy Indian or Indians he or they shall so kill, to be paid out of the Treasury, any law, usage, or custom to the contrary notwithstanding.

14. *Provided, always,* that any person claiming the said reward, before he be allowed or paid the same, shall produce to the Assembly the scalp of every Indian so killed, and make oath or otherwise prove that he was the person who killed, or was present at the killing, of the Indian whose scalp shall be so produced. . . . And as further encouragement, shall also have and keep to his or their own use or uses all plunder taken out of the possession of any enemy Indian or Indians, or within twenty miles of any of the Cherokee towns, or any Indian town at war with any of his Majesty's subjects.

Treaties of peace followed this conflict. Commissioners from South Carolina met with representatives of the Cherokee on May 20, 1777; and two months later a Virginia commission with North Carolina commissioners, Avery, Sharpe, Winston, and Lenoir, had a similar meeting. By these treaties a considerable area of country was ceded by the Indians to the states, and boundaries were determined. The North Carolina legislature ruled that "no person shall enter or survey any lands within the Indian hunting grounds, or without the limits heretofore ceded by them." Throughout the period of the Revolution, however, the Cherokee remained allies of the English and continued this opposition to the colonists until 1792.

During these years there were many encounters and stirring adventures. One narrative of this period tells how a boy aged sixteen, Joseph Brown, and his two young sisters, were captured at Nickajack Town while descending the Tennessee on a flatboat. The father and other men of the party, about ten in all, were killed in the skirmish, and the mother and several other children were taken to various Indian towns, some of them going to the Creeks, who had aided the Cherokee in this raid. Young Brown was first condemned to death, but was rescued by a white man living in the town and was afterward adopted into the family of the chief, in spite of the warning of an old Indian woman that if allowed to live he would one day guide an army to destroy them. The warning was truly prophetic, for it was Brown who guided the expedition that finally destroyed the Chicamauga town a few years later. When rescued he was in Indian costume, with shirt, breechclout, scalp lock, and holes bored in his ears. His little sister, five years old, had become so attached to the Indian woman who had adopted her that she refused to go to her own mother and had to be pulled away by force. The mother and another daughter had been previously ransomed from the Creeks.

A treaty concluded on the banks of Holston River near the mouth of the French Broad on July 2, 1791, and proclaimed on February 7, 1792, contained among numerous provisions the following:

1. Perpetual peace declared between the United States and the Cherokee Nation.

2. Cherokees to be under sole protection of the United States and to hold no treaty with any state or individuals.

3. Cherokees and the United States to release mutually prisoners captured from one another.

4. Boundary between the United States and the Cherokees defined. . . .

7. The United States solemnly guarantee to the Cherokees all their lands not herein ceded.

8. Citizens of the United States or others not Indians settling on Cherokee lands to forfeit protection of the United States and be punished as the Indians see fit.

9. Inhabitants of the United States forbidden to hunt on Cherokee lands, etc.

14. Cherokees to be furnished with useful implements of husbandry. The United States to send four persons to reside in Cherokee country to act as interpreters.

15. All animosities to cease and treaty to be faithfully carried out.

In 1799 Abraham Steiner and F. C. von Schweinitz, of the Moravian settlement in North Carolina, made a journey to the Cherokee country in Tennessee in an attempt to interest the Cherokee in receiving Moravian missionaries. The two men spent some time at Tellico and made visits to Indian towns along the Tennessee River and then went up the Tellico River to the Hiwassee.

In his interesting hundred-page account of the country and its inhabitants, Steiner reports Knoxville as a town of about one hundred houses, five stores, and no churches. Government officials had splendid control of the country. They arrested or chased away any white men who mistreated the Indians or caused trouble. Some time before his arrival the Indians had come to the Tellico

Block House for the annual distribution of presents from the government. Over four thousand Indians were present, and $6,000 worth of goods was distributed. The Indians would bring cattle, fruit, and many other provisions to the fort for sale.

Steiner describes the beautiful pipes the Indians made from green pipestone. One had made a pipe about six inches long, "with a neatly made head, at the other end a dove, and in the middle the figure of a man, about two inches high, with a brandy keg between his knees. He intends to send this pipe to Princeton College."

Signs of transition in the Indians' manner of living were apparent to the travelers. Improved methods of farming were spreading, spinning wheels were found in several Indian homes, cattle raising was making progress. The Indians seemed to realize that they must adapt themselves to the ways of their neighbors. There were no schools, but there were expressions of desire for learning. Dartmouth and Princeton colleges had sent investigators with the aim of promoting education.

Before returning home Steiner and his companion visited Nashville. Forty-five miles west of Knoxville, at South West Point, began a fifty-mile stretch of desolate country known as "the wilderness." It was the hunting land of the Indians. In winter the journey across the wilderness was difficult, but the great road was well traveled by pioneers on the way to the West. Nashville had about fifty houses and one church (Presbyterian), at which the minister preached once a month. Steiner added, "He also preaches every four weeks on his plantation, but the people say that the attendance there is more for horse trading than for preaching, for he is one of the best horse-traders." Observant Steiner wrote of the Nashville region:

Of antiquities, one finds many graves over all the land. These graves are of different sizes, and are found especially on the streams where flat stones abound. If they are dug up, bones are found of grown persons and of children; some are of giant size. From what race they come is unknown.[1]

[1] See Gates P. Thruston, *Antiquities of Tennessee* (Cincinnati, 1897).

DEALINGS WITH THE UNITED STATES GOVERNMENT

The beginning of negotiations with the United States opened a long and involved series of dealings between the Cherokee and the Federal Government. Tract after tract of land was ceded by the Indians. The government appropriated various sums in attempt to satisfy the tribesmen. Boundary disputes were interminable; disgruntled factions of Indians could not be reconciled; encroachments of white settlers continued. Presidents, from Washington to Van Buren, sought in vain for a solution of the problem. Additional troubles arose when other southern tribes claimed land that was being ceded to the government by the Cherokee. The states, too, were clamoring for their share, and sought to enlarge their boundaries at the expense of the Indians.

As early as 1803 President Jefferson had suggested the desirability of the removal of the southern tribes to territory beyond the Mississippi River. An act of Congress in 1804 approved this suggestion and appropriated $15,000 to enable the President to effect the desired project. The subject was presented to a delegation of Upper Cherokee who visited Washington in 1808, and met with some approval. The next year a party of the Indians visited the western country, and, upon hearing their report, large numbers—said to be about two thousand—signified their desire for removal. As the government was unprepared to defray expenses of so large a migration, the plan was not carried out.

About 1785 small groups began a westward migration, and prior to the treaty of 1817 as many as two thousand Indians departed for the new home. This treaty made provision for the acquisition by the government of another great tract of Cherokee country, with the allotment to the Indians of an equal amount along the Arkansas River. Among other provisions it was determined that "the United States agree to give all poor warriors who remove a rifle, ammunition, blanket, and brass kettle or beaver trap each, as full compensation for improvements left by them, etc. . . . Each head of a Cherokee family residing on lands herein or hereafter ceded to the United States who elects to become a citizen of the United States shall receive a reservation of 640 acres, etc."

General Andrew Jackson in 1816 voiced his opinion that the Cherokee would shortly make a tender of their whole territory to the United States in exchange for lands on the Arkansas River. Later he backed his opinion with vigorous action. General Jackson had availed himself of the aid of the Cherokee in the Creek War, and the battle of Horseshoe Bend had been turned in his favor by the bold advance of his four hundred Cherokee allies. The old chief, Junaluska, among those distingushed for bravery in the battle, later said, "If I had known that Jackson would drive us from our homes, I would have killed him that day at the Horseshoe."

Although their lands were continually being ceded to the government and their home territory was rapidly diminishing, a large majority of the Indians were opposed to removal. A memorial bearing the signatures of sixty-seven chiefs of the tribe declared their protest. Those Indians who favored the proposal to migrate were bitterly opposed by others who wished to hold their ancestral lands. Opposition was carried to the extent of persecution. Hatred engendered by this division caused dissension and strife long after the tribe had removed to their new home beyond the Mississippi. So serious had become the questions involved in the sale of Indian lands that in 1820 the Cherokee Nation passed a law declaring that to enter into any negotiation for the sale of tribal lands without the consent of the national council would be considered treason punishable with death.

After more conference and controversy another treaty was made in 1828, which included among other provisions:

Grant to the Cherokees of seven million acres of land in Arkansas River region; reimbursement for value of improvements abandoned in their removal; payment of $50,000 as the difference in value between their old and new lands; $500 to George Guess, the discoverer of the Cherokee alphabet, as well as the right to occupy a saline; an annuity of $2,000 for ten years to be expended in the education of Cherokee children; $1,000 for the purchase of printing press and type; each head of a Cherokee family east of the Mississippi desiring to remove to be furnished with a good rifle, a blanket, a kettle, five pounds of tobacco, and compensated for all improvements he may abandon.

For nearly twenty years Return J. Meigs, a veteran of the Revolutionary War, had been the United States agent for the Cherokee Nation. "He had, by his faithful, intelligent, and honest administration of the duties of his office as Indian agent, secured the perfect confidence of his official superiors through all the mutations of administration. He had acquired a knowledge of and familiarity with the habits, character, and wants of the Cherokees such as was perhaps possessed by few, if indeed by any other man." His views deserved consideration. Since the government had been exercising supervision over the Indians and had provided them with implements and other means of obtaining a livelihood, they had made considerable headway towards becoming an agricultural and pastoral people. In the opinion of Agent Meigs:

The point had been reached where the Cherokee people should begin to fight their own battles of life, and that any further contributions to their support, either in the shape of provisions or tools, would have only a tendency to render them more dependent upon the Government and less competent to take care of themselves. Those who were already advanced in the arts of civilized life should be the tutors of the more ignorant. They possessed a territory of perhaps 10,000,000 acres of land, principally in the States of Georgia, North Carolina, and Tennessee, for the occupation of which they could enumerate a little more than 10,000 souls or 2,000 families. If they were to become an agricultural and pastoral people, an assignment of 640 acres of land to each family would be all and more than they could occupy with advantage to themselves. Such an allotment would consume but 1,280,000 acres, leaving more than 8,000,000 acres of surplus land which might and ought to be sold for their benefit, and the proceeds [which he estimated at $300,000, to be paid in fifty annual installments] applied to their needs in the erection of houses, fences, and the clearing and breaking up of their land for cultivation. The authority and laws of the several States within whose limits they resided should become operative upon them, and they should be vested with the rights, privileges, and immunities of citizens of those States.

The state of Georgia at this time began a vigorous campaign to remove the Cherokee and to possess their lands. The pleasant habitation of the tribe had become more alluring on account of the discovery of gold within their territory. A sharp contest arose between the state of Georgia and the Federal Government. Already fourteen million acres of land from the Creeks and one million acres from the Cherokee had been added to that state at an expense to the United States of a million dollars and an exchange of a million acres of land. President Monroe believed that there was no obligation on the part of the Federal Government to remove the Indians by force. The Cherokee were indignant at the attitude of Georgia, and Georgia at the attitude of the President. An alarming situation faced the next president, John Quincy Adams.

To deviate from the tangle of conflicting interests, rooted in racial differences and developed largely into a wrangle over land, we may turn to an estimate of Cherokee development:

The Rev. David Brown, who in the fall of 1825 made an extended tour of observation through their nation, submitted, in December of that year, for the information of the War Department, an extended and detailed report of his examination, from which it appeared that numberless herds of cattle grazed upon their extensive plains; horses were numerous; many and extensive flocks of sheep, goats, and swine covered the hills and valleys; the climate was delicious and healthy and the winters were mild; the soil of the valleys and plains was rich, and was utilized in the production of corn, tobacco, cotton, wheat, oats, indigo, and potatoes; considerable trade was carried on with neighboring States, much cotton being exported in boats of their own to New Orleans; apple and peach orchards were quite common; much attention was paid to the cultivation of gardens; butter and cheese of their own manufacture was seen upon many of their tables; public roads were numerous in their nation and supplied at convenient distances with houses of entertainment kept by the natives; many and flourishing villages dotted the country; cotton and woolen cloths were manufactured by the women and home-made blankets were very common; almost every family grew sufficient cotton for its own consumption; industry and commercial enterprises were extending themselves throughout the nation; nearly all the merchants were native Cherokee; the population was rapidly increasing, a census just taken showing 13,563 native citizens, 147 white men and 73 white women who had intermarried with the Cherokees, and 1,277 slaves; schools were increasing every year, and indolence was strongly discountenanced; the nation had no debt, and the revenue was in a flourishing condition; a printing press was soon to be established, and a national library and museum were in contemplation.

It must not be forgotten that the influence of the missionaries was profoundly felt. This was the only tribe of North Carolina and contiguous territory where sustained mission work was carried on. Earnest messengers of the Gospel came early among them. From the Moravian settlement in North Carolina in 1799, and from other parts of the country later, went consecrated and cultured apostles to the Cherokee. These faithful sowers of the Word planted their seed in hope and saw that it bore good fruit. They had no little share in promoting the advance of the Cherokee shown in the above description.[2]

Much of the advance in civilization was due also to intermarriage with white men, chiefly traders of the pre-Revolutionary period, and a few Americans from the frontier. Most of this admixture was from good stock. Important families in Cherokee history are Doughertys, Galpins, and Adairs of Irish descent; Rosses, Vanns, and McIntoshes of Scottish origin; Waffords and others from the Carolinas and Georgia. The father of Sequoya was said to be Nathaniel Gist, son of Christopher Gist.

The government found that it was no longer dealing with a savage tribe. Remnants of barbarity persisted (who can say how long they persist, even in the best of civilizations?), but here was a well-defined superstructure. The Cherokee had reached a level where they could share many of the best things of their neighbors. They demanded a right to fair and humane treatment. George Guess, known as Sequoya, invented an alphabet for his people and in 1821 submitted it to the chief men of his nation. Within a few months thousands were able to read and write their language. Chief John Ross debated with members of Congress. In 1837 a general convention of delegates of the nation, held at New Echota,

---

[2] The first Cherokee convert was a warrior who had been captured in the Delaware-Cherokee War. He had been brought into the neighborhood of the Moravian mission station at Schoenbrunn, established by David Zeisberger in eastern Ohio. At the close of the war he had been granted permission to return, but he did not wish to at that time. He remained in the vicinity and married a Delaware woman. He was baptized on July 4, 1773, receiving the baptismal name Noah. The location of the Moravian settlement in North Carolina, which he said was in the neighborhood of Pilot Mountain, was familiar to him. He said that his tribe could be reached by going down the Ohio and up the Kanawha rivers. See George Henry Loskiel, *History of the Mission among the Indians* (English edition, London, 1794) and John Gottlieb Erastus Heckewelder, *An Account of the History, Manners and Customs of the Indian Nations Who Once Inhabited Pennsylvania and the Neighboring States* (Philadelphia, 1918).

adopted a constitution, assuming sovereignty and independence. These forward steps, however, hastened the decision of the momentous question. The governor of Georgia sent a copy of the "presumptuous" constitution to the President, and a new legal battle began.

Secret agents had been appointed and money had been authorized to be expended in purchasing the influence of chiefs in favor of removal. Burdensome laws were laid upon the Indians, such as these: "No contract between a white man and an Indian, either verbal or written, should be binding unless established by the testimony of two white witnesses." "No Indian or descendant of an Indian residing within the Creek or Cherokee nations of Indians, shall be deemed a competent witness in any court of this state to which a white person may be a party" (Georgia Code). Under these drastic measures the North Carolina Cherokee and many others resolutely refused to be moved.

A delegation of the Cherokee, with John Ross at their head, was quartered in Washington the greater part of the winter of 1832-33, pleading the cause of their nation. The President urged that they consent to the proposed removal. Ross made a diplomatic reply, asking whether, if the doctrine that Indian tribes could not exist contiguous to a white population should prevail and they should be compelled to remove to the West, anything would prevent a similar removal in later years for the same reason.

The following year Chief Ross presented a memorial to Congress, a document worthy of recording in these pages:

The memorial of the Cherokee Nation respectfully showeth, that they approach your honorable bodies as the representatives of the people of the United States, intrusted by them under the Constitution with the exercise of their sovereign power, to ask for protection of the rights of your memorialists and redress of their grievances.

They respectfully represent that their rights, being stipulated by numerous solemn treaties, which guaranteed to them protection, and guarded as they supposed by laws enacted by Congress, they had hoped that the approach of danger would be prevented by the interposition of the power of the Executive charged with the execution of treaties and laws; and that when their rights should come in question they would be finally and authoritatively decided by the judiciary, whose decrees it would be the duty of the Executive to see carried into effect. For many years these their just hopes were not disappointed.

The public faith of the United States, solemnly pledged to them, was duly kept in form and substance. Happy under the parental guardianship of the United States, they applied themselves assiduously and successfully to learn the lessons of civilization and peace, which, in the prosecution of a humane and Christian policy, the United States caused to be taught them. Of the advances they have made under the influence of this benevolent system, they might a few years ago have been tempted to speak with pride and satisfaction and with grateful hearts to those who have been their instructors. They could have pointed with pleasure to the houses they had built, the improvements they had made, the fields they were cultivating; they could have exhibited their domestic establishments, and shown how from wandering in the forests many of them had become the heads of families, with fixed habitations, each the center of a domestic circle like that which forms the happiness of civilized man. They could have shown, too, how the arts of industry, human knowledge, and letters had been introduced amongst them, and how the highest of all the knowledge had come to bless them, teaching them to know and to worship the Christian's God, bowing down to Him at the same seasons and in the same spirit with millions of His creatures who inhabit Christendom, and with them embracing the hopes and promises of the Gospel.

But now each of these blessings has been made to them an instrument of the keenest torture. Cupidity has fastened its eye upon their lands and their homes, and is seeking by force and by every variety of oppression and wrong to expel them from their lands and their homes and to tear them from all that has become endeared to them. Of what they have already suffered it is impossible for them to give the details, as they would make a history. Of what they are menaced with by unlawful power, every citizen of the United States who reads the public journals is aware. In this their distress they have appealed to the judiciary of the United States, where their rights have been solemnly established. They have appealed to the Executive of the United States to protect these rights according to the obligations of treaties and the injunctions of the laws. But this appeal to the Executive has been made in vain. In the hope that by yielding something of their clear rights they might succeed in obtaining security for the remainder, they have lately opened a correspondence with the Executive, offering to make a considerable cession from what had been reserved to them by solemn treaties, only upon condition that they might be protected in the part not ceded. But their earnest supplication has been unheeded, and the only answer they can get, informs them, in substance, that they must be left to their fate, or renounce the whole. What that fate is to be unhappily is too plain.

The State of Georgia has assumed jurisdiction over them, has invaded their territory, has claimed the right to dispose of their lands, and has actually proceeded to dispose of them, reserving only a small portion to individuals, and even these portions are threatened and will no doubt, soon be taken from them. Thus the nation is stripped of its territory and individuals of their property without the least color of right, and in open violation of the guarantee of treaties. At the same time the Cherokees, deprived of the protection of their own government and laws, are left without the protection of any other laws, outlawed as it were and exposed to indignities, imprisonment, persecution, and even to death, though they have committed no offense whatever, save and except that of seeking to enjoy what belongs to them, and refusing to yield it up to those who have no pretense of title to it. Of the acts of the legislature of Georgia your memorialists will endeavor to furnish copies to your honorable bodies, and of the doings of individuals they will furnish evidence if required. And your memorialists further respectfully represent that the Executive of the United States has not only refused to protect your memorialists against the wrongs they have suffered and are still suffering at the hands of unjust cupidity, but has done much more. It is but too plain that, for several years past, the power of the Executive has been exerted on the side of their oppressors and is cooperating with them in the work of destruction. Of two particulars in the conduct of the Executive your memorialists would make mention, not merely as matters of evidence but as specific subjects of complaint in addition to the more general ones already stated.

The first of these is the mode adopted to oppress and injure your memorialists under color of enrollments for emigration. Unfit persons are introduced as agents, acts are practiced by them that are unjust, unworthy, and demoralizing, and have no object but to force your memorialists to yield and abandon their rights by making their lives intolerably wretched. They forbear to go into particulars, which nevertheless they are prepared, at a proper time, to exhibit.

The other is calculated also to weaken and distress your memorialists, and is essentially unjust. Heretofore, until within the last four years, the money appropriated by Congress for annuities has been paid to the nation, by whom it was distributed and used for the benefit of the nation. And this method of payment was not only sanctioned by the usage of the Government of the United States, but was acceptable to the Cherokees. Yet, without any cause known to your memorialists, and contrary to their just expectations, the payment has been withheld for the period just mentioned, on the ground, then for the first time assumed, that the annuities were to be paid, not as hitherto, to the nation, but to the individual Cherokees, each his own small fraction, dividing the whole according to the numbers of the nation. The fact is, that for the last four years the annuities have not been paid at all.

The distribution in this new way was impracticable, if the Cherokees had been willing thus to receive it, but they were not willing; they have refused and the annuities have remained unpaid. Your memorialists forbear to advert to the motives of such conduct, leaving them to be considered and appreciated by Congress. All they will say is, that it has coincided with other measures adopted to reduce them to poverty and despair and to extort from their wretchedness a concession of their guaranteed right. Having failed in their efforts to obtain relief elsewhere, your memorialists now appeal to Congress, and respectfully pray that your honorable bodies will look into their whole case, and that such measures may be adopted as will give them redress and security.

In February, 1835, two rival delegations of the Cherokee were in Washington. One party, headed by John Ross, long the principal chief, was bitterly opposed to surrender of their territory and removal. The other, led by John Ridge, a subchief of considerable influence, though formerly in accord with the Ross party, sensed the futility of continued opposition and saw an opportunity to obtain increased power by seeking governmental favor. The Ridge party effected a treaty which was rejected by the Cherokee later in full council.

Negotiations continued and another treaty was proposed. A council was called at New Echota. Only a few hundred Indians assembled. John Ross, whose delegation was in Washington, was held a prisoner without any charge against him. The Cherokee national newspaper had been suppressed previously. Thus a delegation of less than five hundred men, women, and children out of a total population of more than sixteen thousand was used by the government to make binding a treaty with the Cherokee Nation, which gave the final blow towards their dispossession. The treaty, signed in 1835 and proclaimed in 1836, stipulated among its provisions that $5,000,000 be allowed for cession of territory, and that $600,000 be allowed to defray expenses of removal.

The number of Cherokees affected by the treaty is shown in the census report of 1835:

	Cherokees	Slaves	Whites inter-married with Cherokees
In Georgia	8,946	776	68
In North Carolina	3,644	37	22
In Tennessee	2,528	480	79
In Alabama	1,424	299	32
	16,542	1,592	201

There is a touch of sentiment in the visit of John Howard Payne, of "Home, Sweet Home" remembrance, to the one-room log cabin of John Ross a few weeks before this final treaty council.[3] The year before, while Ross was away in Washington, his beautiful home in Georgia had been drawn in the state lottery, and his family evicted. (At this time the daughter of John Ross was a pupil in Salem Academy in North Carolina.)

Elias Boudinot, one of the ablest and most cultured members of the tribe, editor and publisher of a newspaper printed in both English and Cherokee, defended the treaty in opposition to John Ross. Many leading citizens of the United States, however, were bold in their expressions of indignation. Major William A. Davis, appointed to enroll the Cherokee and to appraise the value of their improvements, wrote to the Secretary of War: "Sir, that paper called a treaty is no treaty at all, because not sanctioned by the great body of the Cherokees and made without their participation or assent." Henry Clay expressed his sympathy with the Cherokee people for the wrongs and sufferings they had experienced and regretted not only that injustice had been done, but also that a deep wound had been inflicted on the character of the American people. Henry A. Wise of Virginia, member of the House of Representatives, made an earnest denunciation of the treaty, declaring that in order to make treaties binding the assent of both parties must be obtained. Of the Indians he said, "There are proofs around us in this city of the high advancement in civilization which characterizes the Cherokees." He would tell the

[3] See Grant Foreman, *Indian Removal* (Norman, Oklahoma, 1932).

gentleman from Georgia that a statesman from his own state, who occupied a high and honorable post in this government, would not gain greatly by a comparison, either in civilization or morals, with a Cherokee chief whom he could name. He would institute such a comparison between John Ross and John Forsyth of Georgia. Daniel Webster in addressing the Senate said, "There is a strong and growing feeling in the country that great wrong has been done to the Cherokees by the treaty of New Echota." Other denunciations of government policy were made by Edward Everett, David Crockett, and numerous other statesmen. Crockett, who was from Tennessee, declared before the House of Representatives that the treatment of the Indians was unjust, dishonest, and cruel.

THE CHEROKEE REMOVAL

President Van Buren proposed to allow an extension of two years' time for removal but the decisive step had already been taken. The terms of the treaty were being enforced, and the westward movement was under way. By the end of the year 1837, Cherokees to the number of 2,103 had been removed, of whom 1,282 had been permitted to remove themselves. Reports reached the President that caused him to fear that the greater part of the Cherokee would not leave their homes. He ordered General Winfield Scott to proceed with a regiment of artillery, a regiment of infantry, and six companies of dragoons, and further authorized that militiamen and volunteers not exceeding four thousand in number be called from the states if necessary. On reaching the Cherokee country, General Scott issued a proclamation:

The President of the United States has sent me with a powerful army to cause you, in obedience to the treaty of 1836, to join that part of your people who are already established in prosperity on the other side of the Mississippi. Unhappily the two years . . . allowed for that purpose you have suffered to pass away . . . without making any preparation to follow, and now . . . the emigration must be commenced in haste. . . . The full moon of May is already on the wane, and before another shall have passed away every Cherokee, man, woman, and child . . . must be in motion to join their brethren in the West. . . . This is no sudden determination on the part of the President. . . . I have come to carry out that determination. My troops occupy many positions . . . and thousands and thousands are approaching from every quarter to render resistance and escape alike hopeless. . . . Will you then by resistance compel us to resort to arms? . . . Or will you by flight seek to hide yourselves in mountains and forests and thus oblige us to hunt you down? Remember that in pursuit it may be impossible to avoid conflicts. The blood of the white man or the blood of the red man may be spilt, and if spilt, however accidentally, it may be impossible for the discreet and humane among you, or among us, to prevent a general war and carnage.

Of the sad farewell of the Cherokee to their ancestral mountain homes, James Mooney has written:

The history of this Cherokee removal of 1838, as gleaned by the author from the lips of the actors in the tragedy, may well exceed in weight of grief and pathos any other passage in American history. Even the much-sung exile of the Acadians falls far behind it in its sum of death and misery. Under Scott's orders the troops were disposed at various points throughout the Cherokee country, where stockade forts were erected for gathering in and holding the Indians preparatory to removal. From these, squads of troops were sent out with rifle and bayonet to every small cabin hidden away in the coves or by the sides of the mountain streams, to seize and bring in as prisoners all the occupants, however or wherever they might be found. Families at dinner were startled by the sudden gleam of bayonets in the doorway and rose up to be driven with blows and oaths along the weary miles of trail that led to the stockade. Men were seized in their fields or going along the road, women were taken from their wheels and children from their play. In many cases, on turning for one last look as they crossed the ridge, they saw their homes in flames, fired by the lawless rabble that followed on the heels of the soldiers to loot and pillage. So keen were these outlaws on the scent that in some instances they were driving off the cattle and other stock of the Indians almost before the soldiers had fairly started the owners in the other direction. . . . A Georgia volunteer, afterwards a colonel in the Confederate service, said: "I fought through the Civil War and have seen men shot to pieces and slaughtered by thousands, but the Cherokee removal was the cruelest work I ever knew."

To prevent escape the soldiers had been ordered to approach and surround each house, as far as possible, so as to come upon the occupants without warning. One old patriarch when thus surprised, calmly called his children and grandchildren around him, and kneeling down, bid them pray with him in their own language, while the astonished soldiers looked on in silence. A woman, on finding the house surrounded, went to the door and called up the chickens to be fed for the last time, after which, taking her infant on her back and her two other children by the hand, she followed her husband with the soldiers.

All were not thus submissive. One old man named Tsali, "Charley," was seized with his wife, his brother, his three sons and their families. Exasperated at the brutality accorded his wife, who, being unable to travel fast, was prodded with bayonets to hasten her steps, he urged the other men to join with him in a dash for liberty. As he spoke in Cherokee, the soldiers, although they heard, understood nothing until each warrior suddenly sprang upon the one nearest and endeavored to wrench his gun from him. The attack was so sudden and unexpected that one soldier was killed and the rest fled, while the Indians escaped to the mountains. Hundreds of others, some of them from the various stockades, managed also to escape to the mountains from time to time, where those who did not die of starvation subsisted on roots and wild berries until the hunt was over. Finding it impracticable to secure these fugitives, General Scott finally tendered them a proposition, through (Colonel) W. H. Thomas, their most trusted friend, that if they would surrender Charley and his party for punishment, the rest would be allowed to remain until their case could be adjusted by the government. On hearing of the proposition, Charley voluntarily came in with his sons, offering himself as a sacrifice for his people. By command of General Scott, Charley, his brother, and the two elder sons were shot near the mouth of the Tuckasegee, a detachment of Cherokee prisoners being compelled to do the shooting in order to impress upon the Indians the fact of their utter helplessness. From these fugitives thus permitted to remain originated the present eastern band of Cherokee.[4]

Nearly seventeen thousand Indians had been assembled in the various stockades when the work of removal began in June, 1838. Disease, privation, and other hardships of the western trail claimed many victims among the broken-spirited emigrants. Hundreds were left dead along the way. At least 10 per cent (some estimates are as high as 25 per cent) of the tribe perished before the end of the journey. The last party of Cherokee emigrants began

[4] Mr. Mooney stated: "The notes on the Cherokee round-up and Removal are almost entirely from the author's information as furnished by actors in these events, both Cherokee and white."

their march on December 4, 1838. Those who offered resistance to the end fled to the wild mountain country of western North Carolina, and in their strong native fortress more than a thousand hid themselves to make their last stand. These were the ancestors of the surviving Eastern Band now living on the Oconaluftee River and neighboring country.

Into their new home in the West the emigrant Indians carried the bitterness of earlier dissensions. Three factions existed: the "Old Settler" party, composed of first emigrants, the "Treaty" or "Ridge" party, and the "Government" or "Ross" party. Violence followed. John Ridge, Major Ridge, his father, and Elias Boudinot were murdered. In tribal fashion, Stand Watie killed James Foreman, a member of the Ross party implicated in the Ridge murders. The feud continued for years.

At the outbreak of the Civil War the Southern Confederacy sought to secure the sympathy of the Cherokee Nation for the Southern cause. A considerable number of the Cherokee were slaveholders. Many of these, with Stand Watie as leader, readily responded to the overtures made by the Confederacy. Another party, headed by John Ross, refused to enter into any agreement, insisting on strict neutrality. As the agitation continued, Ross and his party wavered, and the sentiment of the Cherokee Nation for a time was strongly pro-Confederate. A regiment was enlisted and was commanded by Stand Watie. Another regiment previously raised by Chief Ross, ostensibly as home guards, was also placed at the service of the Confederate States. These troops operated with the Southern forces until the battle of Pea Ridge, in 1862. After this battle Colonel Wier of the Union Army, commanding neighboring Indian troops, sent a proposal to John Ross on behalf of the United States Government. Ross declined this, declaring loyalty to the South.

The Cherokee troops were unpaid and poorly cared for by the Confederacy. In July, 1862, when the Union Army invaded the Indian territory and the Southern cause languished, the discontented and unfed Cherokee soldiers reversed their allegiance. The regiment raised by Ross and commanded by Colonel Drew went over almost to a man to the ranks of the Federals. Ross was escorted out of the Cherokee country and retired to Philadelphia. He remained away from his home for three years.

The United States Government meanwhile sought to re-establish the refugees who had left their homes and to restore tranquillity in the troubled Nation. But Stand Watie and his regiment of 700 soldiers plundered the country. The losses in stock alone amounted to more than 300,000 head. When the war ended, the Cherokee Nation was destitute.

John Ross was too ill to take part in the treaty of 1866 and died on August 1 of that year at the age of seventy-seven years, fifty-seven of which he had given to the service of his people.[5] In a brief eulogy of the Chief, Charles Royce wrote:

He was in many respects a remarkable man. Though of Scotch-Indian parentage he was the champion of the full-blood against the mixed-blood members of the nation, and for nearly half a century had been a prominent figure in all the important affairs of the Cherokee Nation. Notwithstanding his many opportunities for immense gains he seems to have died a poor man and his family were left without the necessaries of life. His sixty slaves, and everything he possessed in the way of houses, stock, and other like property, were swept away during the war.

. . . .

We must now conclude the story of the Western Cherokee, who surrendered 81,000,000 acres, or nearly 127,000 miles, of territory for their new home beyond the Mississippi, where they dwell today. A fitting epilogue is furnished by Dr. Royce:

Their history has been an eventful one. For two hundred years a contest involving their very existence has been maintained. . . . By degrees they were driven from their ancestral domain to an unknown and inhospitable region. The country of their fathers was peculiarly dear to them. It embraced the head springs of many of the most important streams of the country. From the summit of their own Blue Ridge they could watch the tiny rivulets on either side of them dashing and bounding over their rocky beds in their eagerness to join and swell the ever increasing volume of waters rolling toward the Atlantic Ocean or the Gulf of Mexico: the Tennessee and the Cumberland, the

[5] On February 28, 1867, in the Moravian Chapel in Bethlehem, Pa., Bishop Edmund de Schweinitz "baptized three grandchildren of the late Hon. John Ross, Principal Chief of the Cherokee Nation." They later returned to their home in Indian Territory (*History of the Chapel*, Bethlehem, Pa., 1868).

Kanawha and the Kentucky, the Peedee and the Santee, the Savannah and the Altamaha, the Chattahoochee and the Alabama, all found their beginning within the Cherokee domain. The bracing and invigorating atmosphere of their mountains was wafted to the valleys and low lands of their more distant borders, tempering the heat and destroying the malaria. Much of their country was a succession of grand mountains, clothed with dense forests; or beautiful but narrow valleys, and extensive well watered plains. Every nook and corner of this vast territory was endeared to them by some incident of hunter, warrior, or domestic life. Over these hills and through the recesses of the dark forests the Cherokee hunter had from time immemorial pursued the deer, elk, and buffalo. Through and over them he had passed on his long and vengeful journeys against the hated Iroquois and Shawnee.

.   .   .   .

The removal turned the Cherokees back in the calendar of progress and civilization at least a quarter of a century. The hardships and exposures of the journey, coupled with the fevers and malaria of a radically different climate, cost the lives of perhaps 10 per cent of their total population.

.   .   .   .

Today [1885] their country is more prosperous than ever. They number twenty-two thousand, a greater population than they have had at any previous period, except perhaps just prior to the date of the treaty of 1835, when those east added to those west of the Mississippi are stated to have aggregated nearly twenty-five thousand people.

The Indian Territory which received the Cherokee has become a part of the state of Oklahoma. In the northeast corner of the state the Cherokee reside with the other members of the Five Civilized Tribes as their neighbors. Lands have been apportioned and economic life has been established on an independent basis. The lands of the Cherokee have failed to reveal the rich resources which have become the portion of neighboring Indians. This has proved rather a blessing, for they are said to be for that reason more aggressive and to display a high standard of intelligence.

Although tribal affairs of the Cherokee Nation came to an end in 1914, they still possess a strong tribal consciousness. The Federal Government continues to exercise supervision, which is being relinquished by gradual stages.

The population of the Cherokee Nation as reported by the

Commissioner of Indian Affairs in 1921 was 41,824. These figures include 36,432 full-blood or mixed; 286 by intermarriage; 187 Delawares; 4,919 freedmen, former slaves or their descendants. In 1933 the Commissioner informed the writer that "no statistics showing number of full-blood and mixed-blood Indians have been compiled by this Office for several years."

REFERENCES

The Colonial Records of North Carolina. Edited by William L. Saunders. Vols. VI-VII. Raleigh, 1886.

Foreman, Grant. *Indian Removal.* Norman, Oklahoma, 1932.

Fries, Adelaide L. (ed.). *Records of the Moravians in North Carolina.* Vol. III. Raleigh, 1926.

————. "Report of the Brethren Abraham Steiner and Friedrich Christian von Schweinitz of Their Journey to the Cherokee Nation in the Cumberland Settlements in the State of Tennessee, from 28th October to 28th December, 1799," *North Carolina Historical Review,* XXI (1944), 330-375.

Lindquist, G. E. E. *The Red Man in the United States.* New York, 1923.

Mooney, James. "Myths of the Cherokee," *Nineteenth Annual Report of the Bureau of American Ethnology,* Washington, 1900, Part I, pp. 3-548.

Poe, Clarence H. "Indians, Slaves and Tories: Legislation Regarding Them," *North Carolina Booklet,* Vol. IX, No. I. Raleigh, 1909.

Royce, Charles C. "The Cherokee Nation of Indians," *Fifth Annual Report of the Bureau of American Ethnology,* Washington, 1887, pp. 121-378.

THE CHEROKEE

PART III

THE EASTERN CHEROKEE

ABOUT ONE HALF of the fugitives hiding in the mountains of western North Carolina attached themselves to a leader named Utsala, or "Lichen," and established themselves in the wild region of the upper Oconaluftee River. Pursuit of these refugees was both a difficult and a hazardous undertaking, and attempts to capture them proved unsuccessful. After Charley and his sons made their dash for freedom, General Scott saw in this incident an opportunity for compromise. He engaged William H. Thomas, a trader among the Cherokee for fifty years who possessed their full confidence, to carry to Utsula the proposal that if Charley and his party were surrendered, the remainder of the fugitives might remain unmolested until efforts could be made to adjust matters with the government. Colonel Thomas many years afterwards told Mr. Mooney how this mission was accomplished:

The trader with a couple of Indians followed the secret paths to Utsula's hiding place. He submitted the proposition to the chief, informing him that if Charley and his party be delivered, the rest of the fugitive band could remain in peace; if this was not done, the 7,000 troops would set out upon an expedition to hunt down the Indians in their hiding places. Utsula turned the proposition in his mind long and seriously. His heart was bitter, for his wife and little son had starved to death on the mountain side, but he thought of the thousands who were on the march to the west, and of his own little band of followers. If only they might stay, even though a few must be sacrificed, it was better than that all should die—for they had sworn never to leave their country. He consented and Thomas returned to General Scott.

Now occurred a remarkable incident which shows the character of Thomas and the masterly influence which he already had over the Indians, although as yet he was hardly more than thirty years old. It was known that Charley and his party were hiding in a cave of the Great Smokies, at the head of Deep Creek, but it was not thought likely that he could be taken without bloodshed and a further delay which might prejudice the whole undertaking. Thomas determined to go to him and try to persuade him to come in and surrender. Declining Scott's offer of an escort, he went alone to the cave, and, getting between the Indians and their guns as they were sitting around the fire near the entrance, he walked up to Charley and announced his message. The old man listened in silence and then said simply, "I will come in. I don't want to be hunted down by my own people." They came in voluntarily and were shot, as has been already narrated, one only, a mere boy, being spared on account of his youth. This boy, now an old man (1900), is still living, Wasituna, better known to the whites as Washington.

Thomas next went to Washington to represent the cause of the 1,046 Indians scattered about in the mountains of North Carolina and Tennessee. For six years he labored on this mission and finally obtained permission for them to remain. He also secured for them their share of money due for improvements and for confiscation of their land.[1] Under authority as their trustee he bought for them with the funds a number of tracts of land on Oconalufty River and Soco Creek within the present Swain and Jackson counties, together with several detached tracts in neighboring territory. The main body of land came to be known as Qualla Reservation, taking the name from Thomas' principal trading place and agency headquarters. As the state of North Carolina refused to recognize Indians as landowners within the state until 1866, Thomas, as their agent, held the deeds in his own name. He laid off the land purchased for them into five districts or towns, which he named Bird Town, Paint Town, Yellow Hill, and Big Cove, the first three being names of Cherokee clans. [There is also Wolf Town, named for another clan.] He also drew up a form of government, which was under his direction assisted by an able Cherokee named Yonaguska until the latter's death, after which the Eastern Band knew no other chief than Thomas until his retirement from active life.[2]

The claim is made that "to Colonel William Holland Thomas the East Cherokee of to-day owe their existence as a people, and for half a century he was as intimately connected with their history as was John Ross with that of the main Cherokee Nation." He deserves more than passing notice in the annals of the North Carolina Indians. He was born in 1805 on Raccoon Creek near Waynesville. Shortly before the child's birth his father was drowned. When only twelve years of age he tended a trading post on Soco Creek owned by Felix Walker, son of the congressman of the same name who made a national reputation by "talking for Buncombe."[3] His contract for three years' service was $100

[1] By act of Congress, a census was taken in 1849, which listed 1,717 eastern Cherokee, increased by later additions to 2,133. Appropriation of $53.33 1/3 was allowed each, the same amount as for those who moved West, with interest at 6% from May 23, 1836.

[2] James Mooney, "Myths of the Cherokee." Information in this part of the chapter is drawn largely from this source, reprinted with permission of the Bureau of American Ethnology. Another important later study is *The Eastern Cherokees*, by William H. Gilbert, Jr. (Bulletin 133, Bureau of American Ethnology, Washington, 1943).

[3] Buncombe County, N. C. Congressman Walker's repeated praise of this county brought into popular usage the word *Buncombe*, which has been shortened to "bunk," a term applied by a prominent industrialist to history.

and expenses, but his employer spent so much time with law studies that he became involved in debt, and at the close of his contract Thomas was obliged to accept a number of secondhand law books for his payment. Of these he made good use, as shown by his service later in the state senate and in other official capacities.

As a store boy he attracted the notice of Yonaguska, or Drowning-Bear, acknowledged chief of all the Cherokee then living near the waters of Tuckasegee and Oconaluftee. The chief formally adopted the fatherless boy, who was henceforth known as Wil-Usdi, or Little Will, since he was of small stature. From his Indian friends, particularly a boy of the same age who was his companion in the store, he learned their language. In his declining years it dwelt in memory more strongly than his mother tongue.

Thomas later set himself up in business at Qualla. Although most of the neighboring Indians moved away as their lands were sold, many continued to trade with their friend and counselor. At the time of the removal Thomas was proprietor of four other trading places besides his headquarters at Qualla. He continued his study of law and took an active part in politics. In 1848 he was elected to the state senate and continued to serve in that capacity until the outbreak of the War Between the States. He inaugurated a system of road improvements and became known as the Father of the Western North Carolina Railroad. Resigning from the Senate in order to recruit troops for the Confederacy, in 1862 he organized the Thomas Legion, consisting of two regiments of infantry, a battalion of cavalry, a company of engineers, and a field battery, he himself commanding as colonel, although then nearly sixty years of age. Four companies were made up of his own Cherokee. At the close of the war he returned home and unofficially took charge of the affairs of the Indians. He attended them during a smallpox epidemic which came shortly after the war ended, and in the ensuing period of distress he gave himself freely in their service.

His own affairs had suffered grievously during the war. His resources had been swept away. In addition to these losses, the hardships of his three years in military service at his advanced age proved too great a strain. He suffered a physical and mental collapse from which he never rallied except at intervals. He died in 1893. Among the Cherokee the name Wil-Usdi is still honored as that of a father and a great chief.

The retirement of Thomas by reason of his infirmity was a great blow to the Indians. For years the affairs of the tribe on their reservation were disturbed. The Indian lands had been held in the name of Thomas as agent, and through his insolvency these lands, not fully paid for, were offered for sale. Only when the United States Government came to the aid of the Indians were their lands recovered for them.

Yonaguska, the father of Thomas by adoption, was a prominent figure in the history of the Cherokee of the East. He was more noted as a peace chief than as a war leader. He is described as being tall, strikingly handsome, and a great orator. When about sixty years of age he had a severe sickness, terminating in a trance, during which his friends thought him dead. At the end of twenty-four hours, however, he returned to consciousness and announced that he had been to the spirit world, where he had talked with friends who had gone before, and with God, who had sent him back with a message to the Indians, promising to call him again at a later time. From that day until his death his words were reverentially listened to by all hearers. Although formerly addicted to liquor, he now, upon the recommendation of Thomas, quit drinking and organized a temperance society which included the whole tribe. Thomas wrote the pledge, which was signed first by the chief and then by each one of the council, and from that time until after Yonaguska's death whiskey was unknown among the Eastern Cherokee.

He resisted every persuasion to move west. While counseling peace and friendship with his neighbors, he always held to the Indian faith and was extremely suspicious of missionaries. Someone brought him a Bible translation of the book of Matthew, but Yonaguska would not allow it to be read to his people until it had first been read to him. After listening to one or two chapters the old chief dryly remarked, "Well, it seems to be a good book—strange that the white people are not better, after having had it so long." Shortly before his death he had his friends carry him to the town house where, lying on his couch, he made a last talk to

Plate 49

View from Newfound Gap in the Great Smoky Mountains, Home of the Eastern Cherokee

Photograph by courtesy of Elliot Lyman Fisher

Plate 50

Jutaculla Rock, a Notable Pictograph in Jackson County

(An Indian legend says that the rude carvings on the rock are scratches made by the giant Jutaculla [Tsulkalu] in jumping from the mountain to the creek below.)

Photograph by courtesy of the State Department of Archives and History

Plate 51

The Nikwasi (Nucasse) Mound at Franklin, N. C., Macon County
Photograph by courtesy of the State Department of Archives and History

Plate 52

Excavation of Peachtree Mound and Village Site,
Hiwassee River, near Brasstown

Courtesy of the Smithsonian Institution, U. S. National Museum

Plate 53

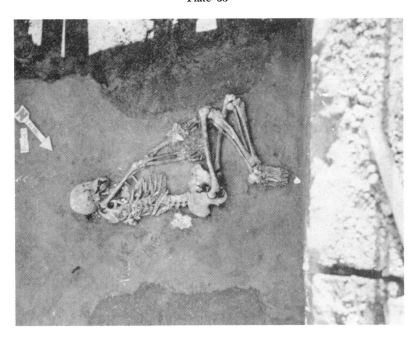

Burials at Peachtree Mound, Hiwassee River, near Brasstown

Courtesy of the Smithsonian Institution, U. S. National Museum

Plate 54

Sequoya
Copy from a Painting, 1828

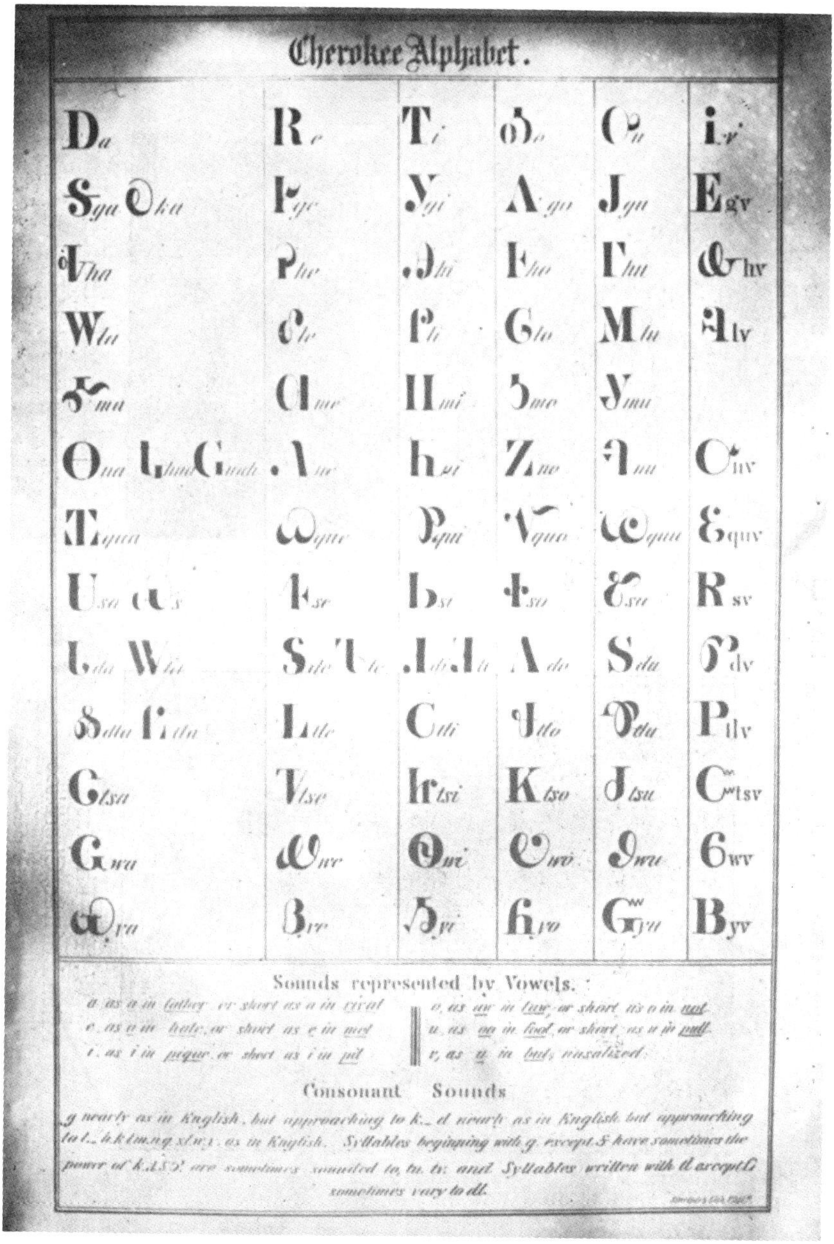

Plate 55

The Cherokee Alphabet of Sequoya

Photograph by courtesy of the Bureau of American Ethnology

Plate 56

Cherokee Chief John Ross

Photograph by courtesy of Dr. John R. Swanton and
the Bureau of American Ethnology

W. H. Thomas
Friend of the Cherokee

By courtesy of the Bureau of American Ethnology

Plate 57

Stone Pipes, Piedmont and Western North Carolina

(Several of these were associated with burials.)

Photograph by Roy J. Spearman

Plate 58

Walini, a Cherokee Woman, 1888

Photograph by courtesy of the Bureau of American Ethnology

Plate 59

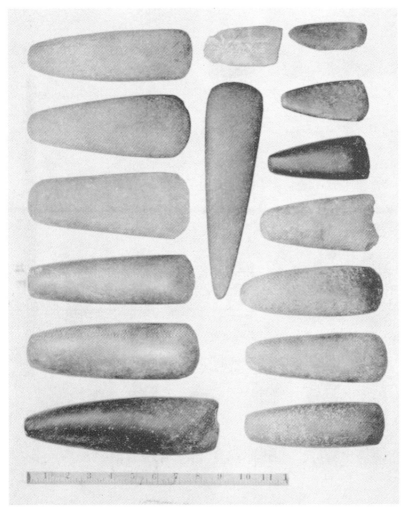

Polished Stone Celts

Photograph by Roy J. Spearman

Plate 60

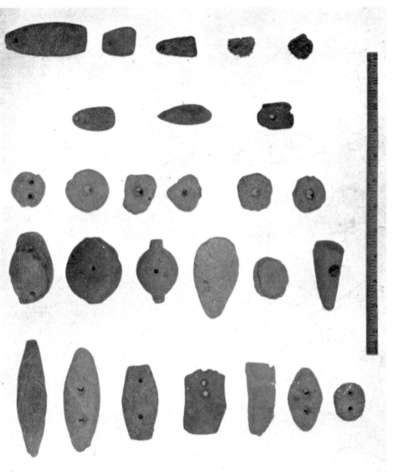

Stone Gorgets, Pendants, and Other Perforated Stones

Photograph by Roy J. Spearman

Plate 61

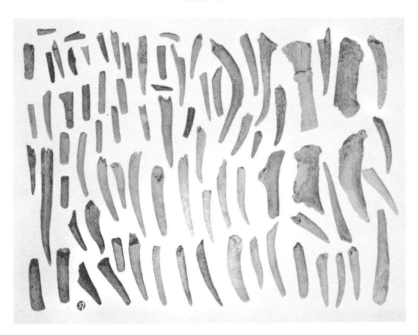

Fragments of Deer Antlers from Donnaha Village Site

Photograph by Roy J. Spearman

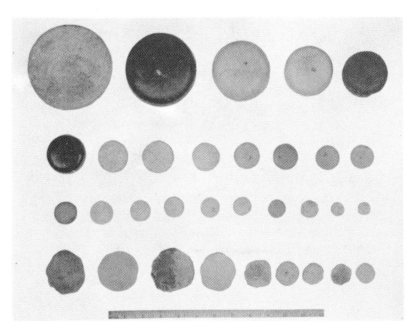

Discoidal Stones and Circular Pottery Pieces

Photograph by Roy J. Spearman

Plate 62

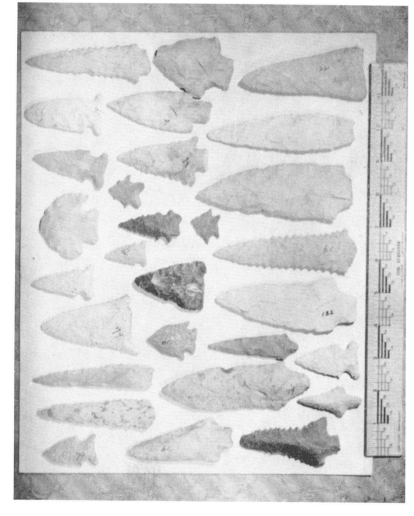

Chipped-Stone Artifacts from Davie County (79) and Randolph County (122)

Photograph by Herman Dezern

Plate 63

Presbyterian Mission School at Elm Springs, Indian Territory

Plate 64

Israel, Chief Member of the Spring Creek Moravian Mission,
Cherokee Nation

his people, commending Thomas to them as their chief and again warning them earnestly against ever leaving their own country. Then, wrapping his blanket around him, he quietly lay back and died. He left two wives and considerable property, including an old Negro slave named Cudjo, who was devotedly attached to him.

Early in 1862 an agent appeared among the North Carolina Cherokee to enlist them in the Confederate Army. This agent was an Indian with a reputation for reckless daring. Thomas feared that he would lead his Indians into needless hazards, and to prevent it he mustered them into his legion. They would thus be kept out of the path of the great armies, and could serve effectively as scouts in the mountain regions. They earned the commendation that "they did good work and service for the South." The war brought out their old-time nature. A grand war dance was engaged in before the troops set out, and the warriors were painted and feathered in good style. Before starting, every man cousulted an oracle stone to learn whether or not he might return in safety. They carried with them the love of ball play, and on one occasion a detachment left to guard a bridge were so intent upon a ball game that they narrowly escaped being captured by a sudden attack of the enemy. In the sharpest engagement one of their lieutenants was killed, and the Indians could not be restrained from scalping one or two of the dead soldiers of the opposing forces, for which ample apologies were given by their officers.

When physical and mental disability removed Thomas from leadership, Nimrod Jarrett Smith became chief of the band. During his administration schools were established and other notable advances were made. It has been said of Smith that "with frequent opportunities to enrich himself at the expense of his people, he maintained his honor and died a poor man."

A government agent had been previously appointed, but served only one year. In 1882 the agency was re-established.

After long-standing litigation over the status of the Indian lands, matters were adjusted in 1894 when the necessary government approval and supervision were obtained. The exact legal status of the Eastern Cherokee is still obscure. They are wards of the Government, citizens of the United States, and a corporate body of the state, all at the same time. Under their tribal constitution they are governed by a principal and an assistant chief, elected for a term of four years, with an executive council appointed by the chief, and sixteen councilors elected by the various settlements for a term of two years.

From 1881 to 1892 a boarding school for Indian children was conducted by the Friends, who also carried on religious work on the reservation.

The Indian agency and school are now administered by a Federal officer, who also handles the money of the members of the tribe and keeps a check on the tribal funds. He has no control otherwise over the Indians, who are subject to state authority. Individual Indians hold land as tenants of the corporation. The reservation is a community of small farmers. Some members of the tribe make baskets and pottery and weave rugs. There is a Farm Society with a membership of over three hundred members. In the fall a fair is held annually; farm products and cattle are exhibited, and objects of Indian handicraft are on sale; usually the ancestral ball game is played, though lacking in its former ceremonial accompaniments.

There are several churches on the reservation. The school, with a capacity of four hundred pupils, is under excellent supervision. There is also a hospital with a full-time physician and three nurses, including a visiting nurse. In 1933 an examination of nearly one thousand Indians, directed by the State Health Department, made a favorable showing of health status.

The report of the Commissioner of Indian Affairs for 1932 gave the population of the Eastern Cherokee as 3,230, of whom 2,811 resided on the reservation. William Harlen Gilbert, Jr., in *The Eastern Cherokees*, published in 1943, states that

the total native population of the Eastern Cherokee Reservation numbers scarcely 1,900 persons, and of these about 1,000 are still native enough to have clan affiliations. . . . The speech of the home is still native although most, if not all, of the Cherokees speak or understand English.

In recent years Tahquette, Sampson Owl, Henry Bradley, Saunooke, and Jarrett Blythe (twice) have been chiefs.

Members of the tribe who served in the First World War organized an all-Indian post of the American Legion. In the Second World War the Cherokee responded with a full quota.

SOME PROMINENT CHARACTERS

Attakullakulla—Also known as Little Carpenter, born about 1700.[4] He was one of a delegation taken to England in 1730 by Sir Alexander Cuming. In 1753, at a conference called by Governor Glen in South Carolina, he was the chief speaker for his people, although being at that time second in power in his tribe. It is stated that through his influence Fort Dobbs was built. At the massacre of Fort Loudon he rescued Captain Stuart, as already narrated. He was instrumental in arranging the treaty of 1761 and in securing the appointment of Stuart as British agent for the southern tribes. Notwithstanding his friendship for Stuart, however, and the fact that a majority of his people were allies of the English, he raised a force of five hundred warriors which he offered to the colonists. In 1763 a prominent Indian trader from Virginia, named Boyer, visiting in Wachovia, told "many things about the Cherokees, especially about Altakullakulla, or Little Carpenter, who, he said, had as good an idea of a future state as any white man. The Chief wished better instruction for his people, and would ask the Government for a minister for them."[5]

In 1765 the Chief escorted white teachers to the Cherokee Nation. Although he had become sedate, dignified, and somewhat taciturn in maturer years, he was, according to the report of a South Carolina historian, fond of the bottle in his younger days and often inebriated. He died about 1780.

Nancy Ward—A kinswoman of Attakullakulla. She resided at Echota, where she held the office "Beloved Woman," or "Pretty Woman," by virtue of which she was always entitled to speak in councils and to decide the fate of captives. She distinguished herself by her constant friendship for the white settlers, using her best efforts to bring about peace between them and her own people, and often befriending the white settlers in time of danger. Her appearance was described as "queenly and commanding." Her

---

[4] The studies of James Mooney, published by the Bureau of American Ethnology, have supplied most of the material applied to these characters.

[5] See Adelaide L. Fries, *Records of the Moravians in North Carolina*, Vol. I.

influence was effectual in elevating the condition of her people in their new western home.

Sequoya—Also known as George Guess or Gist, was born about 1760. He became a hunter and trader in furs. He was also a craftsman in silver work and an ingenious mechanic. He invented an alphabet and system of writing suitable to the language of his people. Strangely enough, this distinguished Cherokee never attended school and in all his life never learned to speak, read, or write the English language. Nor did he ever abandon his native religion, although from frequent visits to the Moravian Mission he became imbued with a friendly feeling toward the new civilization. He was crippled for life by a hunting accident, and this handicap afforded him an opportunity for study. By a chance conversation in 1809 he was led to reflect upon the ability of the white men to communicate their thoughts by writing. For years he labored patiently in discouragement and repeated failure, unmindful of the ridicule of his tribesmen.[6] As his home country about Echota had passed from control of his people by one of the numerous cessions of land, he was living in upper Alabama when in 1821 he submitted his alphabet to the chief men of his nation. Within a few months thousands of illiterate Cherokees were able to read and write their own language, teaching each other in cabins and along the roadside. The following year Sequoya visited Arkansas, and a year later settled there. In the fall of the same year, 1823, John Ross, the president of the national committee, in the name of the national council presented him with a silver medal bearing an inscription in both languages. The invention of the alphabet had an immediate and wonderful effect on Cherokee development.

Parts of the Bible were printed in 1824, and four years later a newspaper, the *Cherokee Phoenix*, appeared printed in Cherokee and English. Sequoya was for several years a member of the

---

[6] When Sequoya, the inventor of the Cherokee alphabet, was trying to introduce it among his people, about 1822, some of them opposed it on the grounds that Indians had no business with reading. They said that when the Indian and the white man were created, the Indian, being the elder, was given a book, while the white man received a bow and arrows. Each was instructed to take good care of his gift and make the best use of it, but the Indian was so neglectful of his book that the white man stole it from him, leaving the bow in its place, so that books and reading now belong of right to the white man, while the Indian ought to be satisfied to hunt for a living (*Cherokee Advocate*, October 26, 1844).

national council of the Western Cherokee. He died in Mexico in 1843 while seeking scattered bands of Cherokee who had migrated southwest.

John Ross—Born in 1790. Attended school in Tennessee. He was sent on a mission to the Cherokee in Arkansas by Agent Meigs in 1809, and from that time until the close of his life he remained in public service of his nation. He was adjutant of the Cherokee regiment in the war against the Creeks. As president of the national committee from 1819 to 1826 he was instrumental in the introduction of school and mechanical training among his people and had a large share in the development of the government of his people as embodied in their national constitution. From 1828 until the removal of the tribe he was principal chief of the nation and ably defended his people before the government of the United States. He was chosen chief of the united Cherokee Nation in Indian Territory and he held that office until his death.

The national council of the Cherokee Nation included this tribute in its resolutions:

Blessed with a fine constitution and a vigorous mind, John Ross had the physical ability to follow the path of duty wherever it led. No danger appalled him. He never faltered in supporting what he believed to be right, but clung to it with a steadiness of purpose which alone could have sprung from the clearest convictions of rectitude. He never sacrificed the interests of his nation to expediency. He never lost sight of the welfare of the people. For them he labored daily for a long life, and upon them he bestowed his last expressed thoughts. A friend of the law, he obeyed it; a friend of education, he faithfully encouraged schools throughout the country, and spent liberally his means in conferring it upon others. Given to hospitality, none ever hungered around his door. A professor of the Christian religion, he practiced its precepts. His works are inseparable from the history of the Cherokee people for nearly half a century, while his example in the daily walks of life will linger in the future and whisper words of hope, temperance, and charity in the years of posterity.

Junaluska—Whose name means "he tried repeatedly, but failed," a noted chief of the Eastern Cherokee in North Carolina. In the Creek War he led a detachment of warriors to the support of General Jackson and did good service in the bloody battle of

Horseshoe Bend. Having boasted on setting out that he would exterminate the Creeks, he was obliged to confess on his return that some of that tribe were still alive; whence the name jokingly bestowed upon him by his friends. He went West in the removal of 1838, but returned to North Carolina. As a special recognition of his services he was granted rights of citizenship and a tract of land near the present town of Robbinsville. He died in 1858.[7]

James D. Wafford—In youth he attended the mission school conducted by the Rev. Evan Jones. He held many positions of trust among his people. From him was secured much information about the history, geography, linguistics, and customs of his tribe.

Nimrod Jarrett Smith—For a number of years Chief of the Eastern Band residing on the reservation in North Carolina. He was born near Murphy about 1838. At the beginning of the War Between the States he enlisted with a considerable number of the Eastern Cherokee in the Thomas Confederate Legion and served to the close of the war as sergeant of his company. He was an active worker on behalf of his people. Through his efforts the first schools were established among the Eastern Cherokee, and the landed interests of the tribe were secured on a sound basis. He died in 1893. Mr. Mooney furnished this description:

In person Chief Smith was a splendid specimen of physical manhood, being six feet four inches in height and built in proportion, erect in figure, with flowing black hair curling down over his shoulders, a deep musical voice, and a kindly spirit and natural dignity that never failed to impress the stranger.

REFERENCES

Fries, Adelaide L. (ed.). *Records of the Moravians in North Carolina*. Vol. I. Raleigh, 1922.

Gilbert, William Harlen, Jr. *The Eastern Cherokee*. Bulletin 133, Bureau of American Ethnology. Washington, 1943.

Kelsey, Rayner W. *Friends and the Indians, 1655-1917*. Philadelphia, 1917.

Mooney, James. "Myths of the Cherokee," *Nineteenth Annual Report of the Bureau of American Ethnology*, Washington, 1900, Part 1, pp. 3-548.

[7] A monument marks the tomb of Junaluska, and the assembly grounds of the Methodist Church bear his name.

CHAPTER XV

Sacred Formulas of the Cherokee

The Cult of the Shamans

IN 1887-88 James Mooney lived among the Cherokee of North Carolina. During this time he gathered several hundred sacred formulas of the tribe. These were exceedingly difficult to obtain, since they were the property of surviving shamans, or of descendants of shamans, and were closely guarded. He was fortunate, however, in his attempts and gathered material which reveals much concerning the religious beliefs of the tribe, the functions of the priestly class, and the methods employed by the conjurers. Such a collection could not possibly have been secured from any other tribe, as the Cherokee alone had a written language which could be employed in recording their formulas in such a manner that translation was possible. The story of how these secrets of the cult were obtained is a fascinating narrative. Many of them came directly from the hands of shamans who still practiced their profession. Leading contributors to the collection were Ayunini, or Swimmer, then living, and the late Gatigwanasti, Gahuni, and Enola. The last named had been a licensed Methodist minister known as the Reverend Black Fox, but he seemed to have carried on his ancient profession as a side line.

The formulas, or sacred charms, covered a wide range. Probably half of them pertained to medicine. When the unemotional character of the Indian is considered, the number of love charms is surprising. In addition, hunting, fishing, war, self-protection, defeat of enemies, witchcraft, crops, council, ball play, and numerous other subjects were represented.

Before examining some of these formulas it may be well to review accounts of Mr. Mooney's findings in Cherokee mythology and theology.[1]

[1] The ensuing section of this chapter, including the formulas, is reprinted

Origin of Disease and Medicine

In the old days quadrupeds, birds, fishes, and insects could all talk, and they and the human race lived together in peace and friendship. But as time went on the people increased so rapidly that their settlements spread over the whole earth and the poor animals found themselves beginning to be cramped for room. This was bad enough, but to add to their misfortunes man invented bows, knives, blowguns, spears, and hooks, and began to slaughter the larger animals, birds, and fishes for the sake of their flesh or their skins, while the smaller creatures, such as the frogs and worms, were crushed and trodden upon without mercy, out of pure carelessness or contempt. In this state of affairs the animals resolved to consult upon measures for their common safety.

The bears were the first to meet in council in their townhouse in Kuwahi, the "Mulberry Place" (one of the high peaks of the Smoky Mountains, on the Tennessee line, near Clingman's Dome), and the old White Bear chief presided. After each in turn had made complaint against the way in which man killed their friends, devoured their flesh, and used their skins for his own adornment, it was unanimously decided to begin war at once against the human race. Some one asked what weapons man used to accomplish their destruction. "Bows and arrows, of course," cried all the bears in chorus. "And what are they made of?" was the next question. "The bow of wood and the string of our own entrails," replied one of the bears. It was then proposed that they make a bow and some arrows and see if they could not turn man's weapons against himself. So one bear got a nice piece of locust wood and another sacrificed himself for the good of the rest in order to furnish a piece of his entrails for the string. But when everything was ready and the first bear stepped up to make the trial it was found that in letting the arrow fly after drawing back the bow, his long claws caught the string and spoiled the shot. This was annoying, but another suggested that he could overcome the difficulty by cutting his claws, which was accordingly done, and on a second trial it was found that the arrow went straight to the mark. But here the chief, the old White Bear, interposed and said that it was necessary that they should have long claws in order to be able to climb trees. "One of us has

---

with permission of the Bureau of American Ethnology. See James Mooney, "Myths of the Cherokee," *Nineteenth Annual Report of the Bureau of American Ethnology* (Washington, 1900), Part 1, pp. 3-548; and "Sacred Formulas of the Cherokee," *Seventh Annual Report of the Bureau of American Ethnology* (Washington, 1891), pp. 301-397.

already died to furnish the bow, and if we now cut off our claws we shall all have to starve together. It is better to trust to the teeth and claws which nature has given us, for it is evident that man's weapons were not intended for us."

No one could suggest any better plan, so the old chief dismissed the council and the bears dispersed to their forest haunts without having concerted any means for preventing the increase of the human race. Had the result of the council been otherwise, we should now be at war with the bears, but as it is, the hunter does not even ask the bear's pardon when he kills one.

The deer next held a council under their chief, the Little Deer, and after some deliberation resolved to inflict rheumatism upon every hunter who should kill one of their number, unless he took care to ask their pardon for the offense. They sent notice of their decision to the nearest settlement of Indians and told them at the same time how to make propitiation when necessity forced them to kill one of the deer tribe. Now, whenever the hunter brings down a deer, the Little Deer, who is swift as the wind and can not be wounded, runs quickly up to the spot and bending over the blood stains asks the spirit of the deer if it has heard the prayer of the hunter for pardon. If the reply be "Yes" all is well and Little Deer goes on his way; but if the reply be in the negative he follows on the trail of the hunter, guided by the drops of blood on the ground, until he arrives at the cabin in the settlement, when the Little Deer enters invisibly and strikes the neglectful hunter with rheumatism, so that he is rendered on the instant a helpless cripple. No hunter who has regard for his health ever fails to ask pardon of the deer for killing it, although some who have not learned the proper formula may attempt to turn aside the Little Deer from his pursuit by building a fire behind them in the trail.

Next came the fishes and reptiles, who had their own grievances against humanity. They held a joint council and determined to make their victims dream of snakes twining about them in slimy folds and blowing their fetid breath in their faces, or to make them dream of eating raw or decaying fish, so that they would lose appetite, sicken, and die. Thus it is that snake and fish dreams are accounted for.

Finally the birds, insects, and smaller animals came together for a like purpose, and the Grubworm presided over the deliberations. It was decided that each in turn should express an opinion and then vote on the question as to whether or not man should be deemed guilty. Seven votes were to be sufficient to condemn him. One after another denounced man's cruelty and injustice toward the other animals and voted in favor of his death. The Frog spoke first and said: "We must do something to check the increase or the race of people will become so numerous that we shall be crowded from off the earth. See how man has kicked me about because I'm ugly, as he says, until my back is covered with sores"; and here he showed the spots on his skin. Next came the Bird, who condemned man because "he burns my feet off," alluding to the way in which the hunter barbecues birds by impaling them on a stick set over the fire, so that their feathers and tender feet are singed and burned. Others followed in the same train. The Ground Squirrel alone ventured to say a word in behalf of man, who seldom hurt him because he was so small; but this so enraged the others that they fell upon the Ground Squirrel and tore him with their teeth and claws, and the stripes remain on his back to this day.

The assembly began to devise and name various diseases, one after another, and had not their invention finally failed them not one of the human race would have been able to survive. The Grubworm in his place of honor hailed each new malady with delight, until at last they had reached the end of the list, when some one suggested that it be arranged so that ailments peculiar to woman should sometimes prove fatal. On this he rose up in his place and cried: "Watan! Thanks! I'm glad some of them will die, for they are getting so thick that they tread on me." He fairly shook with joy at the thought, so that he fell over backward and could not get on his feet again, but had to wriggle off on his back, as the Grubworm has done ever since.

When the plants, who were friendly to man, heard what had been done by the animals, they determined to defeat their evil designs. Each tree, shrub, and herb, down even to the grasses and mosses, agreed to furnish a remedy for some one of the diseases named, and each said: "I shall appear to help man when he calls upon me in his need." Thus did medicine originate, and the plants, every one of which has its use if we only knew it, furnish the antidote to counteract the evil wrought by the revengeful animals. When the doctor is in doubt what treatment to apply for the relief of a patient, the spirit of the plant suggests to him the proper remedy.

CHEROKEE THEOLOGY

The religion of the Cherokee, described by Mr. Mooney, like that of most North American tribes, was zootheism, or animal worship, with the survival of an earlier stage which included the worship of all tangible things, and the beginnings of a higher system in which the elements and great powers of nature were

deified. Among the animal gods insects and fishes occupy a sub-
ordinate place, while quadrupeds, birds, and reptiles are invoked
constantly. The mythic great horned serpent, the rattlesnake, and
the terrapin, the various species of hawk, and the rabbit, the squirrel, and the dog are the principal animal gods. The spider also
occupies a prominent place in the love and life-destroying formulas,
his duty being to entangle the soul of his victim in the meshes of
his web or to pluck it from the body of the doomed and drag it
away to the Darkening Land.

Among what may be classed as elemental gods the principal are
fire, water, and the sun, all of which are addressed under figurative
names. The sun is called "Apportioner," just as our word *moon*
originally meant "Measurer." The sun is invoked chiefly by the
ball player, whereas the hunter prays to the fire; but every important ceremony—whether connected with medicine, love, hunting, or the ball play—contains a prayer to the "Long Person," the
formulistic name for water, or, more strictly speaking, the river.
Wind, storm, cloud, and frost are also invoked.

Few inanimate gods are included, the principal being the
Stone, to which the shaman prays while endeavoring to find a lost
article by means of swinging a pebble suspended by a string; the
Flint, invoked when the shaman is about to scarify a patient with a
flint arrowhead before rubbing on medicine; and the Mountain,
which is addressed in one or two formulas.

There are a number of personal deities, the principal being the
Red Man. He is one of the greatest of the gods, hardly subor-
dinate to the elemental deities. Another god invoked in the hunting songs is "Slanting Eyes," a giant hunter who lives in one of
the great mountains of the Blue Ridge and owns all the game.
Others are the Little Men, probably the two Thunder Boys; the
Little People, fairies who live in the rock cliffs; and one diminutive sprite who holds the place of our Puck.

The personage invoked is always selected in accordance with
the theory of the formula and the duty to be performed. Thus,
when a sickness is caused by a fish, the Fish Hawk, the Heron, or
some other fish-eating bird is implored to come and seize the intruder and destroy it, so that the patient may find relief. When
the trouble is caused by a worm or an insect, some insectivorous

bird is called in for the same purpose. When a flock of redbirds is pecking at the vitals of the sick man, the Sparrow-Hawk is brought down to scatter them, and when the rabbit, the great mischief-maker, is the evil genius, he is driven out by the Rabbit-Hawk. Sometimes after the intruder has been expelled, "a small portion still remains," in the words of the formula, and accordingly the Whirlwind is called down from the treetops to carry away the remnant to the uplands and there scatter it so that it shall never reappear. The hunter prays to the fire, from which he draws his omens; to the reed, from which he makes his arrows; to "Slanting Eyes," the great lord of game, and finally addresses in songs the very animals which he intends to kill. The lover prays to the Spider to hold fast the affections of his beloved one in the meshes of his web, or to the Moon, which looks down upon him in the dance. The warrior prays to the Red War-club, and the man about to set out on a dangerous expedition prays to the Cloud to envelop him and conceal him from his enemies.

Each spirit of good or evil has its distinct and appropriate place of residence. The Rabbit is declared to live in the broom sage on the hillside, the Fish dwells in a bend of the river under the pendant hemlock branches, the Terrapin lives in the great pond in the West, and the Whirlwind abides in the lofty treetops. It should be stated that the animals of the formulas are not the ordinary, everyday animals, but their great progenitors, who live in the upper world above the arch of the firmament.[2]

The chief color symbolism is as follows:

East—red—success; triumph
North—blue—defeat; trouble
West—black—death
South—white—peace; happiness

INCANTATIONS

FOR A SNAKE BITE

Dunuwa, dunuwa, dunuwa, dunuwa, dunuwa, dunuwa.
Sge! Ha-Walasigwu tsunluntaniga.

[2] See L. E. Hinkle, "The Cherokee Language," *Bulletin of the Archaeological Society of North Carolina*, II (April, 1935), 1-9. Dr. Hinkle has observed that there are words of the formulas which have lost their meaning, but that these words are retained and pronounced with even more reverential awe than words understood. This religious adherence to form is not confined to the Indians.

Dayuha, dayuha, dayuha, dayuha, dayuha, dayuha.
Sge! Ha-Walasigwu tsunluntaniga.

Dunuwa appears to be an old verb, meaning "it has penetrated," probably referring to the fang of the reptile.

Translation of the second and fourth lines:

Listen! Ha! It is only a common frog which has passed by and put it (the intruder) into you.

Listen! Ha! It is only an Usugi which has passed by and put it into you.

(Prescription)—Now this at the beginning is a song. One should say it twice and also say the second line twice. Rub tobacco (juice) on the bite for some time, or if there be no tobacco, just rub on saliva once. In rubbing it on, one must go around four times. Go around toward the left and blow four times in a circle. This is because in lying down the snake always coils to the right and this is just the same as uncoiling it.

The rattlesnake is regarded as a supernatural being whose favor must be propitiated, and great pains are taken not to offend him. Whenever the ailment is of a serious character, the shaman always endeavors to throw contempt upon the intruder and convince it of his own superior power by asserting the sickness to be the work of some inferior being. Here the ailment caused by the rattlesnake, the most dreaded of the animal spirits, is ascribed to the frog, one of the least importance.

MOVING PAINS IN THE TEETH [NEURALGIA?]

Listen! In the sunland you repose, O Red Spider. Quickly you have brought and laid down the red path. O great adawehi, quickly you have brought down the red threads from above. The intruder in the tooth has spoken and it is only a worm. The tormentor has wrapped itself around the root of the tooth. Quickly you have dropped down the red threads, for it is just what you eat. Now it is for you to pick it up. The relief has been caused to come. Yu! Etc. etc.

The disease spirit is called "the intruder" and "the tormentor" and is declared to be a mere worm, which has wrapped itself around the base of the tooth. This is the regular toothache theory. The shaman prays first to the Red Spider, and then in turn to the

Blue Spider in the north, the Black Spider in the west, and the White Spider above, to let down the threads and take up the intruder, which is just what the spider eats.

HUNTING BIRDS

Listen! O Ancient White, where you dwell in peace I have come to rest. Now let your spirit arise. Let it (the game brought down) be buried in your stomach, and may your appetite never be satisfied. The red hickories have tied themselves together. The clotted blood is your recompense. . . .

O Ancient White, put me in the successful hunting trail. Hang the mangled things upon me. Let me come along the successful trail with them doubled up (under my belt). It (the road) is clothed with mangled things.

O Ancient White, O Kanati, support me continually, that I may never become blue. Listen!

This formula is recited by the bird hunter in the morning while standing over the fire at his hunting camp before starting out for the day's hunt. On the way to the hunting ground he shoots away at random a short blowgun arrow and carries along the remaining six of regulation size.

A favorite method with the bird hunter during the summer season is to climb a gum tree, which is much frequented by the smaller birds on account of its berries, where, taking up a convenient position amid the branches with his noiseless blowgun and arrows, he deliberately shoots down one bird after another until his shafts are exhausted; then climbs down, draws out the arrows from the bodies of the dead birds, and climbs up again to repeat the operation.

The prayer is addressed to the "Ancient White" (Fire), the spirit most frequently invoked by the hunter. The "clotted blood" refers to the blood-stained leaves upon which the fallen game has lain. The hunter gathers these up and casts them into the fire, in order to draw omens for the morrow from the manner in which they burn. "Let it be buried in your stomach" refers also to the offering made to the fire. By the "red hickories" are meant the strings of hickory bark which the bird hunter twists about his waist for a belt. The dead birds are carried by inserting their heads under this belt. "The mangled things" are the wounded birds.

For Catching Large Fish

Listen! Now you settlements have drawn near to hearken. Where you have gathered in the foam you are moving about as one. You Blue Cat and the others. I have come to offer you freely the white food. Let the paths from every direction recognize each other. Our spittle shall be in agreement. Let them (your and my spittle) be together as we go about. They (the fish) have become a prey and there shall be no loneliness. Your spittle has become agreeable. I am called Swimmer. Yu!

Spitting on the bait to attract big fish is evidently a very ancient custom. According to Swimmer's instructions, the fisherman must first chew a small piece of a plant which catches insects and spit it upon the bait and also upon the hook. He will be able to pull out the fish at once, or if the fish are not about at the moment, they will come in a very short time.

LOVE

Ku! Listen! In Alahiyi you repose, O Terrible Woman, O you have drawn near to hearken. There in Elahiyi you are at rest, O White Woman. No one is ever lonely with you. You are most beautiful. Instantly and at once you have rendered me a white man. No one is ever lonely when with me. Now you have made the path white for me. It shall never be dreary. Now you have put me into it. It shall never become blue. You have brought down to me from above the white road. . . . I am very handsome. You have put me into the white house. I shall be in it as it moves about and no one with me shall ever be lonely. Verily, I shall never become blue. . . .

And now there in Elahiyi you have rendered the woman blue. Now you have made the path blue for her. Let her be completely veiled in loneliness. Put her into the blue road. And now bring her down. Place her standing upon the earth where her feet are now and wherever she may go. Let loneliness leave its mark upon her. Let her be marked out for loneliness where she stands.

Ha! I belong to the (. . Wolf . .) clan, that one alone which was allotted for you. No one is ever lonely with me. I am handsome. Let her put her soul into the very center of my soul, never to turn away. Grant that in the midst of men she shall never think of them. I belong to the one clan alone which was allotted for you when the seven clans were established.

Where (other) men live it is lonely. They are very loathsome. The common polecat has made them so like himself that they are fit only for his company. They have become mere refuse. They are very loathsome. The common opossum has made them so like himself that they are fit only to be with him. They are very loathsome. Even the crow has made them so like himself that they are fit only for his company. They are very loathsome. The miserable rain-crow has made them so like himself that they are fit only to be with him.

The seven clans all alike made one feel very lonely in their company. They are not even good looking. They go about clothed with mere refuse. They even go about covered with ordure. But I—I was ordained to be a white man. I stand with my face toward the Sun Land. No one is ever lonely with me. I am very handsome. I shall certainly never become blue. I am covered by the everlasting white house wherever I go. No one is ever lonely with me. Your soul has come into the very center of my soul, never to turn away. I (.. name ..) take your soul. Sge!

In a somewhat similar strain there were formulas designed to fix affections. Here is a fragment from such a charm:

Listen! "Ha! Now the souls have met, never to part," you have said, O Ancient One above. O Black Spider, you have been brought down from on high. You have let down your web—Her soul you have wrapped up in your web. . . . May you hold her soul in your web so that it shall never get through the meshes.

I HAVE LOST SOMETHING

Listen! Ha! Now you have drawn near to hearken, O Brown Rock; you never lie about anything. Ha! Now I am about to seek for it. I have lost a hog and now tell me about where I shall find it. For is it not mine? My name is. . . .

This charm is addressed to a small water-worn pebble suspended by a string held between the finger and thumb of the shaman, who is guided in his search by the swinging of the pebble, which, according to the theory, will swing farther in the direction of the lost article than in the contrary direction.

REFERENCES

Hinkle, L. E. "The Cherokee Language," *Bulletin of the Archaeological Society of North Carolina,* II (April, 1935), 1-9.

Mooney, James. "Myths of the Cherokee," *Nineteenth Annual Report of the Bureau of American Ethnology,* Washington, 1900, Part 1, pp. 3-548.

——. "Sacred Formulas of the Cherokees," *Seventh Annual Report of the Bureau of American Ethnology,* Washington, 1891, pp. 301-397.

——.*The Swimmer Manuscript, Cherokee Sacred Formulas and Medicinal Prescriptions.* Revised, completed, and edited by Frans M. Olbrechts. Bulletin No. 99, Bureau of American Ethnology. Washington, 1932.

CHAPTER XVI

Myths of the Cherokee

THE MOONEY COLLECTION

MUCH OF OUR information about the Indian has come to us secondhand. We have gathered his artifacts and speculated on their use; we have read historical accounts of his contact with the colonists; we have legends, spurious stories, and moving pictures. What did the Indian really think? What was his belief? What was the mental attitude of the Indian? The revelation of the inner life, the psychological and philosophical content, has been provided for us by the Cherokee in a way that is denied us by most other tribes. For this we have to thank James Mooney. During his residence among the Carolina Cherokee, Mr. Mooney succeeded in collecting a large number of myths and legends of the tribe. The Eastern Band held closely to the traditions of their people. Secluded in the mountains, they were not exposed to the influences of the outside world, as were their brothers in the West. The collected material falls into the divisions of sacred myths, animal stories, local legends, and historical traditions. The sacred myths were entrusted to the priestly class. Other stories and legends were common property of the numerous storytellers. Three-fourths of the stories collected by Mr. Mooney came from an aged medicine man named Ayunini, or "Swimmer." Other sizable contributions were made by John Ax, Suyeta, Tagwadihi (Catawba Killer), and Chief Nimrod Jarrett Smith.

Instead of beginning with the familiar introduction, "Once upon a time," the Cherokee storyteller announces, "This is what the old men told me when I was a boy."

Several of the myths follow:[1]

[1] James Mooney, "Myths of the Cherokee," *Nineteenth Annual Report of the Bureau of American Ethnology* (Washington, 1900), Part 1, pp. 3-548. The selection of myths is reprinted with permission of the Bureau of American Ethnology.

How the World Was Made

The earth is a great island floating in a sea of water, and suspended at each of the four cardinal points by a cord hanging down from the sky vault, which is of solid rock. When the world grows old and worn out, the people will die and the cords will break and let the earth sink down into the ocean, and all will be water again. The Indians are afraid of this.

When all was water, the animals were above in Galunlati, beyond the arch; but it was very much crowded, and they were wanting more room. They wondered what was below the water, and at last Dayunisi, "Beaver's Grandchild," the little Water-beetle, offered to go and see if it could learn. It darted in every direction over the surface of the water, but could find no firm place to rest. Then it dived to the bottom and came up with some soft mud, which began to grow and spread on every side until it became the island which we call the earth. It was afterward fastened to the sky with four cords, but no one remembers who did this.

At first the earth was flat and very soft and wet. The animals were anxious to get down, and sent out different birds to see if it was yet dry, but they found no place to alight and came back again to Galunlati. At last it seemed to be time, and they sent out the Buzzard and told him to go and make ready for them. This was the Great Buzzard, the father of all the buzzards we see now. He flew all over the earth, low down near the ground, and it was still soft. When he reached the Cherokee country, he was very tired, and his wings began to flap and strike the ground, and wherever they struck the earth there was a valley, and where they turned up again there was a mountain. When the animals above saw this, they were afraid that the whole world would be mountains, so they called him back, but the Cherokee country remains full of mountains to this day.

When the earth was dry and the animals came down, it was still dark, so they got the sun and set it in a track to go every day across the island from east to west, just overhead. It was too hot this way, and Tsiskagili, the Red Crawfish, had his shell scorched a bright red, so that his meat was spoiled; and the Cherokee do not eat it. The conjurers put the sun another hand-breadth higher in the air, but it was still too hot. They raised it another time, and another, until it was seven hand-breadths high and just under the sky arch. Then it was right, and they left it so. This is why the conjurers call the highest place Gulkwagine Digalunlatiyun, "the seventh height," because it is seven hand-breadths above the earth. Every day the sun goes along under this arch, returning at night on the upper side to the starting place.

There is another world under this, and it is like ours in everything —animals, plants, and people—save that the seasons are different. The streams that come down from the mountains are the trails by which we reach this underworld, and the springs at their heads are the doorways by which we enter it, but to do this one must fast and go to water and have one of the underground people for a guide. We know that the seasons in the underworld are different from ours, because the water in the springs is always warmer in winter and cooler in summer than the outer air.

When the animals and plants were first made—we do not know by whom—they were told to watch and keep awake for seven nights, just as young men now fast and keep awake when they pray to their medicine. They tried to do this, and nearly all were awake through the first night, but the next night several dropped off to sleep, and the third night, others were asleep, and then others, until, on the seventh night, of all the animals only the owl, the panther, and one or two more were still awake. To these were given the power to see and to go about in the dark, and to make prey of the birds and animals which must sleep at night. Of the trees only the cedar, the pine, the spruce, the holly, and the laurel were awake to the end, and to them it was given to be always green and to be greatest for medicine, but to the others it was said: "Because you have not endured to the end you shall lose your hair every winter."

THE FIRST FIRE

In the beginning there was no fire, and the world was cold, until the Thunders (Ani-Hyuntikwalaski), who lived up in Galunlati, sent their lightning and put fire into the bottom of a hollow sycamore tree which grew on an island. The animals knew it was there, because they could see the smoke rising out at the top, but they could not get to it on account of the water, so they held a council to decide what to do. This was a long time ago.

Every animal that could fly or swim was anxious to go after the fire. The Raven offered, and because he was so large and strong they thought he could surely do the work, so he was sent first. He flew high and far across the water and alighted on the sycamore tree, but while he was wondering what to do next, the heat had scorched all his feathers black, and he was frightened and came back without the fire. The little Screech-owl (Wahuhu) volunteered to go, and reached the place safely, but while he was looking down into the hollow tree a blast of hot air came up and nearly burned out his eyes. He managed to fly home as best he could, but it was a long time before he could see well, and his eyes are red to this day. Then the Hooting Owl (Uguku) and the Horned Owl (Tskuli) went, but by the time they got to the hollow tree the fire was burning so fiercely that the smoke nearly blinded them, and the ashes carried up by the wind made white rings about their eyes. They had to come home again without the fire, but with all their rubbing they were never able to get rid of the white rings.

Now no more of the birds would venture, and so the little Uksuhi snake, the black racer, said he would go through the water and bring back some fire. He swam across to the island and crawled through the grass to the tree, and went in by a small hole at the bottom. The heat and smoke were too much for him, too, and after dodging about blindly over the hot ashes until he was almost on fire himself he managed by good luck to get out again at the same hole, but his body had been scorched black, and he has ever since had the habit of darting and doubling on his track as if trying to escape from close quarters. He came back, and the great blacksnake, Gulegi, "The Climber," offered to go for fire. He swam over to the island and climbed up the tree on the outside, as the blacksnake always does, but when he put his head down into the hole the smoke choked him so that he fell into the burning stump, and before he could climb out again he was as black as the Uksuhi.

Now they held another council, for still there was no fire, and the world was cold, but birds, snakes, and four-footed animals, all had some excuse for not going, because they were all afraid to venture near the burning sycamore, until at last Kananeski Amaiyehi (the Water Spider) said she would go. This is not the water spider that looks like a mosquito, but the other one, with black downy hair and red stripes on her body. She can run on top of the water or dive to the bottom, so there would be no trouble to get over to the island, but the question was, How could she bring back the fire? "I'll manage that," said the Water Spider; so she spun a thread from her body and wove it into a tusti bowl, which she fastened on her back. Then she crossed over to the island and through the grass to where the fire was still burning. She put one little coal of fire into her bowl, and came back with it, and ever since we have had fire, and the Water Spider still keeps her tusti bowl.

How They Brought Back the Tobacco

In the beginning of the world, when people and animals were all the same, there was only one tobacco plant, to which they all came for their tobacco until the Dagulku geese stole it and carried it far away to the south. The people were suffering without it, and there was one old woman who grew so thin and weak that everybody said she would soon die unless she could get tobacco to keep her alive.

Different animals offered to go for it, one after another, the larger ones first and then the smaller ones, but the Dagulku saw and killed every one before he could get to the plant. After the others the little Mole tried to reach it by going under the ground, but the Dagulku saw his track and killed him as he came out.

At last the Hummingbird offered, but the others said he was entirely too small and might as well stay at home. He begged them to let him try, so they showed him a plant in a field and told him to let them see how he would go about it. The next moment he was gone and they saw him sitting on the plant, and then in a moment he was back again, but no one had seen him going or coming, because he was so swift. "This is the way I'll do," said the Hummingbird, so they let him try.

He flew off to the east, and when he came in sight of the tobacco the Dagulku were watching all about it, but they could not see him because he was so small and flew so swiftly. He darted down on the plant—tsa!—and snatched off the top with the leaves and seeds, and was off again before the Dagulku knew what had happened. Before he got home with the tobacco the old woman had fainted and they thought she was dead, but he blew the smoke into her nostrils, and with a cry of "Tsalu!" (Tobacco!) she opened her eyes and was alive again.

The Milky Way

Some people in the south had a corn mill, in which they pounded the corn into meal, and several mornings when they came to fill it they noticed that some of the meal had been stolen during the night. They examined the ground and found tracks of a dog, so the next night they watched, and when the dog came from the north and began to eat the meal out of the bowl they sprang out and whipped him. He ran off howling to his home in the north, with the meal dropping from his mouth as he ran, and leaving behind a white trail where now we see the Milky Way, which the Cherokee call to this day Giliutsunstanunyi, "Where the dog ran."

Origin of Strawberries

When the first man was created and a mate was given to him, they lived together very happily for a time, but then began to quarrel, until at last the woman left her husband and started off toward Nundagunyi, the Sun land, in the east. The man followed alone and grieving, but the woman kept on steadily ahead and never looked behind, until Unelanunhi, (the great Apportioner, the Sun), took pity on him and asked him if he was still angry with his wife. He said he was not, and Unelanunhi then asked him if he would like to have her back again, to which he eagerly answered yes.

So Unelanunhi caused a patch of the finest ripe huckleberries to spring up along the path in front of the woman, but she passed by without paying any attention to them. Farther on he put a clump of blackberries, but these also she refused to notice. Other fruits, one, two, and three, and then some trees covered with beautiful red service berries, were placed beside the path to tempt her, but she still went on until suddenly she saw in front a patch of large ripe strawberries, the first ever known. She stopped to gather a few to eat, and as she picked them she chanced to turn her face to the west, and at once the memory of her husband came back to her and she found herself unable to go on. She sat down, but the longer she waited the stronger became her desire for her husband, and at last she gathered a bunch of the finest berries and started back along the path to give them to him. He met her kindly and they went home together.

THE DELUGE

A long time ago a man had a dog, which began to go down to the river every day and look at the water and howl. At last the man was angry and scolded the dog, which then spoke to him and said: "Very soon there is going to be a great freshet and the water will come so high that everybody will be drowned; but if you will make a raft to get upon when the rain comes you can be saved, but you must first throw me into the water." The man did not believe it, and dog said, "If you want a sign that I speak the truth, look at the back of my neck." He looked and saw that the dog's neck had the skin worn off so that the bones stuck out.

Then he believed the dog, and began to build a raft. Soon the rain came and he took his family, with plenty of provisions, and they all got upon it. It rained for a long time, and the water rose until the mountains were covered and all the people in the world were drowned. Then the rain stopped and the waters went down again, until at last it was safe to come off the raft. Now there was no one alive but the man and his family, but one day they heard a sound of dancing and shouting on the other side of the ridge. The man climbed to the top and looked over; everything was still, but all along the valley he saw great piles of bones of the people who had been drowned, and then he knew that the ghosts had been dancing.

The Rabbit Goes Duck Hunting

The Rabbit was so boastful that he would claim to do whatever he saw anyone else do, and so tricky that he could usually make the other animals believe it all. Once he pretended that he could swim in the water and eat fish just as the Otter did, and when the others told him to prove it he fixed up a plan so that the Otter himself was deceived.

Soon afterward they met again and the Otter said, "I eat ducks sometimes." Said the Rabbit, "Well, I eat ducks too." The Otter challenged him to try it; so they went up along the river until they saw several ducks in the water and managed to get near without being seen. The Rabbit told the Otter to go first. The Otter never hesitated, but dived from the bank and swam under water until he reached the ducks, when he pulled one down without being noticed by the others, and came back in the same way.

While the Otter had been under the water the Rabbit had peeled some bark from a sapling and made himself a noose. "Now," he said, "Just watch me;" and he dived in and swam a little way under the water until he was nearly choking and had to come up to the top to breathe. He went under again and came up again a little nearer to the ducks. He took another breath and dived under, and this time he came up among the ducks and threw the noose over the head of one and caught it. The duck struggled hard and finally spread its wings and flew up from the water with the Rabbit hanging on to the noose.

It flew on and on until at last the Rabbit could not hold on any longer, but had to let go and drop. As it happened, he fell into a tall hollow sycamore stump without any hole at the bottom to get out from, and there he stayed until he was so hungry that he had to eat his own fur, as the rabbit does ever since when he is starving. After several days, when he was very weak with hunger, he heard children playing outside around the trees. He began to sing:

> Cut a door and look at me;
> I'm the prettiest thing you ever did see.

The children ran home and told their father, who came and began to cut a hole in the tree. As he chopped away the Rabbit inside kept singing, "Cut it larger, so you can see me better; I'm so pretty." They made the hole larger, and then the Rabbit told them to stand back so that they could take a good look at him as he came out. They stood away back, and the Rabbit watched his chance and jumped out and got away.

How the Terrapin Beat the Rabbit

The Rabbit was a great runner, and everybody knew it. No one thought the Terrapin anything but a slow traveler, but he was a great warrior and very boastful, and the two were always disputing about their speed. At last they agreed to decide the matter by a race. They fixed the day and the starting place and arranged to run across four mountain ridges, and the one who came in first at the end was to be the winner.

The Rabbit felt so sure of it that he said to the Terrapin, "You know you can't run. You can never win the race, so I'll give you the first ridge and then you'll have only three to cross while I go over four."

The Terrapin said that would be all right, but that night when he went home to his family he sent for his Terrapin friends and told them he wanted their help. He said he knew he could not outrun the Rabbit, but he wanted to stop the Rabbit's boasting. He explained his plan to his friends and they agreed to help him.

When the day came all the animals were there to see the race. The Rabbit was with them, but the Terrapin was gone ahead toward the first ridge, as they had arranged, and they could hardly see him on account of the long grass. The word was given and the Rabbit started off with long jumps up the mountain, expecting to win the race before the Terrapin could get down the other side. But before he got up the mountain he saw the Terrapin go over the ridge ahead of him. He ran on, and when he reached the top he looked all around, but could not see the Terrapin on account of the long grass. He kept on down the mountain and began to climb the second ridge, but when he looked up again there was the Terrapin just going over the top. Now he was surprised and made his longest jumps to catch up, but when he got to the top there was the Terrapin away in front going over the third ridge. The Rabbit was getting tired now and nearly out of breath, but he kept on down the mountain and up the other ridge until he got to the top just in time to see the Terrapin cross the fourth ridge and thus win the race.

The Rabbit could not make another jump, but fell over on the ground crying mi, mi, mi, mi, as the Rabbit does ever since when he is too tired to run any more. The race was given to the Terrapin and all the animals wondered how he could win against the Rabbit, but he kept still and never told. It was easy enough, however, because all the Terrapin's friends looked just alike, and he had simply posted one near the top of each ridge to wait until the Rabbit came in sight and then climb over and hide in the long grass. When the Rabbit came on he could not find the Terrapin and so thought the Terrapin was ahead, and if he had met one of the other terrapins he would have thought it the same one because they looked so much alike. The real Terrapin had posted himself on the fourth ridge, so as to come in at the end of the race and be ready to answer questions if the animals suspected anything.

Because the Rabbit had to lie down and lose the race the conjurer now, when preparing his young men for the ball play, boils a lot of rabbit hamstrings into a soup, and sends someone at night to pour it across the path along which the other players are to come in the morning, so that they may become tired in the same way and lose the game. It is not always easy to do this, because the other party is expecting it and has watchers ahead to prevent it.

The Rabbit and the Possum after a Wife

The Rabbit and the Possum each wanted a wife, but no one would marry either of them. They talked over the matter and the Rabbit said, "We can't get wives here; let's go to the next settlement. I'm the messenger for the council, and I'll tell the people that I bring an order that everybody must take a mate at once, and then we'll be sure to get our wives."

The Possum thought this a fine plan, so they started off together to the next town. As the Rabbit traveled faster, he got there first and waited outside until the people noticed him and took him into the townhouse. When the chief came to ask his business, the Rabbit said he brought an important order from the council that everybody must get married without delay. So the chief called the people together and told them the message from the council. Every animal took a mate at once, and the Rabbit got a wife.

The Possum traveled so slowly that he got there after all the animals had mated, leaving him still without a wife. The Rabbit pretended to feel sorry for him and said, "Never mind, I'll carry the message to the people in the next settlement and you hurry on as fast as you can, and this time you will get your wife."

So he went on to the next town, and the Possum followed close after him. But when the Rabbit got to the townhouse he sent out the word that, as there had been peace so long that everybody was getting lazy, the council had ordered that there must be a war at once and that they must begin right in the townhouse. So they all began fighting, but the Rabbit made four great leaps and got away just as the Possum came in. Everybody jumped on the Possum, who had not thought of bringing his weapons on a wedding trip, and so could not defend himself. They had nearly beaten the life out of him when he fell over and pretended to be dead until he saw a good chance to jump up and get away. The Possum never got a wife, but he remembers the lesson, and ever since he shuts his eyes and pretends to be dead when the hunter has him in a close corner.

Why the Possum's Tail Is Bare

The Possum used to have a long bushy tail, and was so proud of it that he combed it out every morning and sang about it at the dance, until the Rabbit, who had had no tail since the Bear pulled it out, became very jealous and made up his mind to play the Possum a trick.

There was to be a great council and a dance at which all the animals were to be present. It was the Rabbit's business to send out the news, so as he was passing the Possum's place he stopped to ask him if he intended to be there. The Possum said he would come if he could have a special seat, "because I have such a handsome tail that I ought to sit where everybody can see me." The Rabbit promised to attend to it and to send some one besides to comb and dress the Possum's tail for the dance; so the Possum was very, very pleased and agreed to come.

Then the Rabbit went over to the Cricket, who is such an expert hair-cutter that the Indians call him the barber, and told him to go next morning and dress the Possum's tail for the dance that night. He told the Cricket just what to do and then went on about some other mischief.

In the morning the Cricket went to the Possum's house and said he had come to get him ready for the dance. So the Possum stretched himself out and shut his eyes while the Cricket combed out his tail and wrapped a red string around it to keep it smooth and straight until night. But all this time, as he would wind the string around, he was clipping off the hair close to the roots, and the Possum never knew it.

When it was night the Possum went to the townhouse where the dance was to be and found the best seat ready for him, just as the Rabbit had promised. When his turn came in the dance he loosened the string from his tail and stepped into the middle of the floor. The drummers began to drum and the Possum began to sing, "See my beautiful tail." Everybody shouted and he danced around the circle and sang again, "See what a fine color it has." They shouted again and he danced around another time singing, "See how it sweeps the ground." The animals shouted more loudly than ever, and the Possum was delighted. He danced around the circle of animals and they were all laughing at him. Then he looked down at his beautiful tail and saw that there was not a hair left upon it, but that it was as bare as the tail of a lizard. He was so much astonished and ashamed that he could not say a word, but rolled over helpless on the ground and grinned, as the Possum does to this day when taken by surprise.

REFERENCES

Mooney, James. "Myths of the Cherokee," *Nineteenth Annual Report of the Bureau of American Ethnology*, Washington, 1900, Part 1, pp. 3-548.

———. *The Swimmer Manuscript, Cherokee Sacred Formulas and Medicinal Prescriptions*. Revised, completed, and edited by Frans M. Olbrechts. Bulletin No. 99, Bureau of American Ethnology. Washington, 1932.

CHAPTER XVII

Cherokee Games

CHUNGKE

NUMEROUS ACCOUNTS of Cherokee games and dances have been recorded. A description of the popular game Chungke, the translation of the name being "running hard labor," has been furnished by Adair:

They have near their state house, a square piece of ground well cleaned, and fine sand is carefully strewed over it, when requisite, to promote a swifter motion to what they throw along the surface.

Only one, or two on a side, play at this ancient game. They have a stone about two fingers broad at the edge, and two spans around; each party has a pole of about eight feet long, smooth, and tapering at each end, the points flat. They set off a-breast of each other at six yards from the end of the play ground: then one of them hurls the stone on its edge, in as direct a line as he can, a considerable distance toward the middle of the other end of the square; when they have run a few yards, each darts his pole anointed with bear's oil, with a proper force, as near as he can guess in proportion to the motion of the stone, that the end may lie close to the stone—when this is the case, the person counts two of the game, and, in proportion to the nearness of the poles to the mark, one is counted, unless by measuring, both are found to be at an equal distance from the stone. In this manner, the players will keep running most part of the day, at half speed, under the violent heat of the sun, staking their silver ornaments, their nose, finger, and ear rings; their breast, arm and wrist plates, and even all their wearing apparel, except that which barely covers their middle. All the American Indians are much addicted to this game, which to us appears to be a task of stupid drudgery; it seems however to be of early origin, when their forefathers used diversions as simple as their manners. The hurling stones they use at present, were time immemorial rubbed smooth on the rocks and with prodigious labour; they are kept with the strictest religious care, from one generation to another, and are exempted from being buried with the dead. They belong to the town where they are used, and are carefully preserved.

BALL PLAY

The ball game of the Cherokee, as played by the Eastern Band in North Carolina, has been described by James Mooney. The game is still played on the Indian reservation and elsewhere, though it has lost much of its ceremonial significance thus recorded by Mr. Mooney:[1]

The ball now used is an ordinary leather-covered ball, but in former days it was made of deer hair covered with deerskin. The ball sticks vary considerably among different tribes. The Cherokee player uses a pair, catching the ball between them and throwing it the same way. The stick is somewhat less than 3 feet in length, and its general appearance closely resembles a tennis racket, or a long wooden spoon, the bowl of which is a loose network of thongs of twisted squirrel skin or strings of Indian hemp. The frame is made of a slender hickory stick, bent upon itself, and so trimmed and fashioned that the handle seems to be of one solid round piece, when, in fact, it is double.

In addition to the athletic training, which begins two or three weeks before the regular game, each player is put under a strict gaktunta or tabu, during the same period. He must not eat the flesh of a rabbit (of which the Indians are generally very fond) because the rabbit is a timid animal, easily alarmed and liable to lose its wits when pursued by the hunter. Hence the player must abstain from it, lest he, too, should become disconcerted and lose courage in the game. He must also avoid meat of the frog (another item on the Indian's bill of fare), because the frog's bones are brittle and easily broken, and a player who should partake of the animal would expect to be crippled in the first inning. For a similar reason he abstains from eating the young of any bird or animal, and from touching an infant. . . . The tabu lasts for seven days preceding the game, but in most cases is enforced for twenty-eight days—i.e. 4 x 7—4 and 7 being sacred numbers. Above all, he must not touch a woman. If a woman even as much as touches a ball stick on the eve of a game, it is thereby rendered unfit for use.

When a player fears a particular contestant on the other side, as is frequently the case, his own shaman (medicine man) performs a spe-

---

[1] James Mooney, "The Cherokee Ball Play," *American Anthropologist*, o.s. III (1890), 105 ff.; see also *Twenty-fourth Report of the Bureau of American Ethnology*. The account of Cherokee ball play is reprinted with permission of the *American Anthropologist* and of the Bureau of American Ethnology.

cial incantation, intended to compass the defeat and even the disabling or death of his rival.

On the night preceding the game each party holds the ball-play dance in its own settlement. On the reservation the dance is always held on Friday night, so that the game may take place on Saturday afternoon, in order to give the players and spectators an opportunity to sleep off the effects on Sunday.

The dance must be held close to the river, to enable the players to "go to the water" during the night, but the exact spot selected is always a matter of uncertainty up to the last moment, excepting with a chosen few. If this were not the case, a spy from the other settlement might endeavor to insure the defeat of the party by strewing along their trail a soup made of the hamstrings of rabbits, which would have the effect of rendering the players timorous and easily confused.

The dance begins soon after dark on the night preceding the game, and lasts until daybreak, and from the time they eat supper before the dance until after the game, on the following afternoon, no food passes the lips of the players.

[Mr. Mooney selected for illustration the last game which he witnessed on the reservation, in September, 1889. On this occasion the young men of Yellow Hill contended against the team from Raven Town, about ten miles farther up the river, and as the latter place was a large settlement noted for its adherence to the old traditions, a spirited game was expected.]

Each party holds a dance in its own settlement, the game taking place about midway between. The Yellow Hill men were to have their dance up river about half a mile from my house. The spot selected for the dance was a narrow strip of gravelly bottom, where the mountain came close down to the water's edge. Several fires were burning. Around the larger fires were the dancers, the men stripped as for the game, with their ball sticks in their hands and the firelight playing upon their naked bodies.

The ball-play dance is participated in by both sexes, but differs considerably from any other of the dances of the tribe, being a dual affair throughout. The dancers are the players of the morrow, with seven women, representing the seven Cherokee clans. The men dance in a circle around the fire, chanting responses to the sound of a rattle carried by another performer, who circles around on the outside, while the women stand in line a few feet away and dance to and fro, now advancing a few steps toward the men, then wheeling and dancing away from them, but all the while keeping time to the sound of the drum and chanting the refrain to the ball songs made by the drummer, who is seated on the ground on the side farthest from the fire. The rattle is a gourd fitted with a handle and filled with small pebbles, while the drum resembles a small keg with a head of ground-hog leather. The drum is partly filled with water, the head being also moistened to improve the tone, and is beaten with a single stick. Men and women dance separately throughout, the music, the evolutions, and the songs being entirely distinct, but all combine to produce a harmonious whole. The women are relieved at intervals by others who take their places, but the men dance in the same narrow circle the whole night long.

At one side of the fire are set up two forked poles, supporting a third laid horizontally, upon which the ball sticks are crossed in pairs until the dance begins. Small pieces from the wing of the bat are sometimes tied to these poles, and also to the rattle used in the dance, to insure success in the contest. The skins of several bats and swift-darting insectivorous birds were formerly wrapped up in a piece of deerskin, together with the cloth and beads used in the conjuring ceremonies later on, and hung from the frame during the dance. On finally dressing for the game at the ball ground, the players took the feathers from these skins to fasten in their hair or upon the ball stick, to insure swiftness and accuracy in their movements.

Sometimes also hairs from the whiskers of the bat are twisted into the netting of the ball sticks. The players are all stripped and painted, with feathers in their hair, just as they appear in the game. When all is ready an attendant takes down the ball sticks from the frame, throwing them over his arm in the same fashion, and, walking around the circle, gives to each man his own. Then the rattler, taking his instrument in his hand, begins to trot around on the outside of the circle, uttering a sharp "Hi!" to which the players respond with a quick "Hi-hi!" while slowly moving around the circle with their ball sticks held tightly in front of their breasts. Then with a quicker movement, the song changes to "Ehu!" and the responses to "Hahi! Ehu! Ehu! Hahi!" Then, with a prolonged shake of the rattle, it changes again to "Ahiye!" the dancers responding with the same word "Ahiye!" but in a higher key; the movements become more lively and the chorus louder, till at a given signal with the rattle the players clap their ball sticks together, and, facing around, go through the motions of picking up and tossing an imaginary ball. Finally, with a grand rush, they dance up close to the women, and the first part of the performance ends with a loud, prolonged "Hu-u!" from the whole crowd.

In the meantime the women have taken positions in a line a few feet away, with their backs turned to the men, while in front of them the drummer is seated on the ground, but with his back turned toward them and the rest of the dancers. After a few preliminary taps on the drum, he begins a slow, measured beat, and strikes up one of the dance refrains, which the women take up in chorus. This is repeated a number of times until all are in harmony with the tune, when he begins to improvise, choosing words which will harmonize with the measure of the chorus, and at the same time be appropriate to the subject of the dance. As this requires a ready wit in addition to ability as a singer, the selection of a drummer is a matter of considerable importance, and that functionary is held in corresponding estimation. He sings of the game on the morrow, of the fine things to be won by the men of his party, of the joy with which they will be received by their friends on their return from the field, and of the disappointment and defeat of their rivals. Throughout it all the women keep up the same minor refrain, like an instrumental accompaniment to vocal music. As Cherokee songs are always in a minor key, they have a plaintive effect, even when the sentiment is cheerful or even boisterous, and are calculated to excite the mirth of one who understands their language. The impression is heightened by the appearance of the dancers themselves, for the women shuffle solemnly back and forth all night long without ever a smile upon their faces, while the occasional laughter of the men seems half subdued. The monotonous repetition, too, is intolerable to any one but an Indian, the same words, to the same tune, being sometimes sung over and over again for a half hour or more. Although the singer improvises as he proceeds, many of the expressions have now become stereotyped and are used at almost every ball dance.

According to a Cherokee myth, the animals once challenged the birds to a great ball play. The wager was accepted, the preliminaries were arranged, and at last the contestants assembled at the appointed spot—the animals on the ground, while the birds took position in the tree-tops to await the throwing up of the ball. On the side of the animals were the bear, whose ponderous weight bore down all opposition; the deer, who excelled all others in running; and the terrapin, who was invulnerable to the stoutest blows. On the side of the birds were the eagle, the hawk, and the great Tlaniwa—all noted for their swiftness and power of flight. While the latter were preening their feathers and watching every motion of their adversaries below, they noticed two small creatures, hardly larger than mice, climbing up the tree on which was perched the leader of the birds. Finally they reached the top and humbly asked to be allowed to join in the game. The captain looked at them a moment, and, seeing that they were four-footed, asked them why they did not go to the animals where they properly belonged. The little things explained that they had done so, but had been laughed at and rejected on account of their diminutive size. On hearing their story the bird captain was disposed to take pity on them, but there was one serious difficulty in the way—how could they join the birds when they had no wings? The eagle, the hawk, and the rest now crowded around, and, after some discussion it was decided to try and make wings for the little fellows. But how to do it! All at once, by a happy inspiration, one bethought himself of the drum which was used in the dance. The head was made of ground-hog leather, and perhaps a corner could be cut off and utilized for wings. No sooner suggested than done. Two pieces of leather taken from the drumhead were cut into shape and attached to the legs of one of the small animals, and thus originated Tlameha, the bat. The ball was now tossed up, and the bat was told to catch it, and his expertness in dodging and circling about, keeping the ball constantly in motion and never allowing it to touch the ground, soon convinced the birds that they had gained a most valuable ally. They next turned their attention to the other little creature; and now behold a worse difficulty! All their leather had been used in making wings for the bat, and there was no time to send for more. In this dilemma it was suggested that perhaps wings might be made by stretching out the skin of the animal itself. So two large birds seized him from opposite sides with their strong bills, and by tugging and pulling at his fur for several minutes succeeded in stretching the skin between the fore and hind feet until at last the thing was done and there was Tewa, the flying squirrel. Then the bird captain, to try him, threw up the ball, when the flying squirrel, with a graceful bound, sprang off the limb, catching it in his teeth, carried it through the air to another tree-top a hundred feet away.

When all was ready, the game began, but at the very outset the flying squirrel caught the ball and carried it up a tree, and then threw it to the birds, who kept it in the air for sometime, when it dropped; but just before it reached the ground the bat seized it, and by his dodging and doubling kept it out of the way of even the swiftest of the animals until he finally threw it in at the goal, and thus won the victory for the birds. Because of their assistance on this occasion, the ball player invokes the aid of the bat and the flying squirrel and ties a small piece of the bat's wing to his ball stick or fastens it to the frame on which the sticks are hung during the dance.

At a certain stage of the dance a man, especially selected for the purpose, leaves the group of spectators around the fire and retires a short distance into the darkness in the direction of the rival settlement. Then, standing with his face turned in the same direction, he raises his hand to his mouth and utters four yells, the last prolonged into a peculiar quaver. He is answered by the players with a chorus of yells —or rather yelps, for the Indian yell resembles nothing else so much as the bark of a puppy. Then he comes running back until he passes the circle of dancers, when he halts and shouts out a single word, which may be translated, "They are already beaten!" Another chorus of yells greets this announcement. The man is called talala, or woodpecker, on account of his peculiar yell, which is considered to resemble the sound made by a woodpecker tapping on a dead tree trunk. According to the orthodox Cherokee belief, this yell is heard by the rival players in the other settlement—who, it will be remembered, are having a ball dance of their own at the same time—and so terrifies them that they lose all heart for the game. The fact that both sides alike have a talala in no way interferes with the theory.

At frequent intervals during the night all the players, accompanied by the shaman and his assistant, leave the dance and go down to a retired spot at the river's bank, where they perform the mystic rite known as "going to water," hereafter to be described. While the players are performing this ceremony, the women, with the drummer, continue the dance and chorus. The dance is kept up without intermission, and almost without change, until daybreak. At the final dance green pine tops are thrown upon the fire, so as to produce a thick smoke, which envelops the dancers. Some mystic properties are ascribed to this pine smoke, but what they are I have not yet learned, although the ceremony seems to be intended as an exorcism, the same thing being done at other dances when there has recently been a death in the settlement.

At sunrise, the players, dressed now in their ordinary clothes, but carrying their ball sticks in their hands, start for the ball ground, accompanied by the shamans and their assistants. The place selected for the game, being always about midway between the two rival settlements, was in this case several miles above the dance ground and on the opposite side of the river. On the march each party makes four several halts, when each player again "goes to water" separately with the shaman. This occupies considerable time, so that it is usually afternoon before the two parties meet on the ball ground. While the shaman is busy with his mysteries in the laurel bushes down by the water's edge, the other players, sitting by the side of the trail, spend the time twisting extra strings for their ball sticks, adjusting their feather ornaments, and discussing the coming game. In former times the player during these halts was not allowed to sit upon a log, a stone, or anything but the ground itself; neither was it permissible to lean against anything except the back of another player, on penalty of defeat in the game, with the additional risk of being bitten by a rattlesnake.

On coming up from the water after the fourth halt, the principal shaman assembles the players around him and delivers an animated harangue, exhorting them to do their utmost in the coming contest, telling them that they will undoubtedly be victorious, as the omens are all favorable, picturing to their delighted vision the stakes to be won and the ovation awaiting them from their friends after the game, and finally assuring them in the mystic terms of the formulas that their adversaries will be driven through the four gaps into the gloomy shadows of the Darkening Land, where they will perish forever from remembrance. The address, delivered in rapid, jerky tones like the speech of an auctioneer, has a very inspiriting effect upon the hearers and is frequently interrupted by a burst of exultant yells from the players. At the end, with another chorus of yells, they again take up the march.

On arriving in sight of the ball ground, the talala again comes to the front and announces their approach with four loud yells, ending with a long quaver, as on the previous night at the dance. The players respond with another yell, and then turn off to a convenient sheltered place by the river, to make final preparations.

The shaman then marks off a small space upon the ground to represent the ball field, and, taking in his hand a small bundle of sharpened stakes about a foot in length, addresses each man in turn, telling him the position which he is to occupy in the field at the tossing up of the ball, after the first inning, and driving down a stake to represent each player until he has a diagram of the whole field spread out upon the ground.

The players then strip for the final scratching. This painful operation is performed by an assistant, in this case an old man named Standing Water. The instrument of torture is called a kanuga and resembles a short comb with seven teeth, seven being also a sacred number with the Cherokees. The teeth are made of sharpened splinters from the leg bone of a turkey and are fixed in a frame made from the shaft of a turkey quill, in such a manner that by a slight pressure of the thumb they can be pushed out to a length of a small tack. Why the bone and feather of the turkey should be selected I have not yet learned, but there is undoubtedly an Indian reason for the choice.

The players having stripped, the operator begins by seizing the arm of a player with one hand while holding the kanuga in the other, and plunges the teeth into the flesh at the shoulder, bringing the instrument down with a steady pressure to the elbow, leaving seven white lines which become red a moment later as the blood starts to the surface. He now plunges the kanuga in again at another place near the shoulder, and again brings it down to the elbow. Again and again the operation is repeated until the victim's arm is scratched in twenty-eight lines above the elbow. It will be noticed that twenty-eight is a combination of four and seven, the two sacred numbers of the Cherokee. The operator then makes the same number of scratches in the same manner on the arm below the elbow. Next the other arm is treated in the same way; then each leg, both above and below the knee, and finally an X is scratched across the breast of the sufferer, the upper ends are joined by another stroke from shoulder to shoulder, and a similar pattern is scratched upon his back. By this time the blood is trickling in little streams from nearly three hundred gashes. None of the scratches are deep, but they are unquestionably very painful, as all agree who have undergone the operation. Nevertheless the young men endure the ordeal willingly and almost cheerfully, regarding it as a necessary part of the ritual to secure success in the game. To cause blood to flow more freely, the young men sometimes scrape it off with chips as it oozes out. The shaman then gives to each player a small piece of root, to which he has imparted magic properties by the recital of certain secret formulas. The men chew these roots and spit out the juice over their limbs and bodies, rubbing it well into the scratches; then going down to the water, plunge in and wash off the blood, after which they come out and dress themselves for the game.

The modern Cherokee ball costume consists simply of a pair of short trunks, ornamented with various patterns in red and blue cloth, and a feather charm worn upon the head. Formerly the breechcloth alone was worn, as is still the case in some instances, and the strings with which it was tied were purposely made weak, so that if seized by an opponent in the scuffle the strings would break, leaving the owner to escape with the loss of his sole article of raiment. The ornament worn in the hair is made up of an eagle's feathers, to give keenness of sight; a deer tail, to give swiftness; and a snake's rattle, to render the wearer terrible to his adversaries. The player also marks his body in various patterns with paint or charcoal. The charcoal is taken from the dance fire, and whenever possible is procured by burning the wood of a tree which has been struck by lightning, such wood being regarded as peculiarly sacred and endowed with mysterious properties. According to one formula, the player makes a cross over his heart and a spot upon each shoulder, using pulverized charcoal procured from the shaman and made by burning together the wood of a honey-locust tree and of a tree which has been struck by lightning, but not killed. The charcoal is pulverized and put, together with a red and black bead, into an empty cocoon from which one end has been cut off. This paint preparation makes the player swift like the lightning and invulnerable as the tree that defies the thunderbolt, and renders his flesh as hard and firm to the touch as the wood of the honey-locust. Just before dressing, the players rub their bodies with grease or the chewed bark of the slippery elm or the sassafras, until their skin is slippery as that of the proverbial eel.

Sometimes a player applies to the shaman to conjure a dangerous opponent, so that he may be unable to see the ball in its flight, or may dislocate a wrist or break a leg. The shaman draws upon the ground an armless figure of his rival with a hole where his heart should be. Into this hole he drops two black beads, covers them with earth and stamps upon them, and thus the dreaded rival is doomed, unless (and this is always the saving clause) his own shaman had taken precautions against such a result, or the one in whose behalf the charm is made has rendered the incantation unavailing by a violation of some one of the interminable rules of the gaktunta.

The players having dressed, are now ready to go to water for the last time, for which purpose the shaman selects a bend of the river where he can look toward the east while facing upstream. This ceremony of going to water is the most sacred and impressive of the whole Cherokee ritual, and must always be performed fasting, and in most cases also is preceded by an all-night vigil. It is used in connection with prayers to obtain a long life, to destroy an enemy, to win the love of a woman, to secure success in the hunt and the ball play, and for recovery from a dangerous illness, but is performed only as a final resort or when the occasion is one of special importance.

The men stand looking down upon the water, with their ball sticks clasped upon their breasts, while the shaman stands just behind them, and an assistant kneeling at his side spreads out upon the ground the cloth upon which are placed the sacred beads. These beads are of two colors, red and black, each kind resting upon a cloth of the same color, and corresponding in number to the number of players. The red beads represent the players for whom the shaman performs the ceremony, while the black beads stand for their opponents, red being symbolic of power and triumph, while black is emblematic of death and misfortune. All being ready, the assistant hands to the shaman a red bead, which he takes between the thumb and finger of his right hand; and then a black bead, which he takes in the same manner in his left hand. Then, holding his hands outstretched, with his eyes intently fixed upon the beads, the shaman prays on behalf of his client to Yuwi Gunahita, the Long Man, the sacred name of the river. "O, Long Man, I come to the edge of your body. You are mighty and most powerful. You bear up great logs and toss them about where the foam is white. Nothing can resist you. Grant me such strength in the contest that my enemy may be of no weight in my hands—that I may be able to toss him in the air or dash him to the earth." In a similar strain he prays to the Red Bat in the Sun Land to make him expert in dodging; to the Red Deer to make him fleet of foot; to the great Red Hawk to render him keen of sight; and to the Red Rattlesnake to render him terrible to all who oppose him.

Then, in the same low tone and broken accents in which all the formulas are recited, the shaman declares that his client (mentioning his name and clan) has now ascended to the first heaven. As he continues praying he declares that he has now reached the second heaven (and here he slightly raises his hands); soon he ascends to the third heaven, and the hands of the shaman are raised still higher; then, in the same way, he ascends to the fourth, the fifth, and the sixth heaven, and finally, as he raises his trembling hands aloft, he declares that the spirit of the man has now risen to the seventh heaven, where his feet are resting upon the Red Seats, from which they shall never be displaced.

Turning now to his client, the shaman, in a low voice, asks him the name of his most dreaded rival on the opposite side. The reply is given in a whisper, and the shaman, holding his hands outstretched as before, calls down the most withering curses upon the head of the doomed victim, mentioning him likewise by name and clan. He prays to the Black Fog to cover him so that he may be unable to see his way; to the Black Rattlesnake to envelop him in his slimy folds; and at last to the Black Spider to let down his black thread from above, wrap it about the soul of the victim and drag it from his body along the black trail to the Darkening Land in the west, there to bury it in the black coffin under the black clay, never to reappear. At the final imprecation he stoops and, making a hole in the soft earth with his finger (symbolic of stabbing the doomed man to the heart), drops the black bead into it and covers it from sight with a vicious stamp of his foot; then with a simultaneous movement each man dips his ball sticks into the water, and bringing them up, touches them to his lips; then, stooping again, he dips up the water in his hand and laves his head and breast.

This ceremony ended, the players form in line, headed by the shaman, and march in single file to the ball ground, where they find awaiting them a crowd of spectators—men, women and children—sometimes to the number of several hundred, for the Indians always turn out to the ball play, no matter how great the distance, from old Big Witch, stooping under the weight of nearly a hundred years, down to babies slung along at their mothers' backs. The ball ground is a level field by the river side, surrounded by the high timber-covered mountains. At either end are the goals, each consisting of a pair of upright poles, between which the ball must be driven to make a run, the side which makes 12 home runs being declared the winner of the game and the stakes. The ball is furnished by the challengers, who sometimes try to select one so small that it will fall through the netting of the ball sticks of their adversaries; but as the others are on the lookout for this, the trick usually fails of its purpose. After the ball is once set in motion it must be picked up only with the ball sticks, although after having picked up the ball with the sticks the player frequently takes it in his hand, and, throwing away the sticks, runs with it until intercepted by one of the other party, when he throws it, if he can, to one of his friends farther on. Should a player pick up the ball with his hands, as sometimes happens in the scramble, there at once arises all over the field a chorus of "Uwayi Guti! Uwayi Guti!" "With the hand! with the hand"—equivalent to our own "Foul! foul!"—and that inning is declared a draw.

While our men are awaiting the arrival of the other party, their friends crowd around them, and the women throw across their outstretched ball sticks the pieces of calico, the small squares of sheeting used as shawls, and the bright red handkerchiefs so dear to the heart of the Cherokee, which they intend to stake upon the game. Knives, trinkets, and sometimes small coins, are also wagered. But these Cherokee to-day are poor indeed. Hardly a man among them owns a horse, and never again will a chief bet a thousand dollars upon his favorites, as was done in Georgia in 1834. To-day, however, as then, they will risk all they have.

Now a series of yells announces the near approach of the men from Raven Town, and in a few minutes they come filing out from the bushes—stripped, scratched, and decorated like the others, carrying their ball sticks in their hands, and headed by a shaman. The two parties come together in the center of the ground, and for a short time the scene resembles an auction, as men and women move about, holding up the articles they propose to wager on the game and bidding for stakes to be matched against them. The betting being ended, the opposing players are drawn up in two lines facing each other, each man with his ball sticks laid together upon the ground in front of him, with the heads pointed toward the man facing him. This is for the purpose of matching the players so as to get the same number on each side; and should it be found that a player has no antagonist to face him he must drop out of the game. Such a result frequently happens, as both parties strive to keep their arrangements secret up to the last moment. There is no fixed number, the common quota being from nine to twelve on a side.

During the whole time that the game is in progress the shaman, concealed in the bushes by the water side, is busy with his prayers and incantations for the success of his clients and the defeat of their rivals. Through his assistant, who acts as messenger, he is kept advised of the movements of the players by seven men, known as counselors, appointed to watch the game for that purpose. Every little incident is regarded as an omen, and the shaman governs himself accordingly.

An old man now advances with the ball, and standing at one end of the lines, delivers a final address to the players, telling them that Unelanuhi, the Apportioner—the sun—is looking down upon them, urging them to acquit themselves in the games as their fathers have done before them; but above all to keep their tempers, so that none may have it to say that they got angry or quarreled, and that after it is over each one may return in peace along the white trail to rest in his white house. White in these formulas is symbolic of peace and happiness and all good things. He concludes with a loud "Ha! Taldu-gwu!" "Now for the twelve!" and throws the ball into the air. Instantly twenty pairs of ball sticks clatter together in the air, as their owners spring to catch the ball in its descent. In the scramble it usually happens that the ball falls to the ground, when it is picked up by one more active than the rest. Frequently, however, a man will succeed in catching it between his ball sticks as it falls, and, disengaging himself from the rest, starts to run with it to the goal; but before he has gone a dozen yards they are upon him, and the whole crowd goes down together, rolling and tumbling over each other in the dust, straining and tugging for possession of the ball, until one of the players manages to extricate himself from the struggling heap and starts off with the ball. At once the others spring to their feet, and, throwing away their ball sticks, rush to intercept him or prevent his capture, their black hair streaming out behind and their naked bodies glistening in the sun as they run. The scene is constantly changing. Now the players are all together at the lower end of the field, when suddenly, with a powerful throw, a player sends the ball high over the heads of the spectators and into the bushes beyond. Before there is time to realize it, here they come with a grand sweep and a burst of short, sharp Cherokee exclamations, charging right into the crowd, knocking men and women to right and left, and stumbling over dogs and babies in their frantic efforts to get at the ball.

It is a very exciting game, as well as a very rough one, and in its general features is a combination of baseball, football, and the old-fashioned shinny. Almost everything short of murder is allowable in the game, and both parties sometimes go into the contest with the deliberate purpose of crippling or otherwise disabling the best players on the opposing sides. Serious accidents are common. In the last game which I witnessed one man was seized around the waist by a powerful adversary, raised into the air, and hurled down upon the ground with such force as to break his collar-bone. His friends pulled him out to one side and the game went on. Sometimes two men lie struggling on the ground, clutching at each other's throats, long after the ball has been carried to the other end of the field, until the drivers, armed with long stout switches, come running up and belabor both over their bare shoulders until they are forced to break their hold. It is also the duty of these drivers to gather the ball sticks thrown away in the excitement and restore them to their owners at the beginning of the next inning.

When the ball has been carried through the goal, the players come back to the center and take position in accordance with the previous instructions of their shamans. The two captains stand facing each other, and the ball is then thrown up by the captain of the side which won the last inning. Then the struggle begins again; and so the game goes on until one party scores 12 runs and is declared the victor and the winner of the stakes.

As soon as the game is over, usually about sundown, the winning players immediately go to the water again with their shamans and perform another ceremony for the purpose of turning aside the revengeful incantations of their defeated rivals. They then dress, and the crowd of hungry players, who have eaten nothing since they started for the dance the night before, make a combined attack on the provisions which the women now produce from their shawls and baskets. It should be mentioned that, to assuage thirst during the game, the players are allowed to drink a sour preparation made from green grapes and wild crabapples.

Although the contestants on both sides are picked men and strive to win, straining every muscle to the utmost, the impression left upon my mind after witnessing a number of games is that the same number of athletic young white men would have infused more robust energy into the play—that is, provided they could stand upon their feet after all the preliminary fasting, bleeding, and loss of sleep.

Before separating, the defeated party usually challenges the victors to a second contest, and in a few days preparations are actively under way for another game.

REFERENCES

Adair, James. *History of the American Indians.* London, 1775.

Gilbert, William Harlen, Jr. *The Eastern Cherokees.* Bulletin 133, Bureau of American Ethnology. Washington, 1943.

Mooney, James. "The Cherokee Ball Play," *American Anthropologist,* o.s. III (1890), 105 ff.; *Twenty-fourth Annual Report of the Bureau of American Ethnology,* Washington, 1907, pp. 575-586.

CHAPTER XVIII

Notes on Indian Life

ALTHOUGH THE INDIANS[1] have been called Red Men, this title is not altogether correct. Their color was more nearly brown or tawny with a tinge of red—a deep sun tan with a blush. Their complexion assumed a darker shade because of frequent anointing with bear's oil in which was mixed other material, like charcoal, or the powder of a scarlet root, etc. This anointing was supposed to enable them to endure better the extremities of the weather. The bear's oil had a prominent part in greasing the hair, supposedly nourishing the scalp (barbers please take note), and, mixed with a powdered root, exterminating lice. This greasing of the hair, and constantly having the head uncovered, may have had something to do with the vigorous growth of the hair—certainly there were never any bald heads. The hair of the head and body was plucked or burned away, among most tribes, with the exception of the scalp lock.[2]

They were well-shaped, clean-made people, chiefly inclined to be tall, though statures varied;[3] very straight, and never stoop-shouldered unless overpowered by old age; muscular and generally slender, lithe, and agile; dexterous with hands and feet, and sure-footed. It is said that an Indian could walk on the ridge of a house or barn and look down as unconcerned as if he were on the ground. Deformity of any kind was very rare. In purebloods eyes and hair were always black. Eyesight was keen. Nails of

[1] The word *Amerind* has been coined to distinguish the American Indian from the natives of India, but has not passed into popular use.

[2] John Lawson furnished much of this information about the Indians of North Carolina. He visited the Siouan tribes in the interior, and resided for a decade as a neighbor of the Tuscarora in eastern North Carolina. His long contact with the latter provided him with the major portion of his material.

[3] Archaeological investigations reveal generally the sound physical condition of the Indians, but evidence of physical defects has been found in skeletal remains. In *The Eastern Cherokees* William H. Gilbert, Jr., states that the average height of the Indians on the reservation in western North Carolina is 5 feet 4 inches.

fingers and toes were allowed to grow unpared, and Europeans were laughed at for paring theirs since it "disarms them of that which nature designed for them."

Although not so robust and strong in body as some of their white neighbors, the Indians were capable of great endurance. In traveling and hunting they were indefatigable; they were good runners and could engage in their strenuous dances several nights in succession without giving out. They could endure great tortures without flinching.

The Indians were expert travelers. In the woods they kept at a constant pace, never striding over a log in the path, but going around it. They had names for eight of the thirty-two points of the compass, and called the winds by their several names. One guide was the moss that grew on the north side of the trees. They acquired accurate knowledge of the country of their travels, and could draw in the ashes of the camp fire, or sometimes on a mat or piece of bark, a map that pleased expert surveyors with its nicety.

Names for the months were given, such as Herring month, Strawberry month, and Mulberry month. Some months were known by the names of the trees which blossomed therein, especially the dogwood tree. Allusion to the time when turkeys gobbled referred to March and April. Changes of the moon were useful in marking divisions of time. They could guess well the time of day by the sun's height. Age was determined by winters.

Lawson's comments upon the good qualities of the Carolina Indians are of interest: "They are as apt to learn any Handicraft as any People that the World affords: they never prove traitors; they are patient under all Afflictions, and have a great many other Natural Vertues; they are really better to us than we have been to them." A stoic people, they were not given to jealousies, and they could endure losses without pain. When the house and all the possessions of a brave were burned, he would laugh the matter off. Worry did not worry him. When faced with death, the Indian bowed his head without a resentful murmur. But the Indians were also considered an importunate people, for it seemed right to them for a man who had given them something to give them something else, and so on ad infinitum.

The various tribes differed in their style of dress. The simplest costume was the loincloth fastened with a girdle. In addition the men wore a cloak or coat of fur or feathers, according to the season. These feather coats, frequently used in the Carolinas, were much admired by the early explorers. Pretty figures wrought in the feathers added to the attractiveness of many. For a long time all Indians were averse to wearing white man's trousers. Moccasins were made from bearskin or buckskin, tanned with the bark of trees in a process in which use was often made of deer's brains. These heelless shoes, which fitted like a glove, were ideal for travel.

Those faithful and industrious workers, the Indian women, have been described as graceful and not without charm in youth, with their bright eyes and pleasant smiles. They wore a short skirt or apron, of deerskin or some woven material, a cloak similar to that of the men, and moccasins. Their hair was bound into a long roll and decorated with shell beads. The men likewise decorated the scalp lock when the occasion seemed proper, using beads, feathers, and the like.

For adornment, shell beads occupied a prominent place. These were used for necklaces, anklets, and headdress. Strings of beads were highly prized and were used as a medium of exchange. Other ornaments were made of shell, notably disks shaped like saucers cut from the outer whorl of the conch shell. On these were usually engraved pretty designs. Copper obtained through trade and mica mined in western North Carolina furnished material for additional ornaments. Deposits of ferruginous material, such as the red and yellow powder found in pockets of sandstone in Moore County, afforded an ample supply of the powdered minerals, which, mixed with bear's grease, made paint for the face and body, used particularly by the men. Much attention was given to cosmetics before tribal dances and war expeditions.

Indian villages were situated along streams, lakes, or coastal waters. The houses, or cabins, were commonly made of bark, reeds, or like material, laid against a framework of saplings set in the ground, with tops tied together to form an oval structure. Southern Indians also employed wattle and daub in housebuilding. There were no windows, only an opening to serve as a door, and another at the top of the house to let out smoke. Mats woven of rushes or cane served as furniture.

The more important towns had a town house, a building larger than the ordinary dwelling, where public affairs were disposed of and near which dances were held and games were played. Often this town house was situated upon a mound. In western North Carolina there are a number of mounds which served for this purpose among the Cherokee, but they were probably begun by another tribe that preceded Iroquoian habitation.

Near the villages were planting grounds, usually on the stream valleys. The Carolina Indians were mostly sedentary agriculturists. They planted corn, beans, pumpkins, potatoes, and some other vegetables and derived therefrom a considerable portion of their food supply. Corn was eaten roasted, or dried for winter use. Parched and pounded, it served as Rockahominy meal, and could be easily carried on travels. Fruits such as wild plums, berries, persimmons, and pawpaws, as well as various roots, acorns, hickory nuts, and other field and forest products, were gathered. Food was stored in earthen pots or wooden bins to serve through the winter.

Game and fish were plentiful. The deer was most prominent as a meat course. Buffaloes were found in this region until after the advent of the settlers. Bear meat was obtained in plentiful supplies and eaten with relish. Panther, wildcat, opossum, raccoon, beaver, and other smaller game were hunted, including rabbit and squirrel, which were roasted whole. Wild turkeys abounded, not our domestic breeds which have been imported, but a brown-colored fowl, large in size and pleasing to the taste. Wild pigeons, ducks, and other fowls could be obtained in large numbers. The Indian was an expert fisherman. He constructed weirs for copious catches. In the rivers two rows of stones were placed to form a V-shaped figure with the point of the V downstream where the weir or trap was placed.[4] One double fall, shaped like a W, is in the Yadkin River south of Salisbury. The fishermen beat the water above the fish-fall and drove the fish into the traps. In the spring great catches of shad were made in the rivers. Many

[4] On a voyage down the Yadkin-Great Peedee River the writer found many of these fish-falls.

of these stone fish-falls may still be traced in the streams, since the later residents in this region have kept them in repair. With considerable skill fish were speared or shot with arrows. Fish hooks of bone have been found.

Fire was procured by rubbing sticks together.

It is sometimes stated that the country occupied by the Indians before the coming of the Europeans was covered with an unbroken forest. Such was not the case. In addition to the usual open spaces in swamp and meadowland, there were frequently to be found large areas burned by the Indian in hunting.

The hunting season began in the late fall. Often large hunting parties journeyed for many miles and set up camp. Sometimes the women and the girls were taken along; they beat the corn in mortars and made bread while the men brought in the game. The hunting season was a time of much jollity. Food was plentiful and feasting was indulged in with great zest. When food was abundant, the Indians ate frequently, sometimes getting up at midnight to partake of a meal. Part of the late crop of beans and other provisions such as dried fruits were carried to the hunting grounds to be enjoyed with the meat supply.

Their division of labor is well seen in the program of the hunting season. The men who were not expert hunters were employed in carrying burdens, in erecting cabins, and in serving as messengers back and forth from the hunting quarters to the towns where the old folks remained. The women brought the loads of grain and other provisions, gathered firewood, and cooked. In spare hours the women wove baskets and mats or made pottery, and the second-rate hunters made bowls and dishes of wooden chips and sometimes made tobacco pipes of clay or stone. Throughout most of the winter the Indians remained in the hunting quarters, returning to their towns in time for spring planting.

Allusion has been made to the hard tasks allotted to the women. It is true that much of the labor was assigned to them, but we must remember that they were free from much of the care and drudgery of housekeeping that is assumed by women to-day. Confinement in store or factory would have been far more irksome than their accustomed employment. They seemed quite willing to accept the home responsibilities and to leave to the men the arduous task of hunting and fishing, a means of livelihood, not recreation, as is usually the case today. Search for food involved toils and dangers, and the hunter was exposed to the rigors of the weather. The men also bore the brunt of warfare. Thus the warrior who provided well for his family through hunting and who exposed himself for their protection from enemies believed that the rightful share of household duties and of primitive agriculture should be left to the womenfolk.

Among the women basketry and pottery-making, as well as the weaving of fabrics, developed into fine arts. Remnants of ancient pottery reveal their skill. Usually the clay was rolled into cylindrical strips and wound, strip on strip, until the vessel was built up. Vessels from one inch to twenty-six inches in height have been found in the Carolina area. The sides of the vessel were rubbed smooth and polished with a small stone or chip. Mrs. Ervin Gordon, a surviving Catawban, uses for this process a small, smooth pebble which has been employed in her family for this purpose for five generations.

Sewing was done by means of bone needles. Leg bones of deer or of the larger fowls were sharpened and used to make perforations for the insertion of woven twine or thongs.

In social relations the Indians were not given to quarreling or fighting within their own tribal group. Their conduct reveals the stern teaching of the school of the forest—that, beset as they were with many common dangers, their proper course was in mutual helpfulness. Nor did they steal from one another. Land claimed by a tribe was considered common property. Many other possessions were thus held. Every effort was made to avoid disputes over property which might so easily arise when the question of ownership was involved. They were accustomed to share willingly with one another, and could not understand the chary attitude of the Europeans. When anyone met with grave misfortune, they were charitable. A woman whose husband had been killed in hunting or at war was considered entitled to support.

Burial customs varied. Usually they were elaborate, including funeral orations, feasting, and considerable lamentation.

Tribal government differed among the various groups. Usually a chief ruled, the succession falling not to the chief's son, but to his sister's son. Assisting the chief was a war captain and counselors chosen from the elder portion of the tribe. They were grave and deliberate in council.

There were no schools as we know them. The Indian youth, however, was subject to strict training in matters that would prove useful to him in making his living and in promoting the welfare of his people. While usually averse to disciplining the children lest there should arise ill feeling that might prove hurtful to the elders in their old age, or lest an ancestral spirit dwelling in the youth should be offended, the parents and other leaders of the tribe sought to fit the young people for a useful life, to inspire them to noble deeds, and to retain their affection.

When a young man had selected a bride, he went to the girl's parents, if living, or if not, to the nearest relatives and made his proposal. They replied that they would consider the matter. A second meeting ensued when the relations on both sides, and sometimes even the chief and the counselors, also debated the matter. If an agreement was reached and the bride gave her consent, the suitor paid for his wife. As Lawson reported:

The handsomer she is, the greater Price she bears. Now, it often happens that the Man has not so much of their Money ready as he is to pay for his wife; but if they know him to be a good Hunter and that he can raise the Sum, agreed for, in some few Moons, or any little time, they agree, she shall go along with him as bethroth'd. . . . The Marriages of these Indians are no farther binding than the Man and Woman agree together. Either of them has Liberty to leave the other upon any frivolous excuse they can make, yet whoever takes the Woman that was another Man's before, and bought by him, as they all are, must certainly pay to her former Husband, whatsoever he gave for her.

More than one wife was permissible, but the additional expenses incurred limited matrimonial ventures to those few who had the sufficient means.

As with most ancient people, the Indians usually set restrictions upon the mother-in-law; she was not allowed to live with or exercise authority in the family of her married children, or even to speak to her son-in-law.

The Indian baby was provided with a cradle a foot broad and two feet long, a flat piece of wood shaped with a hatchet, to which the child was tied securely. A strap was fastened to the upper corners of the board by which the mother carried the cradle on her back. In the rain a mother threw her skin or feather cloak overhead, covering baby also. Among the so-called Flat Head tribes, a weight was placed on the child's forehead to flatten the skull.

All children were given names. The boys, however, when they became warriors, at the age of sixteen or seventeen, or thereabouts, gave names to themselves—Eagle, Panther, Bear, and the like. These names were henceforth retained.

While furs and other commodities were rated as wealth, yet the generally accepted medium of exchange consisted of shell beads, which Lawson called ronoak and peak, and New Englanders called wampum. The peak, or wampum, was a small cylindrical bead ground from ocean shell with a hole bored through. According to Lawson, four or five of these made an inch, although larger beads were in use, and it is said that they were of greater value. Beads of dark-colored shell were worth double value. Lawson also described the making of peak, stating that the Indians ground the shell on a stone and then perforated it with a nail stuck in a reed and rolled continually on the thigh with the right hand while the shell was held in the left hand. How the shell was bored before the Indians had nails, Lawson did not state. He did, however, understand its value, for he recorded: "This is the money with which you may buy Skins, Furs, Slaves, or anything the Indians have; it being the Mammon (as our Money is to us) that entices and persuades them to do anything, and part with everything that they possess, except their Children, for Slaves." Strings of wampum were used not only in trade, but were also employed in negotiating treaties.

Before the intrusion of Europeans the Indians, it is thought, did not frequently engage in war. Conflicts became more common because of disturbances occasioned after the founding of colonies. Nevertheless, they resented injuries; they were a proud people and revengeful. The loss of one of their lowliest tribesmen might bring about a grievous war. They did not engage in open battles, but delighted in surprise attacks. The hour just before dawn was the favorite time for assault.

Cruelties of warfare are well known. Prisoners were put to terrible torture. Even the women and children shared in adding torment to the unfortunate victims. The braver and more renowned captives received the greater persecution. Cruelty was the darkest trait of Indian character.

There was a brighter side to the picture, as was reflected in games and dances. The Indians were enthusiastic sportsmen. They were also inveterate gamblers, sometimes staking all their possessions on the outcome of a game. And they were good losers, for as Lawson observed, "The Loser is never dejected or melancholy at the loss, but laughs and seems no less contented than if he had won." In addition to ball play and chungke there were numerous less strenuous games. One was played with small split reeds, seven inches in length, fifty-one in number. A player would throw a handful of reeds to his opponent and quickly announce his guess as to the number thrown and the number remaining in his hand. A set of these reeds was valued at a dressed doe skin. There were several other such parlor games, one of which was played with persimmon seeds in a manner similar to crap shooting, the side of the seeds falling uppermost determining the gain or loss.

Their several dances were accompanied by music appropriate for the occasion. At the war dance a warlike tune was sung telling "how they will kill, roast, scalp, beat and make Captive, such and such numbers of them, and how many they have destroy'd before" (suggestive of college mass meetings before the big game and of the accompanying football songs). At the peace dances the song related that the Bad Spirit made them go to war and that it should never do so again, but that their sons and daughters should intermarry with the former enemies and the two nations should love one another and become as one people. When the harvest had ended and before spring planting, there were the corn dances, "the one to return thanks to the Good Spirit for the Fruits of the Earth, the other to beg the same blessings for the succeeding year." Lawson observed a rather interesting feature of the ceremony:

And, to encourage the Young Men to labor stoutly, in Planting their Maiz and Pulse, they set a sort of an idol in the field, which is dressed up exactly like an Indian, having all the Indian habits, besides abundance of Wampum, and their Money, made of shells, that hang about his Neck. The Image none of the young Men dare approach; for the Old Ones will not suffer them to come near him, but tell them that he is some famous Indian Warrior, that died a great while ago, and now is come amongst them to see if they work well, which, if they do, he will go to the good Spirit and speak to Him to send them Plenty of Corn and make all the young Men expert hunters and Mighty Warriors. All this While, the King and Old Men sit around the Image, and seemingly pay a profound Respect to the same. One great Help to these Indians in carrying on these Cheats, and inducing the Youths to do what they please is the uninterrupted silence which is ever kept and observed, with all the Respect and Veneration imaginable.

In treatment of disease the Indians have won a reputation for skill which they probably did not deserve. Certainly they had recourse to remedies of roots and herbs which proved efficacious for numerous ailments. Their manner of living, too, was conducive to health except in the case of exposure which brought on rheumatism and kindred ills, and of accidents or violence. A careful search into their prescriptions and methods, however, has robbed them of an enviable reputation. The medicine man, or shaman, was just what his name has come to mean, a sham—a fake.

Haywood wrote in 1823, "In ancient time the Cherokee had no conception of anyone dying a natural death. They universally ascribed the death of those who perished by disease to the intervention or agency of evil spirits and witches and conjurers who had connection with the Shina (Anisgina) or evil spirits."

James Mooney asserted that

in the treatment of wounds the Cherokee doctors exhibit a considerable degree of skill, but as far as any internal ailment is concerned the average farmer's wife is worth all the doctors in the whole tribe. . . . The faith of the patient has much to do with his recovery, for the Indian has the same implicit confidence in the shaman that a child has in a more intelligent physician. The ceremonies and prayers are well calculated to inspire this feeling, and the effects thus produced upon the mind of the sick man undoubtedly react favorably upon his physical organization.

From a scientific standpoint the Indian's knowledge amounted to practically nothing. Consider their treatments: On the old principle that like cures like, for a disease caused by the rabbit, the antidote must be a plant called "rabbit's food," "rabbit's ear," or the like; a decoction of burrs must be a cure for forgetfulness, for nothing will stick like a burr; for worms, a plant resembling a worm must be prescribed; a yellow root must be good when the patient vomits yellow bile, and a black one when dark circles come about the eyes. When these remedies failed, even though the shaman's incantations had been loudly pronounced, the medicine man resorted to other devices. He scratched the patient with a comb made from the fangs of a rattlesnake or lanced the body with a sharp stone, sucking out quantities of blood in his endeavors to drive out the evil spirit. The shaman was a good sleight-of-hand performer in his profession, and carried about him an air of mystery. Lawson related some strange details of the sorcerer's art. On one occasion a medicine man held a string of beads perpendicularly over his patient, and Lawson asserted that the string curled up eel-like into the sorcerer's hand where it remained for a while and then uncurled to its former position. With his religious office and his many weird performances the shaman was able to exercise great power. One of the saddest chapters in the story of any undeveloped peoples deals with the fear of devils and devil-doctors.

The Indians were very religious. According to Mooney:

The Indian is essentially religious and contemplative, and it might be said that every act of his life is regulated and determined by his religious belief. It matters not that some may call this superstition. The difference is only relative. The religion of to-day has developed from the cruder superstitions of yesterday. . . . When we are willing to admit that the Indian has a religion which he holds sacred, even though it be different from our own, we can then admire the consistency of the theory, the particularity of the ceremonial, and the beauty of the expression. So far from being a jumble of crudities, there is a wonderful completeness about the whole system which is not surpassed even by the ceremonial religions of the East.

At the time of his death in 1921, James Mooney was engaged in the task of preparing a bulletin on "The Aboriginal Population

of America North of Mexico." Although he was unable to finish
this work, his researches had extended sufficiently to furnish figures that are exceedingly helpful in estimating Indian population.
Dr. John R. Swanton finished the project begun by Mr. Mooney,
presenting the figures compiled in the course of the study. With
these figures as a basis, the estimate for the North Carolina Indian
population at the time of the first contact with Europeans is as
follows:

Yeopim, Pasquotank, etc.	800
Chowan	1,200
Machapunga, etc.	1,200
Pamlico and Bear River	1,000
Neuse and Coree	1,000
Tuscarora	5,000
Woccon	600
Saura	1,200
Keyauwee	500
Eno, Shoccoree, etc.	1,500
Saxapahaw[5]	800
Cape Fear	1,000
Waxhaw, etc.	1,200
Catawba	5,000
Cherokee (about one fourth of the total 22,000)	6,000
Estimated total	28,000

REFERENCES

Alvarez, Walter C. "The Emergence of Modern Medicine from
Ancient Folkways," *Report of the Smithsonian Institution*, Washington, 1937, pp. 409-430.

Fewkes, Vladimir J. "Catawba Pottery-Making, with Notes on
Pamunkey Pottery-Making, and Coiling," *Proceedings of the
American Philosophical Society*, Vol. LXXXII, No. 2, pp. 69-124.

Gilbert, William Harlen, Jr. *The Eastern Cherokees*. Bulletin No.
133, Bureau of American Ethnology. Washington, 1943.

Haywood, John. *Natural and Aboriginal History of Tennessee*. Nashville, 1823.

[5] There is a duplication, as Shoccoree and Saxapahaw were found to be
identical.

Lawson, John. *History of North Carolina*. London, 1714.

Loskiel, George Henry. *History of the Mission among the Indians.* London, 1794.

Mooney, James. "Sacred Formulas of the Cherokees," *Seventh Annual Report of the Bureau of American Ethnology*, Washington, 1891, pp. 301-397.

———, and Swanton, John R. "The Aboriginal Population of America North of Mexico." *Smithsonian Miscellaneous Collections*, Vol. LXXX, No. 7. Washington, 1928.

Orchard, William C. *Beads and Beadwork of the American Indian.* Museum of the American Indian, Heye Foundation. New York, 1929.

Rights, Douglas L. "The Buffalo in North Carolina," *North Carolina Historical Review*, IX (1932), 242-249.

———. *A Voyage Down the Yadkin-Great Peedee River*. Winston-Salem, 1929.

CHAPTER XIX

Archaeology

UNTIL RECENT years North Carolina has been sadly neglected by archaeologists. The Bureau of American Ethnology, beginning with the year 1882, has engaged in several expeditions, mostly in the western part of the state.[1] The Museum of the American Indian, Heye Foundation, of New York, and several other groups have made excavations. In the *Union Republican*, January 10, 1889, there is an account of an excavation made by Dr. Spainhour, of Morganton.

The first expedition attempted by a North Carolina group was carried out in 1936 in Randolph County by the Archaeological Society of North Carolina. Only partial excavation was made of the site, identified as Keyauwee Town, visited by John Lawson. A mound and the adjoining village area, located on Little River in Montgomery County, were excavated under direction of the Society. Considerable material was found in this investigation. At the invitation of the Society, the owner, L. D. Frutchey, generously donated the site to the state for an archaeological reservation, the first of its kind in the state. The mound, originally more than sixteen feet in height, was called the Frutchey Mound in honor of the donor. Additional acres were purchased and the site was placed under supervision of the Department of Conservation and Development. In 1955 the reservation was transferred to the State Department of Archives and History.

Under the direction of Dr. Joffre L. Coe, the Society also made investigation of the Eno River fields and other sites. At Trading Ford on the Yadkin River, investigation was made by

[1] The work of Frank M. Setzler and Jesse D. Jennings, of the Bureau of American Ethnology, has been particularly noteworthy. See Bulletin 131, Bureau of American Ethnology.

Geiger Omwake, Charles D. Howell, and Donald C. Dearborn, and a report of the excavation was published.

The Archaeological Society of North Carolina, organized in 1933, took the lead in directing the investigation and preservation of archaeological remains in this state. It is affiliated with the Eastern States Archaeological Federation. Since 1949 it has published *Southern Indian Studies*, edited by Dr. Joffre L. Coe. The University of North Carolina has co-operated with the Society and has in recent years given much encouragement to archaeological study. Quarters have been provided for a laboratory and a depository for archaeological material, a course in American Archaeology has been introduced, and surveys and excavations have been made, under direction of Dr. Coe.

Formerly little care was taken in preserving the antiquities of the Indians of North Carolina. Objects found have usually been broken, lost, or traded away.[2] This has resulted in a great loss to the state of material that contributes to knowledge of Indian life. There is growing interest, however, in the preservation of Indian antiquities and the safeguarding of archaeological sites. Traffic in "Indian relics" is frowned upon, and "digging" on archaeological sites without supervision of competent archaeologists is considered extremely detrimental to the study of prehistory.

As for archaeology, the most informing and interesting chapter is yet to be written.

REFERENCES

Coe, Joffre L. "Archaeology in North Carolina," *Bulletin of the Archaeological Society of North Carolina*, IV (May, 1937), 5-6; "Keyawee—A Preliminary Survey," *ibid.*, pp. 8-16.

———. "The Cultural Sequence of the Carolina Piedmont," *Arche-*

---

[2] One old gentleman devised an ingenious method for disposing of the arrowheads he found on his farm. He had gathered a peck of them as he worked in the fields, enjoying his finds over many years. At last he decided that others should enjoy the same thrill of finding arrowheads; so he went about putting the "flints" back where he had found them, taking a pocketful with him as he set out to plow, and pausing from time to time to throw out an arrowhead into the furrows, meditating about the pleasure someone would have some day in turning it up. Like the verse quoted by Cicero, *"Serit arbores ut . . . ,"* he planted arrowheads so that posterity might enjoy them. He did not think about the destructive power of modern agricultural machinery.

ology of the Eastern United States. Edited by James B. Griffin. Chicago, 1952.

Heye, George C. *Certain Mounds in Haywood County, North Carolina.* Museum of the American Indian, Heye Foundation, New York, 1919.

Setzler, Frank M., and Jennings, Jesse D. *Peachtree Mound and Village Site.* Bulletin 131, Bureau of American Ethnology. Washington, 1941.

Stirling, M. W. "Smithsonian Archaeological Projects Conducted under the Federal Emergency Relief Administration, 1933-34," *Annual Report of the Smithsonian Institution for 1934,* Washington, 1935, pp. 371-400 ("North Carolina: Peachtree Mound and Village Site," pp. 392-394).

Thomas, Cyrus. "Burial Mounds of the Northern Sections of the United States," *Fifth Annual Report of the Bureau of American Ethnology,* Washington, 1887, pp. 3-119.

CHAPTER XX

Indian Antiquities

As THIS is the first detailed illustrated account of North Carolina artifacts to be published in this state, it will come far short of complete description, but it should open the way for further advance in this direction. The study of Indian antiquities in North Carolina has been difficult. There has been little careful examination of the field, and there are few collections of authentic material. Most of the material illustrated in this volume is from the collection of the Wachovia Museum in Winston-Salem, assembled by the writer with the help of friends in various parts of the state. It consists largely of surface finds and of salvage from waste of freshets and ravages of plow and harrow. The majority of artifacts in the collection are from Piedmont and western North Carolina. As far as possible it has been carefully catalogued.

Another notable collection of North Carolina-Tennessee material was assembled by Burnham S. Colburn, of Asheville. The State Museum at Raleigh, the Museum of the Cherokee Indian at Cherokee, and the Laboratory of Anthropology and Archaeology of the University of North Carolina at Chapel Hill have important collections.

GEOLOGY OF NORTH CAROLINA

The counties of the eastern shore have little if any native stone. Westward in the coastal plain region are found shell marl, limestone, and sandstone. At the falls line of the streams first is found material suitable for stone artifacts. Upstream in the Piedmont traces of stone work abound. Igneous slate, rhyolite, quartzite, and white quartz are found in outcrops, and thick deposits of tractable material are available.

Near the center of the state have been discovered the most

extensive deposits thus far noted, and signs of quarrying and shaping of blades mark this as an important supply base for raw material of the implement-makers. The volcanic stone of Randolph County was in great demand. The important trails, the Trading Path and the Virginia Trail, crossed near the site of Asheboro, in that county.

Farther west, granite and intrusions of trap rock furnished material for axes and hammers. Soapstone is found, with large deposits in the mountains. The mountain region abounds in stone, especially schists and gneisses, with wide variety of other material, such as Carolina pipestone, greenstone, mica, quartzite, and pure quartz. Workable material for projectiles is not so easily found, as the crystalline rocks are difficult to shape. The abundance of implements made from quartzite pebbles and boulders is notable. As approach is made to the western border of the state, there is increasing appearance of flint chips and implements made from nodules of limestone formations, most of which were probably imported from the Virginia-Tennessee area. Along the Yadkin River jasper is strewn about camp sites for a hundred miles. A jasper quarry in Wilkes County seems to have been the chief source of supply.

In most parts of the state there is sufficient clay to provide for ceramics.

ARTIFACTS

STONE

Arrowheads

Arrowheads are the most common of the objects left by the Indians. They are found in all of the one hundred counties of the state. Several hundred have been found at a single site, and five thousand have been gathered in surface finds along the ten-mile course of a small stream. The writer found one hundred and fifty in a single day on a farm south of Chapel Hill.

For material it seems that the Indians used whatever was available, and the rough stones of crystalline formation show some crude specimens. Preferable, however, was the finer material, and the Indians made long journeys to favorite quarry sites and transported the stone to their villages or hunting lodges. Morgan's Creek in Orange County, Little River in Randolph County, and the Yadkin-Peedee River in Richmond County give evidence of extensive arrowhead manufacture.

The process for making implements such as arrowheads, spears, and knives is described as follows: At the quarry site the stone was broken out with stone hammers or large boulders. The desired material was such that it broke with a conchoidal fracture; that is, when a chip was broken off, a shell- or saucer-shaped shallow depression was left. The rough stone of the quarry was shaped with the hammers into blades, usually leaf-shaped, with a range of from one inch to one foot or more in length. These blanks could be transported, in lots of one hundred or more, conveniently by carriers. Deposits of these have been found where they were buried near camp sites, in caches, to be dug up later for finishing. The blanks were specialized by further chipping. Tools of bone or antler were used for shaping the blades into sharp-pointed and notched implements. Tradition says that the old men of the tribe were the arrow-makers.

Most of the shapes found in other parts of the country are represented here. Along the larger streams the triangular arrow point, sometimes called bird point, is most numerous. So many of these are found near streams that one is led to wonder if they were for fish instead of birds, and perhaps attached to reeds. (In the National Museum is such an arrowhead imbedded in a human vertebra.) A popular form in central North Carolina was the stemmed, shouldered, and barbed arrowhead, one to three inches long. In the Randolph County area there is a small, roughly serrated arrowhead without barbs, made in large quantities from stone found there. Though not so numerous, there are some eccentric forms strangely shaped. In Ashe, Person, Randolph, Yadkin, and some other counties Folsom-like points have been found.

The favorite material was the Randolph igneous stone or similar material. White quartz was much used in Catawba County. Pure quartz arrowheads are found scattered through the Piedmont area and in considerable number in some of the mountain counties, and show the skill of the arrow-makers to advantage. Translucent stone of the mountains seems to have attracted the attention of the Indians for making arrowheads of fine workmanship.

Among the artifacts examined, some are evidently intrusions; Tennessee, Ohio, and Virginia material has been identified.

Spears and Knives

The line of demarcation between arrowheads and spears or knives is not easy to determine. The larger blades or points that are four inches or more in length are presumably too large for convenient use on an arrow shaft. Some of the blades show a well-defined cutting edge.

In various parts of the state caches have been unearthed. Numbers of blades vary from a handful to more than one hundred.

Drills

Implements with wide base and slender body terminating in a point served as drills, or could have been used in making perforations for sewing. A small proportion of these is found.

Scrapers

Short implements shaped like arrowheads, with a wide, blunt edge instead of a point, could be fitted with a handle and used as scrapers. Some of these are merely chunks of flint with finished edge.

Axes

Axes were made by pecking and polishing. Unfinished axes show marks of workmanship in this fashion. Granitic stone, diorite, and other volcanic material predominate. Illustrations show a variety of shapes, with grooves variously placed. Sometimes the under side of the ax has been grooved for tightening on the handle. There are several with double blades. Rough-chipped axes are also represented. Adzes are rare.

Hoes and Spades

Rough-chipped implements that could be fitted with handles for agricultural purposes are found, usually on bottom lands of old Indian fields.

Celts

The series of celts runs from the rough-chipped implement with narrow edge to the finely polished artifact with broad, sharp edge. Material is usually of gray or green stone, with some granitic rock and slate. The rough-chipped specimens are mostly of the arrowhead-type stone. Chisel and gouge shapes are rare.

Discoidals

Many biscuit-shaped stones are found, often classed as hammer stones. A pit on either side of the flat surfaces is usually found. Some are classed as mullers.

While there is probability of such use, many stones, ranging to six inches or more in diameter, are finely finished and formed with concave or convex sides. These probably served as game stones. The North Carolina collection does not show so many beautifully fashioned and polished stones as those of some near-by states. The western part of the state has yielded most of these more artistic forms.

Pestles and Grinding Stones

Bell-shaped and straight pestles were used in preparation of food, Grinding stones without handles served similarly, and small stones of this kind were used in producing paint material.

Mortars, Anvils, and Nutcrackers

Stones with concave depressions show use as mortars. On some stones, scars indicate use as anvils. Stones with pits the size of walnuts have been classed as nutcrackers, and although this classification is regarded as doubtful, experiments show that such use is practicable. Some of the mortars have pits of this kind on the under side.

Game Balls

Spheres in size from marbles to baseballs, a few of hematite, may be classed as game stones, although there is little proof of such use.

Plummets

Both stone and hematite plummet-shaped specimens are represented.

Plugs

Knobbed plugs of stone and clay, resembling bolts, have been found, suggesting ear plugs. Round disk ear plugs were found at the Frutchey mound.

Plate 37

Two-time Chief Jarrett Blythe and Neighbor's Son with Blowgun
and Darts, Eastern Cherokee Reservation

Photograph by Bill Baker, by courtesy of the North Carolina Department of Conservation
and Development

Plate 66

A Cherokee Basket-Maker at Work

Photograph by Bill Baker, by courtesy of the North Carolina Department of Conservation
and Development

Plate 67

The John Owl Family at Home

Photograph by courtesy of the State Department of Archives and History

Plate 68

Pottery-Making Today at the Oconaluftee Indian Village

Photograph by courtesy of Oconaluftee Indian Village, Cherokee, N. C.

Plate 69

Basket-Making Today at Oconaluftee Indian Village

Photograph by courtesy of Oconaluftee Indian Village,
Cherokee, N. C.

Plate 70

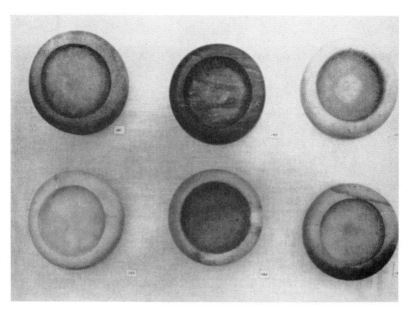

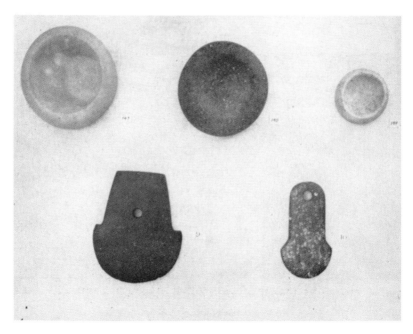

Discoidal Stones and Two Spatulate Forms from the
Cherokee Country

Photographs by courtesy of Burnham S. Colburn

Plate 71

Cherokee Ball Play—The Dance before the Game (1893)
Photograph by courtesy of the Bureau of American Ethnology

The Wolf Town Team All Set and Ready to Go
Photograph by courtesy of the Bureau of American Ethnology

Plate 72

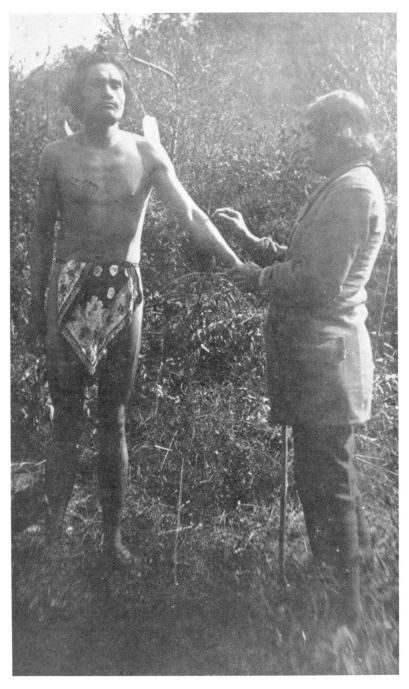

The Shaman Scratches a Player

Photograph by courtesy of the Bureau of American Ethnology

Plate 73

Generations Pass, but Cherokee Ball Play Still Goes On

Photograph by Bill Baker, by courtesy of the North Carolina Department of Conservation and Development

Plate 74

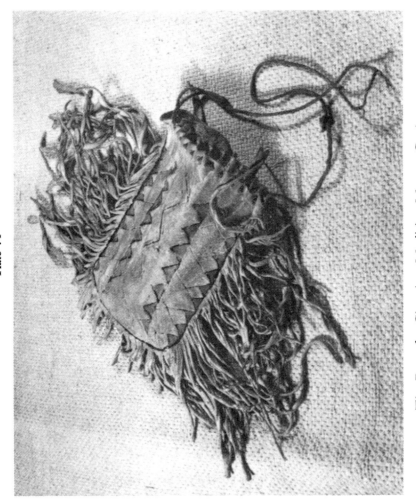

The Bag of a Cherokee Medicine Man or Conjurer,
Sometimes Called a Shaman

Plate 75

Descendants of "Charley," the Cherokee Martyr

Courtesy of J. L. Caton

Plate 76

A Double Fish Fall near High Rock, Yadkin River
Photograph by the Author, 1926

Plate 77

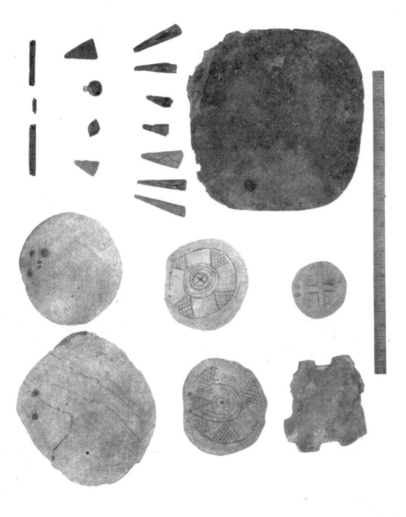

Shell Gorgets, Three Engraved, Showing Rattlesnake and Cross Designs, and Copper Pieces, Including Tubular Beads, Cone-shaped and Flat Triangular Bangles, Hawk's Bell and Fragment, and Breast Plate (Yadkin River)

Photograph by Roy J. Spearman

Plate 78

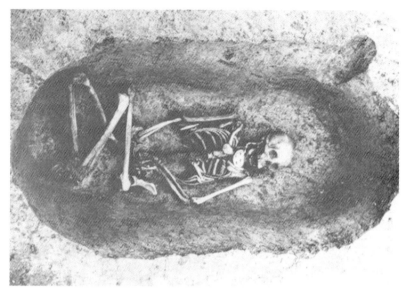

Flexed Burial at Town Creek Indian (Frutchey) Mound
Photograph by courtesy of the State Department of Archives and History

Excavation at Town Creek Indian (Frutchey) Mound
Post holes show outline of walls and entrance of lodge.

Courtesy of the Archaeological Society of North Carolina

Plate 79

Interior of Temple at Town Creek Indian Mound, State Historic Site, Montgomery County

Photograph by courtesy of the State Department of Archives and History

Plate 80

Artist's Drawing of Town Creek Indian Mound Restoration

Photograph by courtesy of the State Department of Archives and History

Sinkers

Soapstone and hardstone specimens, both irregular and symmetric types, have one or more perforations. Some have a groove instead of perforation. They could have served as net sinkers in fishing. There are other perforated stones, the use of which is still regarded as problematical.

Plates (Disks)

Thus far only one carved plate has been found. It was located on the lower Yadkin River. It corresponds with similar plates found in Georgia and Alabama.

Spatulate Forms

Only a few of these have been found in North Carolina. One type has a round handle and another a flat handle, sometimes perforated.

Cones

Iron and stone cones are usually an inch or less in diameter. The use of these is not known.

Hemispheres

Somewhat larger than the cones are iron or stone hemispheres.

Paint Stones

Fragments of paint stones, some traceable to iron formations, are listed.

Pendants

Pendants with perforation near the top for suspension are made of soapstone, slate, and granitic material. Some have notches on the base or sides for decoration.

Banner Stones

Stones with a hole bored for handle are classed as banner stones. A problematical form, this type is regarded as symbolic, an emblem of authority like our modern gavels.

The half-moon or pick-shaped form is the most common, of local material, including banded slate, although some of the specimens are undoubtedly of material imported from beyond the state. A few are boat-shaped.

Winged banner stones, or butterfly stones, are so called according to the shape. The most striking of these are made of quartz or quartzite.

Unfinished banner stones show the method of boring the stone, as the uncompleted boring shows a core. A reed or tube twirled patiently, possibly with the help of a little sand in the opening, could be used for boring.

Gorgets

These stone pieces, presumably ornaments for suspension about the throat or worn on the breast, have two perforations, and the wear of the cords for attachment is plainly indicated on some of the gorgets. Slate is the favorite material, although other stone is noted.

Arrow Shaft-Straighteners

A few stones with grooves have been found, similar to specimens noted elsewhere, and classed as arrow shaft-straighteners.

Abrasive Stones

Some native stone, particularly traprock material, has grooves, suggesting use as abrasive material, and certain specimens show apparent wear.

Tubes

Large tubes of hourglass shape have been found in western North Carolina. Their use is uncertain. There are straight tubes, some identified as broken pipestems. Finished bone objects of similar shape are included, and decoration has been noted. Their use for tobacco smoking and for smoke blowing has been suggested. It is known also that the shamans used instruments for blood-sucking, and the tube form presents itself for consideration.

Bar Amulet

A straight bar of stone with perforations on each end for attachment has shown up in several parts of the state. Just where such a bar was attached and for what purpose are not definitely determined.

Birdstone

This is a straight bar, on one end of which in effigy is the head of a bird, or deer. A few specimens are recorded in North Carolina.

Pictographs

Indian carving on exposed surface of stone *in situ* has been discovered in several regions of North Carolina, particularly in the west. There are a few pictographs in central Carolina.

BONE AND ANTLER

Awls and Needles

Many tools were made of bone and antler. Most numerous are the awls and needles. Deer and wild turkey bones and deer horns provided most material. Ends of the implements were ground down to a point. Many are nicely shaped, although decoration and perforation for suspension are rare.

Arrow Tools

Short plugs of antler, with blunt end, some showing use, are classified among arrow-making tools.

Arrow Tips

A few of the antler forms are similar to arrow tips found in other states.

Jaw Bones

The preservation of jaw bones of the deer and some other animals suggests application for some utilitarian purpose. They could have served as corn-shellers.

Beamers

The leg bone of the deer was shaped into a tool adaptable for use in tanning leather.

Fish Hooks

Fish hooks of bone have been found at several village sites.

Ear Plugs

A pair of antler tubes, shaped like a double bead and perforated, were found together in a fire pit on the Yadkin River. Their shape indicates that they were used for ear plugs.

Animal Teeth

Teeth of bear, beaver, and other animals served as tools; they were also perforated and otherwise specialized as ornaments.

SHELL

Shells are found in abundance on village sites. There are extensive shell mounds along the coast and deposits of shells at sites inland. The marine shells of the mounds include conch, oyster, clam, scallop, and others. The inland deposits, mostly freshwater shells, with mussel and periwinkle predominating, are usually found in refuse pits and sometimes associated with burials. Some of the freshwater shells were used for making shell objects or served the purpose whole as spoons. The larger portion of the specialized shell material, however, was marine in origin. Small shells were pierced for stringing. Olive shells pierced at the end made attractive necklaces, bracelets, and anklets, when strung. Elaborate ornaments were sometimes outlined with the marine shells strung in this way and sewed on garments. Hundreds of such pierced shells were found with one burial at the Keyauwee site. A conch shell, cut to cup shape, was found beside the head of a skeleton at a burial site on the Yadkin-Peedee River. Mussel shells with notches along the edge appear to be diminutive saws.

Pendants

There are some small triangular cutouts of conch shell with a groove near the apex for attaching string. Pierced pendants of the same material have been recorded.

Ear Plugs

Made from both center column and outer surface of the conch shell are ear plugs with knob on end. Some shapes suggest hairpins.

Beads

There are a variety of beads.[1] The two main types of beads are the tubular and the disk. The so-called wampum, already described, belongs to the former, and there are other specimens that range to much greater size in length and in diameter. Disk-shaped beads were generally cut from bivalves and pierced. At the Keyauwee site and in a few other places in the state a flat bead, oblong and usually with squared ends, pierced laterally, shows

[1] On a village site at Donnaha on the Yadkin River the writer found beads made of shell, bone, clay, antler, stone, and copper, and trade beads. Throughout the state trade beads are found in various colors, with white, blue, and green glass beads most numerous.

much skill in manufacture. The perforation is almost as wide as the bead; in fact, at some places the boring instruments struck through the side before completing the perforation.

Gorgets

The shell gorgets, made from the outer whorl of conch shells, follow the types found in other Southern states, though the range is not so wide. They are usually round, although some are squared, and they have two perforations for suspension. On the concave surface some are engraved, and in North Carolina the rattlesnake, the cross, and some other designs have been found. The figures on a few have been designed by cutting away part of the shell.

COPPER

While it has been thought that the copper used by the North Carolina Indians was imported from the region of the Great Lakes, the deposits, with some surface material in evidence, in western North Carolina and eastern Tennessee invite speculation as to whether there was a source of supply made use of in this region. Objects of copper have been found in small numbers in various parts of the state, usually at large village sites. There are preserved a breast plate from the middle Yadkin Valley, spools, elongated, tubular beads, triangular pendants, wooden, copper-coated ear plugs, bangles in a shape that could in some cases pass for conoidal arrow points, and hawk bells of European origin. A copper ax with a fragment of wooden handle was found at the Frutchey mound.

MICA

In the central and western parts of the state pieces of mica have been found at village sites, but there is a dearth of specialized material.

IRON

Of Indian origin are cones, hemispheres, plummets, and some other shapes of iron, including a few axes. Intrusive tools of European origin have been found in several excavations.

POTTERY

Clay Vessels

Fragments of clay vessels are found in all parts of the state, and occasionally whole specimens are uncovered. Such was the case of an urn washed out by the freshet of 1916[2] in a field along the Yadkin River below Badin. When the woman who found the pot in the valley, after the flood, lifted the "lid" (another pot) and discovered the skeleton of an infant, she threw down the "lid" and broke it to pieces, but the larger pot was rescued.

Except in the extreme east, clay was available for pottery making. The Catawba potters continue the art today in the manner of their ancestors, using native clay, rolling it into cylinders, and building up the pot by layers. (Pottery fragments of the old fields show the process.) They do not use tempering material, as did their ancestors. The Cherokee lost the art of pottery making, but have regained it.

The favorite tempering material of the Carolinas was grit, although soapstone fragments and other material have been discovered. In Tennessee, shell was used considerably, but across the North Carolina line the use of shell, strangely enough, fades out and disappears altogether until it reappears near the coast.

The smallest vessels are called paint cups. Although some of them may have served as models such as modern tribes use, some show marks of use. Sizes range from less than an inch in height. Some are pierced for suspension. A pint or more is the next size favored, and vessels run through varying sizes up to twenty-six inches or more in height. There are also saucers, either manufactured per se or borrowed from the bottom of a larger vessel. One of the largest vessels is a storage urn from the Yadkin-Great Peedee River bottom, exposed by a freshet and recovered by H. M. Doerschuk on the Leake plantation in Richmond County.

Unfortunately, it is not possible to enter into detailed descrip-

[2] Two tropical storms met on the crest of the Blue Ridge Mountains in North Carolina in July, 1916, and, as the mountaineers say, "The bottom dropped out." The Yadkin and Catawba rivers rose rapidly and swept down their valleys as destructive floods, tearing through numerous former Indian villages and camp sites and exposing artifacts and skeletal remains. For description of the downpour, see *Yadkin-Peedeɑ River, N. C. and S. C.: Letter from the Secretary of War.* 73rd Congress, 1st Session, House Document No. 68, Washington, 1933.

tion of pottery, which is an inviting subject, and the barest outline must suffice. In shape there are the cone-shaped bottom, popular in the northern part of the state, the round-bottom type more numerous in the southern, and the bowls of the Catawba valley and southern part of the state. A complete water bottle was found on the upper Yadkin near Lenoir.

In decoration the stamped ware, found abundantly in the southeastern states, extends in diminishing quantity to the Virginia line. Clear and beautiful patterns of stamped ware are found in the Catawba and lower Yadkin valleys, and across the mountains into Cherokee County. Fabric-marked, fabric paddle-marked, and plain surfaces are found. The textile-marked ware diminishes to the south.

Designs are incised, notched, and punctate, fillet-banded at top, knobbed, and occasionally provided with handles. Few shards in the state show marks of paint. Holes for bails are frequently found. Almost all the pottery shows absence of legs. Along the Yadkin River, animal or bird effigies are combined with a few pots, and in the west there are human effigies attached as handles, one with a hat, indicating the presence of the explorer.

Stone Vessels

Soapstone was the preferred material. Quarries in Ashe County and other sections of the state have been well preserved and still show marks of Indian industry. The smallest vessels are the paint cups, and the smallest of these is less than an inch in height. One cup, a little larger than a tablespoon, has a short handle. The pint size or larger was popular. In the larger containers, generally two-knobbed vessels, the sizes increase until a capacity of several gallons is reached.

TOBACCO PIPES

Clay

From Indian days North Carolina has been a great tobacco country, and the tobacco pipes of the Indians form an extensive series. Clay pipes range in shape from the straight tubular to the L-shaped. Fragments of pipes or whole specimens have been found in all parts of the state.

Stone

The favorite material was soapstone or Carolina pipestone. The shapes are much the same as those of the clay pipes, with the addition of more decorative types. Illustrations show the wide variety and fine workmanship. Effigy types, not so fully represented, are found at their best in western North Carolina.

Trade Pipes

Clay trade pipes are sometimes found, and fragments are well scattered about the state. Broken stems served as beads.

Tortoise Shell

The terrapin and the turtle shells, with possible use as cups and rattles, are familiar objects met in examination of the Indian village sites.

GOURDS

Gourds were extensively used for containers, masks, rattles, etc.

MASKS

Although the surviving Indians of western North Carolina continued to fashion masks for ceremonials, such objects of considerable age are lacking, because of the perishable material of which they were constructed. A stone mask with face well represented, found near Morganton, is in the National Museum.

BASKETRY AND TEXTILES

The Cherokee still practice the art of basketry with skill, as do the Catawba to a less extent. For knowledge of ancient basketry and making of textiles, little information is available except where fragments preserved by chemical action have been unearthed, and where imprints on clay have been retained on pottery.

REFERENCES

Fowke, Gerard. "Stone Art," *Thirteenth Annual Report of the Bureau of American Ethnology,* Washington, 1896, pp. 47-178.

Holmes, William H. "Aboriginal Pottery of the Eastern United States," *Twentieth Annual Report of the Bureau of American Ethnology,* Washington, 1903, pp. 1-201.

————. "Art in Shell of the Ancient Americans," *Second Annual Report of the Bureau of American Ethnology*, Washington, 1883, pp. 179-305.

————. *Handbook of Aboriginal American Antiquities*. Bulletin No. 60, Bureau of American Ethnology. Washington, 1903.

Orchard, William C. *Beads and Beadwork of the American Indians*. Museum of the American Indian, Heye Foundation. New York, 1929.

Moorehead, Warren K. *The Stone Age in North America*. Boston, 1910.

————. *Stone Ornaments of the American Indian*. Andover, Mass., 1917.

Rights, Douglas L. *The South Fork Indian*. Privately printed, 1925; reprinted in *Bulletin of the Archaeological Society of North Carolina*, III (Sept., 1936), 2-9.

————. "Traces of the Indian in Piedmont North Carolina," *North Carolina Historical Review*, I (1924), 277-288.

Speck, Frank G. *Gourds of the Southeastern Indians*. The New England Gourd Society. Boston, 1941.

Supplement

THE CHEROKEE

THE LANDS of the Eastern Band of Cherokee Indians in North Carolina in 1956 included 29,401 acres in Swain County, 19,347 in Jackson County, and scattered tracts of 5,571 in Cherokee County and 2,158 in Graham County—a total of 56,483 acres.

Population is estimated at 3,300.

Serving as superintendent of the Cherokee Indian Agency is Richard D. Butts, of the U. S. Department of the Interior, Bureau of Indian Affairs. The Tribal Council is composed of Walter Jackson, John McCoy, Peter Reed, Lloyd Owl, Ralph Owl, Carn Sneed, Jim Saunooke, Johnson Catolster, Elizabeth Crowe, Lloyd Sequoyah, Ella West, John Littlejohn (messenger), Arsene Thompson (interpreter), Johnnie Crowe, Jack C. Jackson, Chief Jarrett Blythe, Jarrett Wachacha, George Owl (chairman), Meroney French (vice-chief), and Maggie Wachacha.

Enrolled in the schools were the following: Cherokee elementary 206; Cherokee high school 260; Big Cove 97; Birdtown 99; Snowbird 69; Soco 133; total enrollment 847; average daily attendance 730.9, or 90%.

In the beautiful outdoor mountain-side theater Kermit Hunter's historical drama *Unto These Hills* attracts large audiences on summer nights. In the cast of 130 players, 70 are Cherokees.

The Oconaluftee Indian Village is a recreated Cherokee Indian settlement depicting Indian life and work of two centuries ago, visited daily by throngs of tourists.

Visitors delight in strolling about the lively town of Cherokee and conversing with natives engaged in the business of the trading posts, gaining some impression of aboriginal life in spite of the thick veneer of imported novelties on sale. Among well-known characters are Watty Chiltoskey, Goingback Chiltoskey, and Amanda Crowe, wood-carvers; Mose Owl, maker of bows, arrows, and blowguns; Mrs. Lottie Stamper, Mrs. Nancy Bradley, Mrs. Stacy Catolster, Mrs. Lizzie Youngbird, Lydia Queen, Mrs. Lucy George, Mrs. Katie Reed, Mrs. Agnes Lossiah Welch, Mrs. Bessie Jumper, and Mrs. Lucinda Martin, basket-makers; and Noyah Arch, expert with bow and arrow. One of the most popular characters was Carl Standingdeer, who died in 1954. A maker of bows and arrows and a skilled archer, he posed for thousands of amateur photographers at his post in Cherokee.

There are fourteen Baptist churches on the reservation, two Methodist, and one Protestant Episcopal. McKinley Ross and his quartet have traveled about the state to sing in many church gatherings.

Catawba

Superintendent Richard D. Butts serves also the Catawba Indians, who have now an assigned reservation of 3,434 acres near Rock Hill in South Carolina. There are 457 members of this tribe in 127 family units.

Index

Abbotts Creek, 82, 164

Abrasive stones, 270

A Brief and True Report of the New-found-land of Virginia, 20

Acknowledgments, ix-x

Adair family, 188

Adair, James, 127 139, 151, 233

Adams, President John Quincy, 187

Admirall, ship sent by Raleigh, 11

Adshusheer Indians, joined Eno Indians, 86, 116

Adzes, 267

Alabama: Cherokee residents, 1835, 193; residence of Sequoya, 208

Alabama River, 199

Alamance River, 85, 102

Alaska: Indian remains xi; Indian population, xii

Albany Conference, 41

Albemarle Sound, 16; region, 31, 33, 36, 43, 113

Alexander, Colonel, 135

Algonquian Indians, 4, 28, 145

Allagae, 153

Alligator River, 37

Altamaha River, 199

Altamuskeet (Attamuskeet) Indians, 32. *See* Mattamuskeet Indians

Amadas, Captain Philip, 11, 15

Amerind, 248. *See* Indians, American

Anna Ooka, 45

Anshers, James, 158

Anspach, 164

Antes, Henry, 58

Anvils, 268

Apalatches (Appalachee) Indians, 54

Appachancano, emperor, 33

Appalachian Mountains, 7, 45, 122

Appamattox Indian guide, 33, 67

Aquascogoc: Indian settlement, 15, 16; attacks first colony, 23; forgiveness offered by second colony, 24

Aramanchy (Alamance) River, 102

Ararat River, 162

Archdale, Governor John 37, 43

Archaeological laboratory and depository, Chapel Hill, 264

Archaeological reservation, Montgomery County, North Carolina, 261

Archaeological Society of North Carolina, 63, 83, 86, 261-262

Archaeology, Indian, 261, 262

Arizona, Indian ruins, xi

Arkansas, 208, 209

Arkansas River, 184, 185

Armstrong, James, 131

Arran, Peter, 135

Arrowheads, Indian, 14, 36, 38, 79, 88, 262, 265, 266, 271, 273

Arrow-shaft-straighteners, 270

Arrow tips, 271, 273

Arthur, Gabriel, 67-69, 79, 109

Artifacts: Indian, xii; Harkers Island, 38; Keyauwee, 83, 84; Piedmont and western North Carolina, 264; Tennessee, 264; arrowheads, spears, knives, 265, 266, 267; drills, scrapers, axes, hoes, spades, celts, 267; discoidals, pestles, grinding stones, mortars, anvils, nutcrackers, game balls, plummets, plugs, 268; sinkers, plates, spatulate forms, cones, hemispheres, paint stones, pendants, banner stones, 269; gorgets, arrow-shaft-straighteners, abrasive stones, tubes, bar amulets, birdstones, 270; pictographs, awls, needles, arrow-making tools, arrow tips, jaw bones, beamers, fish hooks, ear plugs, animal teeth, 271; shell, deposits, pendants, ear plugs, beads, 272; gorgets, 273; of copper, mica, iron, 273; pottery, 274-275; stone vessels, 275; tobacco pipes, 275-276; gourds, masks, 276; basketry, textiles, 276

Ashe County, 266, 275

Asheboro, 155, 265

Asheville, 264

Assembly of North Carolina, Acts of, 58, 59, 159

Atkins, Silas, 146

Atlantic Ocean, 28

Attakullakulla (Little Carpenter), chief, 160, 175, 178, 207